The First Ghosts

Irving Finkel

The First Ghosts

Most Ancient of Legacies

HODDER &
STOUGHTON

First published in Great Britain in 2021 by Hodder & Stoughton
An Hachette UK company

I

Copyright © Irving Finkel 2021

The right of Irving Finkel to be identified as the
Author of the Work has been asserted by him in accordance
with the Copyright, Designs and Patents Act 1988.

A CIP catalogue record for this title is available from the British Library

Hardback ISBN 9781529303261
eBook ISBN 9781529303278

Typeset by Palimpsest Book Production Ltd, Falkirk, Stirlingshire

Printed and bound in Great Britain by Clays Ltd, Elcograf S.p.A.

Hodder & Stoughton policy is to use papers that are natural, renewable
and recyclable products and made from wood grown in sustainable forests.
The logging and manufacturing processes are expected to conform
to the environmental regulations of the country of origin.

Hodder & Stoughton Ltd
Carmelite House
50 Victoria Embankment
London EC4Y 0DZ

www.hodder.co.uk

Remember thee!
Ay, thou poor ghost,
While memory holds a seat
In this distracted globe

Hamlet, Act 1, Scene 5

This book is dedicated
to the memory of
W.G. Lambert (1926–2011),
who taught me to read and understand
cuneiform writing

Requiescat

Contents

Author's Note

Let's talk of graves, or worms, and epitaphs;
Make dust our paper

Richard 11, Act 3, Scene 2

I myself have never seen a ghost. I have often wondered about them though, ever since my lifelong friend Peter Blakebrough saw one in, he thinks, about 1958, when he was seven. He first told me about what happened in 1971, and his description made a huge and lasting impression on me. I have kept an optimistic eye open for a ghost ever since, and in some unfathomable way Peter's Lady in Black from those early days became part of my own life memories. Later, my doctoral thesis on Babylonian exorcistic magic contained cuneiform spells for driving ghosts away, the first time that Mesopotamian ghosts in particular reared their heads over the parapet, crooking a bony finger. In all the subsequent decades, however, I have still never seen a ghost for myself, even in the shadier vaults of the British Museum, where the ancient dead can lie peacefully, and many of the living have witnessed strange things. Sometimes I have crouched immobile in the evening darkness at the top level of our Victorian Arched Room library, like a wildlife photographer at a waterhole, waiting in silence for a spectral figure who has, they say, more than once been observed. For me, though, no shady visitor.

I have met many persons of honesty and integrity who tell me that they have seen a ghost in the course of their own modern lives and I cannot find a single reason whatsoever to disbelieve them. When you poke about, in fact, a surprising number of individuals will admit to ghostly experience, as long as they feel secure from ridicule. At a twelve-seater dinner party, for example, the provocative, test-case remark that, 'So-and-So told me the previous day that they'd seen a ghost, and how can people be so daft nowadays?' will be met with the kind of silence during which guests look quickly at one another, until someone says, tentatively, 'Well, you say that, but a strange thing happened to me once years ago . . .' The ice shattered, you learn soon thereafter that someone else's auntie had revealed that, 'before the war, her cousin or was it second cousin, saw her dead father on the garden swing', and then, apparently, 'someone's friend at work's sister was in hospital and, one night when everybody was asleep, she saw, clear as day, a bent figure walk the length of the ward and pass through the wall', and so forth. I dare say that eight out of the given twelve will, thus encouraged, come forth with something comparable that they once heard of or witnessed, never could explain, and ever after tucked away.

Uncounted writers and journalists have turned their attention to ghosts, evaluating testimonies and statements through ghost stories 'real' and invented, chronicling outright sensationalism enlivened by fraud or scientific scepticism. Ghosts are often in the newspapers today. Among such contributions, historical appraisal of the ghost phenomenon is far from plentiful, and the further one goes back in time, the less information tends to be incorporated. Many commercial ghost writers, indeed, have no idea that anything is known of ghosts before, say, the Middle Ages, or even the nineteenth century ad. Few sample the very copious and wonderful evidence in Greek and Latin, or consider the Bible and the cultures of Egypt and Mesopotamia. All these ancient writings stand directly ancestral to beliefs that remain prevalent in our modern, derivative world.

Least well known to the historically inclined ghost-hunter are the written works of the Mesopotamians of ancient Iraq: Sumerians, Babylonians and Assyrians. Using their cuneiform inscriptions, we can look in on – for the first time in history – a complete, functional and in no way alien human system that covers death, burial, afterlife and, above all, *ghosts*. Abundant and surprising details have been preserved in their tablets of clay, almost as if they anticipated our interest to come, millennia after those beleaguered individuals and their spell-brandishing exorcists fell silent in the dust.

This book has been written to breathe life into dry bones and install Mesopotamian ghosts firmly on the historical ghost map. They are, quite literally, the first ghosts in human history that we can really speak about, for we can read and understand the Mesopotamians' own words on the subject today, often more than four thousand years later, from their day-to-day inscriptions excavated out of the ground. There is no book in existence in any modern language that even begins to cover all we know about Mesopotamian ghosts, but there are extraordinary riches within these pages to surprise the interested reader.

I have tried to write with understanding about the people and the ghosts of Mesopotamian antiquity in their own terms: in their world, persons saw ghosts all around them and no one individual disbelieved anyone else. I have translated or retranslated all the cuneiform texts in Sumerian and Akkadian used in this book. The clay tablets on which these messages to us were inscribed are often remarkably durable, but also vulnerable; few survive without some gaps in the wording or broken or unreadable portions. In the translations that follow, three dots indicate either an accidental break in the original, or words or phrases that I have left out for brevity or clarity. I have tried not to burden the text with too many 'strange' words and names, but they *aren't strange at all*, and a handful of terms in Sumerian or Akkadian will soon become perfectly familiar to anyone attracted by the subject of this book. It is quite wonderful that today we can idly bandy about the very names of their once terrifying gods, demons and ghosts, and the mortal practitioners who had to deal with them, considering that their writing and languages have been dinosaur-extinct for over two thousand years. There are many new discoveries and ideas in this work, and I have tried at all times to give these ancient people their voice, since their familiar fears and timeless humanity come down to us unmistakably through their writings from so long ago and will resonate with many a modern reader.

Ghosts, of course, have walked by our side since time immemorial, and did not begin with the ancient Mesopotamians. The belief that the dead can return and interact with the living is so extremely deep-seated and so universally distributed throughout time and geography that it could be classified – were we Martian encyclopaedists armed with pencil and notebook – as one clear component of basic humanity. It is the purpose of this book to seek out, with the help of archaeology and, especially, the most ancient writing, the very first ghosts within our reach.

I

Ghosts at the Beginning

What's past is prologue
                    The Tempest, Act 2, Scene 1

The Belief in Ghosts

This book documents the earliest known evidence in the world for what is conveniently referred to as the 'belief in ghosts'. We can point to the very word for ghost on a tablet of clay from near the beginning of the third millennium bc, some five thousand years ago. This is a fact incontrovertible. Ghosts, therefore, were there already; gratuitous trouble-makers going about their affairs in what we today call the 'Middle East': we can pin them to the spot like a butterfly on a card. One line of cuneiform writing, however, does not mark the beginning of it all, but happens merely to be our earliest flag-post. On the contrary, we must suspect ghostly presences hovering much further back in time, remote indeed beyond imagination. Here, then, we must zoom in for a moment on our ancestral social world, to that stage when *deliberate burial* was first taken for granted.

The First Burials

Palaeontologists at work on the very inception of human evolution think and work in terms of hominins, the wider group of primates among which we *Homo sapiens* came to belong. The essential perspective in this form of science is as long as can be, sweeping back through the archaic members of the genus *Homo*, early *Homo sapiens* and the Neanderthals of the Middle

1

Palaeolithic to the Early and Mid-Upper Palaeolithic and the Late Upper Palaeolithic world. Time here has no concern with our familiar bc and ad but is expressed simply as BP, 'before present', or in nicely rounded MYRs, 'million-years'. The extraordinarily remote evidence for the archaeologist is delicate, elusive and often equivocal.

Crucially, burial is not compelling of itself in our search for ghosts, for there were always many reasons for rapid burial of the dead; it was understood before thought itself what happened to corpses, diseased or otherwise, and there was the question of, say, respect for the dead, or predators. Archaeologically speaking, burial as such carries no implication necessarily different from *waste disposal*. The gradual establishing of deliberate burial in early ancestor communities, however, must have led to significant consequences. Shared ritual tied with mourning would come to teach that individual life itself was finite. With the development of abstract thought and the sharing of language and experience, the great lesson would come to be explicitly, rather than instinctively, understood: all that lives must die, passing through nature to eternity.

Burial, mourning and group social cohesion in the face of death are not, however, exclusively human territory. Paul Pettitt sets the stage for his *Palaeolithic Origins of Human Burial* looking at live modern primates, chimpanzees coping with death. Elephants, the most celebrated of mourners, cover a dead elephant with branches and earth, examining and fondling the bones of their relatives and often returning to them long after, and comparable behaviour in many other species has been recorded. The importance of such evidence is that mourning and burial activity are part of the deep animal world itself, and it is from that remotest of backdrops that pre-human and human ideas have ultimately crystallised. Eventually we come to Neanderthal burials and *Homo sapiens* burials.

Early Homo sapiens *burials*

Following Pettitt's survey, the first examples of *simple inhumation* – the deliberate creation of a space in which to deposit and cover a corpse – are only evident after ~120,000 BP. Down to ~60,000–50,000 BP a good number of early *Homo sapiens* burials are known in the Middle East and Europe that, broadly speaking, pre-date the known Neanderthal burials of the same geographical areas. Certain sites indicate grouped burials and elements that might reflect funerary activity, although it has not always been possible to establish which archaeological features are deliberate and which fortuitous. At the cave site Mugharet-es-Skhul or Mount Carmel, in Israel, for example, the remains of ten individuals were excavated, some if not all of whom had been deliberately buried, lying on their side in a foetal position. Not far away, near Nazareth, thirteen skeletons were found at the cave known as Djebel Qafzeh; one had a mandible of a wild boar placed in the angle between the left forearm and right arm, and another included part of a large bovid cranium.

Early Neanderthal burials

Ironically, it was a famous cluster of dead Neanderthals that brought them disconcertingly back to life, given that they had long been condemned as loping and lugubrious knuckle-trailers, although modern archaeological assessment now increasingly credits them appreciatively with care for the sick, use of symbols, sophisticated communal hunting, some expressions of art and burying their dead. Excavations during the 1950s and 1960s in Shanidar Cave in north-eastern Iraqi Kurdistan uncovered many Neanderthal skeletons, some thought to have been killed by a rock fall from the roof, others apparently *deliberately buried*. That discovery in itself was greeted at the time by substantial publicity, but far more appealing to the media at large was the fact that one grave seemed to have contained flowers, thereby creating a seductive picture of human-like compassion, care for the sick and dying. In 1971 Ralph Solecki, the dig director, published *Shanidar, the First Flower People*, at a time when abundant flower people were alive and kicking to celebrate the news. Later, sadly perhaps, the flowery remains – actually clumps of pollen grains – were shown to be later intrusions due to some meddlesome burrowing rodent, but Solecki's conclusion that 'the first stirrings of social and religious care' are reflected in the whole of the mortuary assembly at Shanidar is nonetheless hard to gainsay. Recent excavations in the same cave, in fact, now confirm deliberate burial at Shanidar by finding an additional skeleton carefully laid out in a grave that had clearly been dug down into a lower layer. The excavators date this individual to between 70,000 and 60,000 years ago. Perhaps the cave was a burial site over a long period to which they returned again and again. We know that Neanderthals and *Homo sapiens* existed contemporaneously, and much-publicised DNA findings show that there was interbreeding. Perhaps burial practice was another form of shared experience.

Neanderthals are accessible to us in some measure from about 400,000 BP until about 40,000 BP, spread from the Atlantic to the Urals, down into south-west Asia, and in Israel and Iraq. *Homo sapiens*, out of Africa in about 100,000 BP, reach Europe in about 40,000 BP. It is perhaps hardly a coincidence that the long-running and hardly changing world of the Neanderthals should come to an end with the arrival of close but different relatives.

Homo sapiens sapiens *Burials with Grave Goods*

Undertakers really got to work in the Upper Palaeolithic, let us say 50,000 years ago, when graves *and* grave goods became commonplace, remaining so, practically speaking, in archaeology ever after. Whoever laid sword or ploughshare next to their father's stilled right thigh in a leaky dugout knew that this was not the complete end.

Afterlife Implications

In the more complex graves of later archaeology a deceased person can be sent off with tools, luxury goods, jewellery, weapons, horses and chariots, servants and gold, all of which imply unmistakeably that the stuff would be needed on arrival, wherever that might be. It is equipment for the coming new existence, modelled inevitably on the old one. In this regard there is no intrinsic difference between one wispy bracelet of cracked beads and the entire contents of Tutankhamun's burial chambers. Grave goods might reflect any number of cultural ideas and traditions, as well as wealth, honour or status, but whenever graves included goods side by side with the deceased, we are entitled to assume an underlying belief that *some part of that individual was believed to be going somewhere*. The 'somewhere' framework, from its very inception, is inevitably predicated on the idea, hunch-like, sketchy or sharply visualised, of an *afterlife*.

From monumental, diverse and complex material over which we can only drift in the slipstream of seasoned palaeontologists and archaeologists, we can distil for the purposes of this enquiry three evolved strands of human belief. They are interwoven and interdependent to such an extent that one can hardly have prevailed without the others. All three are implied by *burial with bits*:

1. Something survives of a human being after death.
2. That something escapes the grasp of the corpse and goes somewhere.
3. That something, if it goes somewhere, can quite reasonably be expected to be capable of coming back.

From this vantage point we should reckon that ghosts arrived on stage by the Upper Palaeolithic, perhaps around 50,000 bc. The simple conception that something recognisable of a dead person might at some time return to human society seems to me neither fanciful nor surprising. Its roots originate at that developmental horizon where burial with goods became the norm for the first time.

In contrast to mourning and burial, it is the deep-seated conception that some part of a person does not vanish forever that separates us absolutely from the whole animal kingdom. No gorilla or bald-headed eagle ever had an inkling of their inner self finishing up somewhere once the proud body had collapsed into chemicals. It is only the early human mind that grew to strive against the prospect of the final annihilation of self, a hallmark rebellion that became hard-wired into, and always an essential element of, human nature. It is the incalculable antiquity of the first stirrings towards post-mortem existence that explains the enduring and universal belief in ghosts. Ghosts have waited in the wings from the beginning and have fluttered persistently as part of human cultural, religious or philosophical baggage ever since. Practically speaking, as a result, they are inexpungible.

The material in the following chapters derives exclusively, I must stress, from written records: we are no longer constrained to theorise and dispute over mute, rescued fragments from the silence of prehistory; we start off on our own journey with the words and ideas of the ancients themselves. It seems to me that human records *en bloc* delineate two phases within what we might call *the ghost business* over the five-thousand-year-span of its trackable history:

Phase 1 is when every individual in a given society believed in ghosts, not as a matter of faith or defiance, but simply because they were just considered to be part of daily life. It was not, in fact, a question of belief, but of acknowledgment. Here, the world of the ancient Mesopotamians is a perfect example.

Phase 2 is when the simplicity of that belief was exposed to and overlaid by religious, philosophical or scientific thinking. This complex of overlay imposed questions, scepticism, outrage and ridicule, eventually reducing the topic to private and chiefly unarticulated belief, but without in any way dislodging its deep-seated hold. Here, modern European society is a perfect example.

It is claimed, and hopefully demonstrated throughout these pages, that long-dead Mesopotamians believed in their ghosts to the point of taking them utterly for granted. The reader embarking on this book might doubt such a proposition, regarding the supposed seeing of ghosts, cohabiting with them or suffering from them, as the sort of nonsense found everywhere in gossipy or superstitious enclaves, not to be taken seriously, and hardly a significant prop in bringing to life a long-vanished culture. The very opposite, in fact, is true.

Taking ghosts for granted in daily life and interacting with them was to be ever after a characteristic shared with peoples and nations round about the world, ancient into modern; it is precisely that which makes documentation of the ghost-belief system in ancient Mesopotamia over four thousand years ago so vital and significant. It is astonishing, in fact, how familiar the long-dead of archaeology emerge to us in this regard. The cynical process of second-guessing the meaning of evidence from antiquity serves no one; my conviction is that the voices that cried out about their ghosts, argued with them and battled against them over nearly three millennia of texts in cuneiform writing must be taken at face value and hearkened to. The important judgement is that their ghosts are not symbols or metaphors but, in their lives, realities.

We bring in Ashurbanipal, King of the World from 669 to 631 bc, to illustrate the point. Ashurbanipal: king of Assyria and the then known world; scholar, politician and warrior; the most exalted individual of the age and one of the great rulers of antiquity. His capital was at Nineveh in the north of what is today's Iraq, and we will encounter him and his library of clay tablets more than once in this book. Ashurbanipal's empire was vast, always requiring rigid control, defence and extension. Assyrian military forces represented a state-of-the-art killing machine that deployed extremes of horror and brutality when lessons needed to be taught, or offences punished. Their unabashed accounts of campaigns and expeditions were committed to permanent record in the form of great clay prisms with columns of cuneiform writing, furnishing modern historians with precious history overlaid with ruthless sadism, shocking for the Assyriological beginner who first translates such narratives.

Here we meet the Assyrian military in the ecstasy of murderous victory over Elamites from over their eastern border, in what is today's Iran, settling old scores, old battles, old histories. Ashurbanipal, as detailed in his great British Museum clay *Prism A* inscription of 643 bc, despatched one of his crack units – as his forces swarmed through the vanquished Elamite capital of Susa – to wreak a very specific kind of vengeance on the Elamites for their earlier affront to his own family:

> *I destroyed and demolished the tombs of their kings, earlier and later, who did not revere Assur and Ishtar, my lords, and had disturbed the kings, my ancestors; and I exposed them to the sun. I took their bones to Assyria and prevented their ghosts from sleeping and deprived them of funerary offerings and water-pouring.*

This is no fluffy, gullible, woo!-woo! ghost superstition. The implacably wolfish Assyrian smarted over the past, and this is dead serious, political reality. Generations of deceased Elamite kings, hitherto perfectly tranquil, would never rest again, with their bones stolen away to be scattered around in the enemy capital. Neither would they receive the crucial offerings on which they depended below in their version of the Netherworld. The Assyrian, like the Elamite, held that disturbing a body in its grave imposed eternal trouble on the individual's ghost even long after death, interment and decay. The reality of the enemy ghost world is identical to his own, and his revenge perpetual.

This round of violence and vandalism was not the end of the story, however. In 612 bc, nearly twenty years after the death of Ashurbanipal, the unthinkable happened: Nineveh the royal fell to the combined forces of Babylonians from the south and Medes from the east. No modern archaeologist working at Nineveh has located Ashurbanipal's grave; perhaps Elamites got their own back during the rampages that attended the fall of Assyria. Victors of either side enacted savage vengeance on the proud royal portraits in stone that lined their enemy's palace walls. Mutilations and cuts inflicted on a statue or image would have the same effect as on the living body and render them powerless.

Relief of Ashurnasirpal II,
Bowdoin College Museum of Art, Brunswick, Maine.

This sculpture, discovered in the 'Central Building' at his capital of Nimrud, depicts the earlier Assyrian king Ashurnasirpal II (883–859 bc). The sculpture as we see it now embodies the story of Assyria's defeat in itself. The king's figure has been substantially and pointedly defaced to powerlessness: his severed right hand, his plucked-out eyes, ears, nose and mouth and his chopped beard; out of view, his feet and Achilles tendons and his bow and bow string are likewise rendered useless. This is revenge personified and perpetuated in stone; the conquerors did to the Assyrians in every way what had been done to them, and left in their assault on the wall-carvings an unmistakable record.

To top up insult with injury, a ghostlike figure has been picked out in the stone to look the tyrannic Assyrian in the eye. The Assyrian specialist Barbara Porter rightly saw in the oddly rounded shape of the back of the figure's head a rude version of the bulbous crown worn by the Elamite kings, with the V-shape facing the king's hand a mocking riposte to the patronising gesture once adopted by the Assyrian overlord. The carving style is connected pockmarks, but both figure and upraised hand were completed by the army sculpture-expert; he was not interrupted at his task, and the representation has his own clear eye, nose and mouth. That the figure looks spectral to our eye is not co-incidental: this is surely the ghost of the ravaged King of Elam come out of the darkness to taunt and haunt the hated Assyrian for evermore.

2

Ancient Mesopotamia:
Home to the First Ghosts

There is a river in Macedon,
and there is a river in Monmouth.
It is called Wye at Monmouth,
but it is out of my prains what is the name
of the other river;
but t'is all one

Henry V, Act 4, Scene 7

The Landscape

Since the ghosts of ancient Mesopotamia are the first whom we can confront face to face we must locate the stage on which they came and went, and the period of time during which they both alarmed and persecuted those about their daily lives. Mesopotamia, or the Land-between-the-Rivers, is the ancient name given by the Greeks to what is now Iraq, with Assyria to the north, Sumer and then Babylonia to the south. Archaeological exploration of that interesting part of the world was already well advanced by the middle of the nineteenth century, and discoveries have come thick and fast ever since. Ancient populations between the Euphrates and Tigris rivers tended to inhabit the same locations for great lengths of time, the result in the Middle East being mountain-like mounds of piled-up, cocooned archaeological material, undisturbed for centuries and awaiting the spade, the laboratory and the library. The first excavations investigated ancient cities whose names were sometimes echoed in the Bible or in classical authors: Nineveh, Nimrud, Babylon. Their archaeological discoveries were spectacular: palaces and temples, major public buildings, walls and city gates. Early progress in reading the cuneiform inscriptions carved into stone walls and impressed into clay bricks brought back the half-forgotten names: Sennacherib, Asnapper (as they called Ashurbanipal) and Nebuchadnezzar. After these first heady days, the scientific aims of archaeology steadily broadened out in every direction; the Mesopotamian archaeologist today commands very extensive and diverse data, and is increasingly concerned with the everyday living conditions of the population at large, over many sites and periods. The reach of these sites stretches from remote prehistoric settlements that preserved the most ancient of lifestyles to bustling and sophisticated cities that, in many ways, anticipated those of the Middle East today. Understanding of daily life three thousand years ago, combining archaeology with inscriptions, can be sometimes astonishing in its detail.

Ghosts are part of all this. It is thanks to the cuneiform writing on tablets of clay from ancient Mesopotamia that we encounter the first ghosts in the world. The Mesopotamians' crucial words for ghost are thus the first in history; in ancient Sumerian it is *gedim*, in ancient Babylonian *eṭemmu*, and we shall have a good look at these terms, for they prove to encapsulate the whole idea of ghosts, forever after, *cap-à-pie*.

History itself was made when the ancient Sumerians, and after them the Assyrians and Babylonians of ancient Iraq, turned to river clay as support for their young writing, well over five thousand years ago, and they never looked back. Clay was the leitmotif of Mesopotamian Man; they wrote on it, they built in it and when it came to the next world, as we shall see, they are even supposed to have been nourished by it. On top of that, it survives in the ground, beautifully, for millennia. For this book, therefore, we have direct evidence about ghosts written in the oldest intelligible writing in the world, underway before 3000 bc, extinct by the second century ad, and only deciphered and rendered intelligible by assorted geniuses in the mid-nineteenth century ad. It is with the help of two dead languages, Sumerian and Akkadian, that we can follow the Mesopotamian dead themselves.

The Writing

Mesopotamian cuneiform, or wedge-shaped writing, allowed words and thoughts to be recorded by impressing syllabic spelling signs made up of different combinations of wedges into tablets of clay. It was almost certainly developed by Sumerians; a giant step that sundered the world from inarticulate prehistory into history, knowledge, ideas and poetry. Even though the earliest inscriptions of which we know were preoccupied with administration – as well as making word lists of the newly minted cuneiform signs before they were forgotten – quite soon thereafter *literature* was also committed to writing, and the great unfolding triumph of the human record was underway. Without it we would have no history, no Keats, no Dostoevsky, no Mills & Boon. Later, cuneiform came to be exported from the heartland between the rivers, taking hold across the Middle East for more than two millennia, resisting and surviving the appearance of the alphabet. To our great fortune, many tens of thousands of these ancient writing tablets, covering many genres, survive today to bring alive that vast stretch of time before the birth of our modern world.

Cuneiform writing changed little over the three millennia of its use. The perfected script, soon after 3000 bc, was flexible enough to record Sumerian – a language unrelated to any other – and Akkadian, a member of the modern Semitic language family. Well-educated scribes knew and thought in both tongues. When they learned a word in one language, they automatically learned it in the other; such as the word for man, Sumerian lú = Akkadian *amēlu*. Huge numbers of paired Sumero–Akkadian words were systematically collected on large clay lexical tablets, the world's first dictionaries.

Hundreds of cuneiform signs had to be mastered, but school-boys who had done their homework were able to spell words fluently in both languages, and indeed other languages too. They wrote with two kinds of signs: those that reproduced sounds in syllables, and those that expressed ideas. For most of our information about the ghost world (as, in fact, about pretty much everything Mesopotamian), we are dependent on writings in cuneiform script. Sumerian words are usually written by us in CAPITALS or plain font; Akkadian, of which there are two dialects, Assyrian and Babylonian, is written in italics. Wherever you look under the surface of these remarkable documents there are wonderful things to be found. The use of writing for literature as well as administration increased and widened out steadily over time. When it comes to ghosts, most of our sources come from the first millennium bc. A high proportion of the inscriptions focused on in this book are written in Akkadian, but individual texts and ideas often hark back to earlier texts written in Sumerian, and, like our ancient predecessors, we will need both.

The Very First Ghost of All

Ancient Mesopotamian tradition complements rather beautifully the idea put forward in the previous chapter that ghosts were there from mankind's very beginning. The Babylonian Flood Story, ancestral to that of the Book of Genesis and named after its hero *Atra-ḫasīs*, explains within its narrative how human spirit came to be created in the first place and what it was made of.

Today we have two versions of this Akkadian cuneiform story, both from the southern Iraqi city of Sippar. One is mid-eighteenth century bc in date, the other written down more than a thousand years later. The creation of *Homo sapiens mesopotamiensis* was the work of the goddess Nintu, whose name means Lady of Birth, who was also known as Belet-ili, Lady of the Gods. Nintu was charged with recycling the body of a deliberately slaughtered god, a former rebel called We-ilu, who possessed the crucial quality of intelligence (in Akkadian *ṭēmu*). Later, this sacrificed god is called Alia, who had the capacity to reason. This divine flesh and blood was to be mixed with clay; the blended outcome is the human spirit (*eṭemmu*).

MAKING MAN: THE *ATRA-ḤASIS* EARLY VERSION
Let the one god be slaughtered (instructed the god Ea), *that all the gods may be cleansed thereby. Let Nintu mix clay with his flesh and blood. Let god and man be blended together in the clay, that forever after we may hear the heartbeat. From the god's flesh let there be spirit. Let it* (the heartbeat) *make known the living as its sign. And that this be not forgotten, let there be spirit.*

They slaughtered We-ilu, who possessed intelligence, in their assembly. Nintu mixed clay with his flesh and blood; Forever [after they heard the heartbeat]. From the god's flesh there was spirit; it (the heartbeat) *made known the living as its sign. And so that this was not forgotten, there was spirit.*

MAKING MAN: THE *ATRA-ḤASIS* LATER VERSION
Let Belet-ili mix his flesh and blood with some clay, so that god and man are mixed together in the clay. Let it beat so that we may hear it for the rest of time; let the spirit be produced from the god's flesh. It shall reveal its sign in a living being, a sign never to be forgotten, the spirit . . .

Belet-ili mixed his flesh and blood with some clay, so that god and man were mixed together in the clay. It beat so that she would hear it for the rest of time; spirit was produced from the god's flesh. It revealed its sign in a living being, a sign never to be forgotten, the spirit.

Homo sapiens mesopotamiensis primus is thus divine flesh and blood mixed with clay, animated by divine intelligence, as is neatly embodied within the ancient Akkadian words in a cosmic-level pun:

We (the god) + *ṭēmu* (intelligence) = (w)*eṭemmu* (spirit).

The *eṭemmu* is that divine element which activates the living Babylonian; what we today would call his *spirit*, if not his soul. When he dies and his flesh and blood return to clay, the *eṭemmu* endures as what we would call his *ghost*. The very stuff of ghosts thus became an inextricable part of the Mesopotamian world life system from Day One on. Note was made of it for us in the *Atra-ḥasis* story four thousand years ago.

The Mesopotamian and His Ghost

That part of a Mesopotamian individual which survived beyond death, then, was his *eṭemmu* or ghost. In very special cases, immortality could be bestowed on man by the gods, but otherwise Mesopotamian persons had to die in the end like everyone else; as Hero Gilgamesh remarked in the story when his own death was approaching,

> *Thus has the bane of mankind come!*

Book-keeping was a favourite Mesopotamian tendency and it is no surprise that a divine record keeper should be in charge of the *Tablet of Destinies*, an important document that features prominently in certain mythological stories. Broadly speaking, a Babylonian's life had its working plan set in place from the moment of his birth by the gods, although the allotted span was not an absolute fixture, and people could certainly die, or be killed, before their time. During the seventh century bc, a pensive Assyrian scribe at Sultantepe near Urfa in Turkey once jotted down this thought-provoking *Ages of Man* framework on a tablet of clay:

50 *short life*
60 *maturity*

70 *long life*
80 *old age*
90 *extreme old age*

The dead were laid to rest with a certain ritual firmness in the natural and reasonable expectation that they would stay where they belonged. This arrangement, however, as elsewhere and afterwards in the world, was by no means foolproof. For any of several reasons that we shall investigate, an individual who had 'crossed over' and 'gone down' might feel compelled to return to the world from which he or she had departed. Mesopotamian ghosts, in as much as we can glimpse them, were insubstantial and flimsy, but often recognisable, and seemingly clothed. They were sure of a reaction when they did come back.

Barring last-minute disaster, or the very unexpected, dead Sumerians and Babylonians were respectfully and properly buried. The default position was under the floor within the area of private houses, or, if the deceased were a new-born or young child, sometimes within the walls. At different times there were cemeteries outside towns or cities, notoriously to be avoided, for they would be populated by unowned and restless ghosts. Archaeological evidence for Mesopotamian burial practice over the three millennia of time is naturally complex and diverse, and it bears directly on the matter of ghosts.

One short and poetic Babylonian spell in cuneiform confronts a ghost who has returned, and it hints at sonorous and impressive injunctions at the moment of burial. It also communicates ghostly nature as a gust of wind, perhaps diaphanous in appearance, for in other cuneiform passages ghosts are described as a shadow:

You are the offspring of the wind
I have laid you in the grave
I have sent you down
Why did you not fear my solemn oath?

Sometimes ghosts came back. Sometimes people saw them. Sometimes they were, quite literally, a pain in the neck.

Forces Seen and Unseen

Judging by cuneiform writings, ghostly entities were plentiful in the cuneiform world. Sometimes they were hardly more than sensed, sometimes all too visible, but their arrival or continuing presence was always loaded with implications. What is more, ghosts were not the only such force to be reckoned with in life, for they co-existed side by side with an assortment of other, entirely *non-human* elements. These were usually invisible, what we typically call devils or demons; evil certainly, with origins that were often obscure but also partly divine. This brigade of dangerous freebooters could also cause trouble, misery and sickness to human beings. They were all around in what Victorians called the ether, and shared with ghosts the feature that, while not necessarily always a problem, they usually were. The type of demon most commonly mentioned in magical texts is the Sumerian udug, Akkadian *utukku*. Everybody knew these two words. The term is generic, in fact, for there were well-known *utukku* demons and others that were practically faceless and hard for us to distinguish other than by name, or to visualise their appearance. The entire malevolent assembly, each member of which could bring trouble and difficulty to the long-suffering Mesopotamian public, came out of quite a different mould from the human-natured ghosts that are the subject of this book. They were, on the whole, harder for the cognoscenti to get rid of, for they could never be 'killed'. We will run into them, too.

Cuneiform Ghost Resources

Surprising features encountered by the cuneiform ghost-hunter are the extent and richness of Mesopotamian source material, for it goes back in time to the third millennium bc, although most of the writings quoted here date from the first millennium bc; with the passage of time, ghost writings certainly proliferate. Accumulated practices and procedures for ghost affairs were carefully systematised into cuneiform manuals. Magical *spells* list the different kinds of persons who would be expected to come back as a ghost and offer escape from their attentions; *omens* cover seeing, hearing, meeting or interacting with ghosts and what that might imply; and *rituals* deal with ghosts when they got out of hand, treating and freeing up patients who were physically or mentally affected for the worse by ghostly attentions.

Ghosts also find their way into other kinds of writing, such as literature and mythology, letters, and, as we have seen already, even royal inscriptions; we will take account of whatever fills out our picture. Crucial within daily life are housing and burial; and how normal people behaved towards their dead, understanding why they should sometimes suffer at their spectral hands. Properly speaking, of course, ghosts went *down* to – and were supposed to *stay* in – the Netherworld. Cuneiform tablets tell us about all that too, and we shall visit below ourselves. First, however, we must consider the question of burial: what they did with their dead.

3

The Death and Burial of Kings

For God's sake let us sit upon the ground
And tell sad stories of the death of kings:
How some have been depos'd, some slain in war
Some haunted by the ghosts they have deposed
Some poisoned by their wives, some sleeping kill'd,
All murthered – for within the hollow crown
That rounds the mortal temples of a king
Keeps Death his court . . .

Richard II, Act 3, Scene 2

Dead Mesopotamian bodies and their constituent parts did not, and do not, as a rule, withstand burial in the ground. It is only in exceptional environments, such as deep wells, that frail organic materials survive from antiquity to reach the bench of the museum conservator or scientist. Archaeologists who work on burials and graves have to accommodate complex and diverse information, for interments are spread over millennia of time across a wide spectrum of archaeological sites, and investigators are often both detective and forensics expert. There are inhumation and crema-tion to consider, and burial within private houses and without. A striking contrast for the working archaeologist is that between ordinary graves and royal graves.

The majority of graves are, obviously, private graves, with contents that only hint at their own back story: the death, mourning and burial of their vanished occupants. Spectacular graves of the rich, replete with skeletons, swords and gold, are often the publicly celebrated part of archaeology, promoted in books and the media, while the bread-and-butter work of the archaeologist wheezing in an ancient cemetery is seldom enlivened by ultra-juicy finds. It is, therefore, ironic that, when museum visitors or readers do encounter ancient Mesopotamia for the first time, it is often via the drop-dead, glamour-packed, third-millennium cemetery at the southern site of Ur, the so-called Ur of the Chaldees. We begin, accordingly, with dead royalty.

Kings and Queens at Ur

The discoveries made at Ur by Sir Leonard Woolley between 1926 and 1932 startled the world, and were even claimed in the press – for a while at least – to rival those of ancient Egypt, although the gold did not quite measure up. Woolley was an exemplary archaeologist, and his professional publications of the work at Ur have stimulated studies and investigations ever since, backed by permanent, iconic displays in the Iraq Museum at Baghdad, Penn Museum in Philadelphia, and the British Museum in London.

Woolley's team of hand-trained workmen uncovered sixteen tombs of the city's élite. Sumerian royal names that came to light, and became satisfactorily famous thereafter, include Meskalamdug, Mesannepada, Akalamdug, A'annepada and their assorted queens, the most famous being Queen Pu'abi, second wife of Meskalamdug (Grave no. 800). The basic plan at Ur was inhumation; a deep pit, with entrance ramp and central tomb chamber. The dead individual was laid out on matting in his or her tomb with a rich assortment of luxurious grave goods. The dead in their subterranean chambers were accompanied round about by the neatly laid out bodies of their former staff, whose lives, rather shockingly, had surely, it seemed, been terminated for the purpose. The greatest number of personnel in one tomb was seventy-nine. Everything was then covered over with matting and filled in. Some tombs were found in a very disturbed state, others surprisingly intact, although the dramatic field photographs from the excavations illustrate the complexity of stratification and identification.

Reconstruction, slightly old-fashioned, of the funeral scene in grave PG 789, one of the kings of Ur. Illustration by Amédée Forestier, 1928.

The grave goods included gold and silver bowls and drinking vessels, elaborately produced musical instruments, decorated items of furniture, carts and a sledge, tools and weapons, jewellery made from precious metals, and costly materials, some imported to Ur from Pakistan, Afghanistan, Iran, Anatolia and Syria, including gold, silver, lapis lazuli, carnelian and agate. And *wonderful* game boards. The finds were, quite simply, a glorious mass of archaeological objects both mundane and startling. The dead retainers lying outside had decorated carts with their draught animals buried with them and the instruments that they had used in the court. Woolley's discoveries brought classical Sumerian taste to public attention, in works which, at their best, made extensive use of the precious materials that had been procured outside and brought to Ur. Surrounding the Royal Tombs, as they are usually called, contemporary, and sometimes later, private graves were clustered about, each with their own – but infinitely less lavish – grave goods. Altogether, over two thousand Sumerian graves were excavated.

No inscriptions from this period survive to inform us about the funerary ritual that must have been enacted prior to and around these burials, or about the underlying beliefs behind the burial system itself. For our purposes, however, the complex of Royal Tombs at Ur locates particular features at this time and place – the middle of the third millennium bc – with unchallengeable certainty:

1.   Ancient Sumerians buried their dead in the belief that they would be going on, or rather down, to the Netherworld, a world obviously in large measure comparable to that from which they had just departed.

2.   Their dead would need material possessions. The nature and content of the Royal Graves are, of course, wonderfully anomalous for the period, but the underlying belief pattern is conventional. There is no question that these buried objects could have been just for the pomp of burial, or the transience of the journey. Full baggage fitted them out with what they cherished when alive and would need in the world beyond, with leisure and scope for, so to speak, served afternoon tea and conversation.

3.   Those in charge during life clearly counted on retaining their previous social standing in the New World, requiring servants and staff quite as much as when they were alive.

4.   The servants, from the apparently peaceful way in which they were laid out, might seem to have accepted their fate, unless, as has periodically been suggested, they were drunk, drugged or poisoned; many a cup lay at hand. Later research on surviving skulls established that some of the males, whose skeletons showed signs of intense physical labour during their working lives and who were hardly effete courtiers of the Versailles type, had also had their heads bashed in from behind, which removes a portion of the easy romantic glamour that first seemed to swirl over the scene. Other bodies,

it is thought, might have undergone heat treatment to delay the onset of decay. Only a few were slim handmaidens attending the highest in the land, sporting wobbly floral headdresses that today make such glorious museum exhibits and party wear.

The 'dead-retainer' procedure as exemplified at Ur was a surprise at its discovery and it still takes a bit of swallowing today. It seems, as one might say, a 'funny thing for Sumerians to do', for otherwise we do not encounter counter-intuitive, 'primitive' Sumerian phenomena, and this kind of sacrificial burial is rare in general. It is significant that in the great sweep of ancient Mesopotamian archaeology, no comparable retainer graves have been found prior to those, or after those, of the Ur cemetery. On present evidence the idea seems to have started up at Ur at one point, and stopped abruptly at Ur at another, never to resurface again in the Land-between-the-Rivers. Some exceptional stimulus must have begun it all, even if it were only plain common sense or social outrage that brought it to a close.

Here, the tantalising Sumerian account we call *The Death of Gilgamesh* sheds light on the question. Gilgamesh, king of the city of Uruk at the start of the third millennium bc, was the ancient Mesopotamian all-time national hero, as we will see. The most famous cuneiform literature of all, the *Epic of Gilgamesh*, recounts his adventures during life, and it is not surprising that the storytelling tradition had something to say about his death too. The *Death of Gilgamesh* tablets that we have, all incompletely preserved, date from about 1800 bc, although the text was likely composed for the Ur III-period court in the city of Ur in about 2050 bc. They preserve the memory of Gilgamesh's funeral some eight hundred years earlier, and the tablet versions incorporate certain interesting variants. In one, the great king was buried in a stone tomb under the River Euphrates; another, recovered from the site of Nippur, describes a scene more than reminiscent of that which was to greet Sir Leonard Woolley under the earth of Ur:

> *His beloved wife, his beloved children, his beloved favourite*
> *and junior wife, his beloved musician, cup-bearer and . . . his*
> *beloved barber, his beloved . . . his beloved palace retainers and*
> *servants and his beloved objects were laid down in their places*
> *as if . . . in the purified palace in the middle of Uruk.*

There were audience gifts for the Netherworld queen Ereshkigal and her spouse Nergal, and surprises for the other gods and goddesses that the dead king would meet, or for dead priests and priestesses, who carried out their former functions below. It seems quite artificial to dissociate this written narrative from the archaeological reality uncovered in the cemetery at Ur, and the connection between them has often been made, but beyond that an explanation can be offered to make sense of it all. Gilgamesh the Great, it seems to me, must have been a ruler and leader in the Alexander the Great mould, matching in that, with both, their lifelong charisma survived their death; which, for the survivors in each case, was intolerable. We might well imagine that his followers would prefer to take drastic steps rather than continue without him, meaning that the burial scene described in the Sumerian text echoed historical reality. Perhaps the burial of conveniently dead or specially despatched retainers was already a deep-seated tradition among the kings of Uruk; but more likely, perhaps, it originated at the very demise of Gilgamesh himself. The tombs of the ancient kings at Uruk, where one would look for a similar tradition, must be buried at the deepest, sub-aqua level. One might fancy that the funerary tradition persisted at Uruk in the case of inevitably lesser dynastic successors. At any rate, all would become explicable if, for example, a prince of the house of Ur had married an Uruk princess, who imported what might have seemed an alien practice into her father-in-law's demesne, where it held sway for a period, ultimately to be terminated for good.

Neighbouring Egyptians, one might reflect, had practised a similar kind of retainer sacrifice during their own First Dynasty at the turn of the fourth millennium bc, but by the time of the Ur cemetery the whole idea had long been abandoned along the Nile, where real humans were sensibly replaced by *ushabti*s. These little mummy-like figurines accompanied the dead by the boxful and were available to work on irrigating the fields beyond for which the deceased might otherwise, once in the world to come, find themselves responsible.

Ur-Namma, King of Ur

Some five hundred years after the Royal Graves, King Ur-Namma, founder of the great Sumerian dynasty at the same city of Ur, architect and judiciary, went to his eternal rest, after eighteen years of rule (2112–2095 bc). The Sumerian composition known today merely as *Urnamma A*, 242 lines in length, describes the king's lamented decline, death and burial, and the mourning that followed. As the end of his life approached, Ur-Namma was likened by the poet to a boat in a storm, a curious echo of the image in Sumerian birth incantations of the unborn baby drifting as a loaded vessel in its mother's womb, seeking to come to harbour. A hazardous journey by chariot was to take the dead king to the Gates of the Netherworld; the royal chariot, in other words, with its donkeys, was buried with him. The roads, says the text, were twisted and they could not hurry, but when Ur-Namma arrived he was met by a tumultuous welcome and a banquet. We see that, in parallel with Gilgamesh long before, he too makes offerings to the gods of the Netherworld, as well as to the seven Chief Doorkeepers and famous dead kings who were already there, while the resident deceased priests and priestesses (originally appointed by omens taken from the liver), told everyone that King Ur-Namma had arrived, and 'the people became tumultuous in the Netherworld'. The king himself acted as host, slaughtering bulls and sheep, for, as he said, 'the food in the Netherworld is bitter and the drink of the Netherworld is salty'; Ur-Namma had evidently known full well what was to be expected once installed in the Netherworld. So, he offered his sacrifices, handing out expensive presents to the important gods who seem to have been clustered around him, including the Netherworld's Queen Ereshkigal herself – a mace, a large bow with quiver and arrows, a multi-coloured leather bag, weapons and more – a generous and open-handed new resident. In this way the narrative details the funerary goods that were buried with the king, and shows that they were not only for his own use but on arrival served as his entrance ticket. Fat animal offerings were diplomatically presented to the Anunna Netherworld gods. This promptly led to their seating Ur-Namma on the Great Dais of the Netherworld and establishing a dwelling-place for him. Henceforth he was to be Judge with his beloved 'brother' Gilgamesh, dealing first off with cases concerning traitors and deserters. A highly satisfactory end to a distinguished mortal career, we might say. Meanwhile, we are told at length, the mourning back at Ur in Sumer continued among the living.

This literary description of Ur-Namma's obsequies thus overlaps suggestively with the Gilgamesh burial account. While chariot burials are known, they are hardly a common phenomenon in the ancient Middle East. One might wonder, in view of this text, whether knowledge or memory of the old royal burials at Ur might not have persisted locally from all that time before, be it in written form or in folk memory. Burying royalty with such riches surrounded by their dead retainers was hardly an operation to be carried out with alacrity or in secrecy. The personal impact of the burials on those who knew of it, or even the people who were interred, must have been substantial, and the subject of stories and speculations thereafter. Locals knew, for sure, where the burial site was located. Woolley thought that graves that were found in chaotic condition had, in fact, been robbed. Who would rob them but individuals who lived in or around Ur? Perhaps those original robbers found a chariot burial together with many bodies like those that met Woolley's team – a discovery that would startle and resonate in Ur long thereafter, with input into developing literature coming to influence, perhaps, how a king in Ur-Namma's time should be properly buried. We are lucky to be able to follow the shade of Ur-Namma into the Netherworld as he met the assembled spectral population; later, we will observe his ghost in action more closely and put two and two together.

The Moment of Death

We can inspect different funereal writings in Sumerian that draw us in closer, even allowing us to peer in at the moment of death. One, dating to about 1900 bc, is written not in standard Sumerian but in the Emesal dialect that is reserved for women and goddesses; the scribe who wrote the tablet included one or two helpful Akkadian translations for the benefit of struggling readers (including us). The god Ashgi lies dead before his sister Egime and it is up to her to deal with everything. Most importantly, she is to declare aloud the formal utterance, *His wind has blown away*, to signify that he is dead.

The poet uses the normal Sumerian word for the wind of nature in referring to the very last breath in the body, exhaled with an audible sigh or rattle, leaving the body dead. The process is that of a modern GP checking the pulse in the neck or holding a mirror to the nostrils and pronouncing that it is all over. What is especially interesting in this early Sumerian tradition is the idea that the *eṭemmu*, the dead person's ghost, remains trapped in the body until released by formula and ritual. Crucial, then, is that suspended interval of time between the moment of death and the point when the dead person's ghost is freed and despatched to the Netherworld.

On the death of her brother, Egime is to fetch a bed and a chair, together with a small, specially made statue. A garment is laid on the chair; the statue is covered. Egime rubs the figure with bread and pours water into the libation pipe, for they are before the grave, and bread and water represent the first funerary offerings that will thereafter be owed to the deceased. The dead

Ashgi is now renamed Lulil, meaning literally *spirit-man*.

This same last-breath idea underpins the Sumerian literary composition sometimes entitled *The Traveller and the Maiden*. The maiden's beloved is dead, and this is how she acts:

> *I dipped bread and wiped him with it;*
> *From a covered bowl that had never been untied,*
> *From a bucket whose rim was unannealed,*
> *I poured out water; the ground drank it up.*
> *I anointed his body with my sweet-smelling oil,*
> *I wrapped up the chair with my new cloth,*
> *Wind had entered him; the wind came out.*
> *My wanderer from the mountains,*
> *henceforth must he lie in the Mountain (the Netherworld).*

Both passages emphasise the three ritual components needed that will enable the ghost to be seen off by means of the liberating pronouncement:

1. A clay effigy of the deceased. This was oiled and dressed and imbued with the identity of the departed, and could or would be symbolically maintained within the family dwelling to provide a focus for remembering them and maintaining their presence within the family.
2. The special chair for the ghost.
3. Grave goods. These consist of what the deceased would need for the journey and when he arrived. The emphasis is on providing food and drink. Once in the Netherworld the sustenance available to the ghosts was, according to some authorities, inferior, and there is no doubt that the persistent emphasis on these offerings reflects sympathetic awareness of this situation.

Contemporary Funeral Administration

The wind ~ spirit (Sumerian im ~ gedim) interplay that comes through from these poems also underpins high-level Sumerian funerary administrative documents from the same time period. Animals for the dead Princess Tezen-mama, period of Shu-Su'en, fourth king of Ur (2037–2028 bc), include one sheep for when the 'wind of Tezen-mama was seized', that is, when she died; eight whole days later, a goat and sheep were listed for the ghost's 'wooden altar' for the performance when the ghost was finally freed to descend to the Netherworld.

Similar account texts cover funeral operations for King Shu-Su'en himself. Animals were offered by boat to several Netherworld gods who recur later in this book, Ninazu, Ereshkigal, Ninshubur and Ningishzida; then more offerings at the great gate of the moon god Nanna; the great gate of the king and of the throne; the gates of the thrones of the earlier Ur kings Shulgi and Amar-Su'en. The whole procedure involves four rituals, in which sacrifices for the gates prepared the way for the king's burial and his entrance into the Netherworld. The successive wooden altars used for the ritual offerings are explicitly labelled, first for the 'breath-ghost', then for the 'seated ghost', then for the ghost itself and finally for ghosts going down or up. This royal ghost, in other words, is tied at first to the body by the last breath; then is seated in the ghost-chair; then is free to go down to the Netherworld. One month after the burial, further offerings are made by his successor, Ibbi-Su'en, to Netherworld gods, and to the late Shu-Su'en himself, at the Shulgi Gate and his own Shu-Su'en Gate, and offerings also at the main Ganzer Gate. There is much attention paid along the way, incidentally, to the long-dead kings of the dynasty.

The traditional system here functioned to ensure the effective passage of a dead person's *eṭemmu*-ghost into the Netherworld: confident in its send-off, secure that needed offerings will follow, and relaxed in that it will never be forgotten.

Fear of Premature Burial Four Thousand Years Ago

As I see it, this careful, ready-for-burial and slightly curious Sumerian ritual of around 2000 bc ultimately reflects the wide-spread and enduring human phobia about being buried alive, and is, very probably, the earliest historical example of it. How otherwise can the long-drawn-out, two-part operation be explained? The same underlying fear of vivisepulture surfaces in Mesopotamia in a seventh-century-bc Assyrian omen, one of a group of ominous predictions that follow a person's seeing a ghost: *If a dead man in his grave comes back to life with people nearby, that city will* . . . I suggest that this identity-aware, analytical thinking about the nature of death and the difference between the corpse and the ghost originated in a remembered horror-laden case when some individual in Sumerian memory had been buried – or almost buried – when not actually dead. Furthermore, the delicate interplay between last-ditch breath and ghost-release that we meet in these passages seems to embody the thinking of Sumerians, for it did not pass into general understanding in later Mesopotamian society: there is no take-up of such ideas in the Akkadian ghost materials sampled in the following chapters. There is, likewise, no mention in later texts of preserving a moulded figure of a deceased family member in the house, although such a tradition would hardly be surprising; we ourselves keep old photographs on a dresser for much the same reason.

The Dead, the Ghost and the Sun God Shamash

One of the characteristic techniques in first-millennium Akkadian banishing magic is to list the types of ghosts that might be causing trouble among the populace in order to pin down the guilty party. An early spell, the *Incantation to Utu*, includes a list of this kind from the second millennium bc, and, like the works we have already examined, is also written in Sumerian. Venerated by the Sumerians under the name of Utu and by the Babylonians as

Shamash, the sun god played an increasingly pivotal role in the world of the dead and their ghosts. In this composition his activities concerning the latter-day fate of the dead are laid out more clearly than can usually be pieced together from later texts and it sets the scene well for us in its covering of ghostly issues.

A long invocation to Utu, laden with epithets, highlights human inability to exist without the sun god. The officiating incantation priest then serves flour and water to Utu, whose divine attendants, the judges, attend to introduce the dead person who is about to face justice. A gracious speech is addressed to Utu, who, we learn, rides four lions across the sky and four across the seas.

The crucial point explicit in this composition is that the ghost's individual case must be decided by Utu. If the proceedings go well, peaceful transition to the Netherworld will follow, and there will be no trouble thereafter for the living. Ghosts, however, cannot receive nourishment until after they have left their bodies, so the offerings must be attended to at the correct moment. The judgement faced by a dead person is referred to in Sumerian as 'the day of the lot of mankind'. An incantation priest is needed to conduct the procedure and address the ghosts on behalf of Utu, for he cannot defend himself.

> Utu, behold . . . Utu, let me speak a word to you: to my word, your ear! Let me go for judgement, may you pay attention to it! Words from heaven reach earth, words from earth reach heaven;
> The word of the living man is precious to the dead man, the word of the dead man is precious to the living man . . .

The dead, from this standpoint, are divided into three categories:

CATEGORY I
The good man, whose name and funeral cult are to be respectfully maintained in perpetuity, as his family well knows. His ghost is

served with food within the family house, which is where the dead body has been laid to rest (see also Chapter 4). Utu is then addressed, and the ghost, like a 'good family ghost', attended to:

> *The rites are set up for him in his grave. On the day of the dark moon, the day of funeral offerings, bread is placed for him, radiance is there . . . in the Netherworld. Through his large libation pipe, honey, beer and fine butter is poured down into it. All the time he is held in respect, let his name be pronounced.*
>
> *On the day he should be present for the sweet things, Any Evil-Doing entity should not be present. The living man shall be present in front of you. The dead man must not be discouraged, must not lose heart, his heart afflicted by evil should not be carried to . . . May Utu absolve his sin, may Utu undo it in front of you. A sin that has not been revoked, a destructive curse that has not been undone . . .*

CATEGORY 2

The man who had committed some unspecified sacrilege with regard to his son. His ghostly progress is held up for judgement and, meanwhile, his ghost can become troublesome:

> *This person, son of his personal god, he whose judgement has not been passed, whose case has not been decided, is a ghost who frightens people in dreams, is a ghost who works evil against men from a place of murder, turning the living man into the ghost of a dead man.*
>
> *Family ghost roaming about at the outskirts of the city, where you receive your verdict, body of a ghost lying in the Netherworld, speak up! Be it a ghost wandering about in the Netherworld, let the family ghost go, let honey and butter be cut off!*
>
> *If it is a hostile ghost that has not been released. As long as you have not been taken away from your body, as long as you*

*have not been removed from your body, and if the ghost is like
a good family ghost, let food be cut off! Let water be cut off!
Let water be cut off from his water pipe!*

Reflected here is an annual celebration of the family's relations
with their dead, conducted within the family house. Undecided
cases were presumably those who had died in the interim and
had to wait. Such a Category 2 man will be absolved in due
course of his wrongdoing towards his son and receive his funeral
offerings:

*The dead man who committed sacrilege to his son, on that day
his sin should be absolved before Utu. Let the dead man eat in
front of his house, let him drink in front of his house, let him
sleep in the shade of his house. May his son pour water into
the sacred pipe for him, may he place food on his grave, may
he pour water into his grave.*

CATEGORY 3

The man who, in doing evil to his son – we get no details – trans-
gressed some limit ordained by the gods. His name should be
obliterated forever and he be a restless ghost for all time to come:

*After he has overstepped the borders of the gods . . . To pass
judgement on that man, let it be in your mind! Let food be cut
off from him, let water be cut off from him! Let no libation
water be poured into his large libation pipe. Do not let the
body of the family ghost be approached, let it roam about. Let
the Anunna-gods wipe out his name.*

After this gruesome verdict comes the crucial list of the kinds
of ghosts who also face eternal punishment. The idea, and its
detailed breakdown of the ranks of miserable ghosts, was very
persistent. These are the sort of marauding, troublesome characters faced by the Mesopotamian ghost specialist:

> *Be it a ghost roaming about in the Netherworld . . . or an evil*
> *ghost, or an evil god, or evil Lamashtu or a girl caught by a*
> *storm, or a ghost who has no one to take care of him, or a*
> *ghost who has neither father nor mother, or a ghost who has*
> *no one to invoke his name, or a ghost who has no one to pour*
> *water for him, or a wind-man who had no spouse, or a girl*
> *who had neither husband nor child, or a man whose name was*
> *destroyed in the steppe, or a man born on the plain, or a man*
> *whose name was destroyed on the plain, or someone not covered*
> *by a grave, or a hostile ghost roaming about . . .*

The rather-easy-to-visualise 'Let-me-enter-and . . .' ghosts that
follow, who obviously trade on people's good nature to sponge
off them, do *not* in contrast seem to crop up later:

> *Be it a 'Let-me-enter' . . .*
> *Be it a 'Let-me-enter, let me eat with you'*
> *Be it a 'Let-me-enter, let me drink with you'*
> *Be it an 'I am hungry, let me eat with you'*
> *Be it an 'I am thirsty, let me drink beer /pour water with you'*
> *Be it an 'I am freezing, let me get dressed with you'.*

Lastly, the text beseeches Utu to, as it were, *hurry up*, so that
the great gods can engineer the safe passage of the ghost who
has successfully passed judgement:

> *After Ningishzida, Throne Bearer of the Netherworld, has let*
> *him pass, after the hand of Biti [Neti], Doorkeeper of the*
> *Netherworld, has seized him, Biti, Doorkeeper of the*
> *Netherworld, makes him enter the multitude of those taken*
> *care of . . .*

He has arrived in the Land-of-Non-Return.
Three types of Mesopotamian man are judged shortly after
death by Utu with regard to their significant post-mortem future,

for a great deal is at stake. It is a very localised kind of judgement. Importantly, the sun god's verdict does not evaluate a man's morals as had been exhibited throughout his life in general, nor does it ordain a suitable Netherworld fate on the basis of past deeds and misdeeds. Underpinning the system is the importance of the right behaviour between father and son, binding family structure and cohesiveness, the Sumerian line, strong from remote times, stretching into the future.

It will have been observed that offerings to the family dead by the living are a concern in all the passages quoted so far, and they are a constant preoccupation of cuneiform ghost literature. Post-mortem care in terms of food and drink was undoubtedly already a very ancient and deeply established social system by the time this Utu composition was written, around 1800 bc, and it remained entrenched in family life until the end of the cuneiform period.

Royal Ghosts

Although royal graves are not common in Mesopotamian archaeology, we can complete this chapter with the help of three dead Assyrian queens and one dead Assyrian king, whose ghosts had special status in the Netherworld. The queenly graves were discovered some years ago by Iraqi archaeologists at the sister capital site of Nimrud in the north of Iraq, the splendour of which, as earlier with the finds from Ur, hit the media. Here, too, there was a sumptuous abundance of gold, precious metals and jewellery. Buried in a communal crypt under a vaulted complex and below the harem area of the North-West Palace lay the partly disturbed dead queens Yabâ, wife of Tiglath-Pileser III (744–727 bc), Banītu, wife of Shalmaneser V, and Ataliya, wife of Sargon II (722–705 bc). An archaeological dream. Amy Gansell, in her study of these queens' graves, suggested that the lavish quantities of jewellery might have included gifts to smooth the royal ghost's passage into the world to come:

Shafts in the floors of separate rooms provided access to the queens' vaulted mudbrick tombs. Each shaft gave way to stairs that led to an ante-room, which was blocked off from the chamber that held the sarcophagus. The primary function of the tombs was to shelter the dead, but the tombs also served as social and ritual sites, beginning with the event of the funeral. Evincing ritual activity, niches in the walls variously held lamps, vessels, and cuneiform tablets naming the dead and threatening intruders . . .

and summarises her analysis of the finds:

Whether as a corpse at the funeral, a denizen of the netherworld, or possibly a ghost among the living, the women buried in the Queens' Tombs were eternally dressed for engagement with the living (including us), the dead, and the divine.

A forbidding curse statement protected Queen Yabâ in her unknown future. It was deeply inscribed on a tablet of stone set in a niche in the right-hand wall of the space leading to the burial chamber of her tomb:

At the command of Shamash, Ereshkigal and the Anunnaki, great gods of the Netherworld, mortal destiny caught up with Queen Yabâ in death, and she travelled the path of her ancestors. Anyone, in time to come, whether a queen who sits on the throne or a palace lady of the Palace who is a royal favourite, who removes me from my tomb, or places anybody else with me, or lays his hand on my jewellery with evil intent or breaks open the seal of this tomb: Above, beneath the rays of the sun, may his spirit roam abroad in thirst. Below he is not to receive, with the Anunnaki, any offering of libation of water, beer, wine or meal, but rather may Ningishzida and Chief Doorkeeper Biduh [Nedu], great gods of the Netherworld, inflict his corpse and spirit (ziqīqu) with eternal restlessness.

Forensic evidence suggested that Queen Atalia's body, as apparently earlier with certain of the bodies from the Ur cemetery, had been subjected to post-mortem heating, thought by scientists to be in the attempt to delay decay; if, for example, the queen had died some distance away from the capital and her body had to be brought there. Queens, it seems, while buried together, were kept separate from their kings.

In conclusion, we can also look in at the climax of the seventh-century interment of an Assyrian king himself at Nineveh, probably King Esarhaddon (681–669 bc), Ashurbanipal's father. The tablet with the narrative is still incomplete despite several joined-on helpful fragments. The account gives us no hint of state religious procedure, mourning ceremonies, processions or organised outpourings of grief that must have gone on during the days running up to the burial itself, which is here reported for us as laconically as by a journalist. It contains part of what must have been a heavily significant poetic lament, followed by lists of grave goods acknowledging the donor or donors, and then a description of the laying-to-rest ritual. The fragmented lament, which was doubtless accompanied by private and professional wailing and trumpets, begins as follows:

The ditches wailed, the canals replying in kind; all trees and fruit turned dark-faced (in mourning). Sparrows wept, insects from the grass . . . exalted . . . the thresholds . . . sighed . . . wailed . . .

The grave goods presented are carefully documented. Those received from the king of Akkad, for example, included a bed, chest and chair inlaid with ivory and silver with sceptre to match, gold and silver cups and drinking bowls; as well as ten horses, thirty oxen and three hundred sheep. Other donations included a statue, a gold Elamite mitre, state robes and garments, a gold-fitted chariot and an umbrella, many more sceptres, weapons, cloaks, and leggings and shoes.

And then come these concluding lines:

I gently laid Father, my begetter, inside that tomb, the secret place, in royal oil. I sealed the opening to the stone coffin, his resting place, with strong copper and reinforced it with a clay sealing.

I made a display before Shamash (the sun god) of the gold and silver paraphernalia proper for a tomb, the symbols of his sovereignty that he loved, and then placed them with Father, my begetter, in the tomb. I offered gifts to the (deceased) Kings, the Anunnaki (Judges) and the gods who inhabit the Netherworld.

Protocol surely dictated who presented goods at such a time, who was expected to, who was allowed to and who would not have dared. One can only imagine what would greet the fortunate archaeologist who discovered an Assyrian royal tomb such as that of the Assyrian king Esarhaddon.

4

Everyday Houses, Burials and Ghosts

Moderate lamentation is the right of the dead,
excessive grief the enemy to the living . . .
                              All's Well that Ends Well,
                                        Act 1, Scene 1

Ghosts, of course, were not the prerogative of human beings royal or rich. In writing this book, the greatest reward has come in following the ghost lives of the humbler inhabitants of ancient Mesopotamia, as far as possible the normal townsfolk. For them, ghosts of the dead were part of life, and to set the scene we must consider the houses of the living as well as the graves of the departed, for the two are closely intertwined.

With everyday graves there are both inhumations and cremations, and burial took place both within private houses and outside, seldom in cemeteries. What is essentially Mesopotamian from our point of view is that family dead were often laid to rest within and below the living quarters. This meant that graves were accessible from above, if need be, for refills. In addition, and more importantly for our purposes, family ghosts, if they returned, would often not stray far from familiar territory and have easy access to their quarry. Ghosts were never far away, in other words. Incantations highlight the vulnerable domestic spots where unwanted visitors lurk, such as the household shrine, house corners and niches, thresholds, and the gate. That the family ghosts who come into focus through this literature seem to be disconcertingly nearby and able to 'pop up' whenever they feel the urge is a direct consequence of two interwoven factors: burial and housing.

Ghosts and the Matter of Housing

With ghosts in mind, therefore, let us look over two examples of what estate agents call 'desirable family houses', for these are where *spectral visitors* were often to be encountered and what sometimes turned into a battlefield.

I. AN EXTENDED OLD BABYLONIAN PROPERTY: PERIOD OF KING HAMMURABI

During the Old Babylonian period, around 1700 bc, both 'linear' and 'square' houses' were in use, the former with rooms on two or three sides of a courtyard, or even without a courtyard, the latter with rooms on all four sides. Archaeological evidence, complemented by written cuneiform from the city of Nippur in the south, suggests that linear houses were for the nuclear, five-individual family, while square houses reflected extended families, although in real life all sorts of individual situations must have been normal. The house plan drawn on a tablet of this period illustrates this lucidly; two linear houses, each with three or four rooms, are combined into a single dwelling with four rows of rooms.

Left: British Museum 86394, Old Babylonian house innovation planned on a clay tablet. Two linear houses enterprisingly combined into one larger property.

Right: Neo-Babylonian house plan from the Merkes quarter at Babylon. After Baker 2014: 15.

2. A NEO-*BABYLONIAN* FAMILY ESTATE HOUSE: PERIOD OF KING NEBUCHADNEZZAR II

This is a typical sixth-century-bc house plan from the city of Babylon, roughly contemporaneous with most of the cuneiform writings about ghosts discussed in this book. It exemplifies a very practical, timeless housing solution, encountered all over the Middle Eastern and Mediterranean worlds in general. The central courtyard is called the *tarbaṣu* in Akkadian, literally 'animal pen', enclosed on all four sides by suites of rooms that, in contemporary legal documents dealing with house sales and alterations, are referred to – rather disconcertingly – as 'north-facing', 'east-facing', and so forth. Access from the outside was by a single entrance, and, as is clear from the plan, privacy was ensured in that no passer-by could see into the interior. Use of rooms in such a Babylonian domestic dwelling can be understood thanks to several scholars who have worked to combine archaeological with written evidence. So, in this house plan, the small west-facing room is probably the kitchen, with the head of the household – or the inheriting older son – installed in the suite of north-facing rooms. Younger brothers would be given the south-facing and east-facing rooms.

We can visualise such a house normally populated by a nuclear three-child family, extended by, at least, unmarried sisters, the widowed mother, and, in wealthy families, slaves. The prevailing system was *virilocal*, meaning that sons ordinarily moved out of their father's house to set up their own households. The oldest son would receive a double share of the inheritance that came to the other children and would thenceforth often reside in his father's house, but it is clear that all efforts were made to retain property within the broader family, and some wealthy families had many houses. Extensions or re-designs of layout are mentioned in cuneiform sale or administrative documents. A larger household that had to accommodate three brothers and their families might easily mean more than fifteen individuals, in any number of local arrangements, but it is helpful to have such a picture in mind when we consider that it is just these individuals, close knit and interconnected, who had to put up with ghosts, and ultimately became ghosts themselves.

Types of Mesopotamian Burial

Burial was not always under the floor. Broadly speaking, there are seven basic types of burial found in Mesopotamia, distributed in great variety over millennia of archaeological sites:

1. Burial within a wall: specifically infants and children.
2. Earth or pit burial: the body wrapped in a reed mat in a pit dug under the floor.
3. Shaft grave: shafts often led to pit graves, or a sarcophagus or a chamber.
4. Jar or double jar burial: one corpse could be buried in a large and lidded, sealed jar, sometimes of domestic type, others specially made. Two jars joined at the mouth are found; it is a question whether such individuals will have died together if they are buried in such a way.
5. Sherd grave: the interred body is covered with a blanket of broken pieces of pottery.
6. Sarcophagus: a Mesopotamian sarcophagus would usually be made of ceramic, and covered over. A characteristic shape is that of the bathtub, with which specimens have occasionally been confused in the past.
7. Specific structures: stone or brick cists beneath the ground, or visible chambers of brick.

The commonest form of burial was to inter the corpse, wrapped in a reed mat beneath the floor, in a simple pit. The more lasting or complicated types of graves such as shaft graves, cists or chambers involved more or less elaborate construction. When family dead were buried under the courtyard floor, the same subterranean chamber could be reused, but the dead might be buried elsewhere for a variety of reasons, including, for example, disease or space. The number of bodies found in such graves shows that not all members of an extended family could or would necessarily be interred there. Sons who moved away would, of course, make arrangement for burials within their own house.

Burial Goods in Graves

Throughout the millennia of Mesopotamian archaeology, as is elsewhere equally the case, the dead were seldom buried without some artefact or another, whatever the form or however humble a tomb. Grave goods buried with the dead embody and encapsulate the understanding that passage to the afterlife follows death, and that the deceased should be equipped with materials from their day-to-day existence in the expectation that they would be needing or enjoying them in their new circumstances.

In certain cases, quite different explanations for excavated grave goods have seemed plausible; items needed in graveside or funerary ritual, or for a send-off banquet meal, or vessels and objects with ritual properties that could not otherwise be thrown away, or even objects that had been contaminated by the dying or dead. In other cases, abundant or outstanding riches, or part of them, have, as we have seen, been considered as tactful gifts for the Netherworld reception committee to secure better facilities on arrival, while plenteous female jewellery in male graves is sometimes interpreted as gifts for goddesses. Such explanations (and others, too) may well be appropriate in certain cases, but can never affect our understanding of the general burial rule; the principle that humanity's grave goods were needed for the next world, where they were all going, is, as I see it, irrefutable.

In this book, the issue has a peculiar vitality. The provision of pots, tools and objects implies that the next world will substantially resemble ours, with the added dimension that pleasure and leisure are often reflected as well as work and labour. What lies ahead, in other words, should, on arrival, be largely familiar, a pale imitation, perhaps with many unknowns; but with downs and ups and all the other qualities familiar to the human being ahead. This is what archaeology suggests, and what Caitlín Barrett calls, in her very informative and important survey *Was Dust Their Food and Clay Their Bread*, the 'pleasant afterlife'. There is no written message to support this conclusion directly, but the verdict is no less convincing for that: it derives directly from what ancient Mesopotamian persons literally took with them. This, as a working understanding of so important an aspect of human belief, is both credible and, as it were, satisfactory. The whole matter will have to be reconsidered later, admittedly, when we come to the description of the *Land-of-no-Return*, and the accounts of those visitors, far and few, who visited it and came back.

On the basis of myriad excavated Mesopotamian graves, we can itemise the basic range of goods recommended for adult burials:

Pottery with or without food
Vessels of stone or metal
Tools or tool models
Weapons
Jewellery
Seals
Figurines
Amulets

While conditions for survival are often unfavourable in ancient Middle Eastern archaeology, this is equally true of the southern Levant, but excavations at Jericho conducted by Kathleen Kenyon in the early 1950s uncovered a particular Middle Bronze Age tomb (Tomb B35, about 1750–1550 bc). Although organic materials also usually decompose in the humid burial conditions of the southern Levant, here such materials had survived in remarkable condition thanks to the tomb's abnormal anaerobic environment. Once unsealed, the tomb revealed wooden furniture including tables and stools, wooden bowls, cups, buttons and combs; reed baskets containing desiccated fruit, seeds and grains; and even a low wooden table on which baskets of food and joints of meat had been left as offerings for the dead. A watercolour drawing made for the dig publication reconstructs an interior domestic view on the basis of the finds, which, in turn, rather ironically, gives a good picture of the grave goods as they were discovered.

Middle Bronze Age House at Jericho, reconstructed after the grave goods in Tomb B35. As it was in life, so after death . . .

Grave goods across time and geography are naturally uneven both in quantity and quality, and the dead might often end up with the bare minimum for the simple reason that useful or precious things could not be so readily spared by the living. In truly élite graves, such as those in the Royal Cemetery at Ur in the previous chapter, ultra-luxurious materials reveal the intention to recreate familiar regal conditions with authority and power preserved, an inflated version of the general model, which is content enough with basic comforts and facilities.

Advice about Tomb-Building

In the end, of course, every mortal had to be laid to rest. For the ancient Mesopotamian – as for all mortals – burial activity was hedged around with emotion, uncertainty and apprehension.

Family tombs would need to be constructed, extended or rebuilt, and important points arising therefrom had to be taken into consideration. Chief among these was the day or time when funereal undertakings should best be instituted. This was not a matter for guesswork or just hoping for the best; there were experts available who could offer seasoned advice, and their expertise derived from their collections of fortune-telling *omens*.

Omens are a primary Mesopotamian phenomenon, an essential hallmark of cuneiform culture and thinking. The omen is a closely structured, one-line framework for prediction on the basis of recorded experience; for noticing, classifying and recording of ominous observations in Mesopotamian society was practically tantamount to a science. Omens take the following format: *If A happens or is observed, B is or might be the consequence.* The system was predicated on a deep, cosmic cause-and-effect and repeat-of-history balance working behind the scenes of the Mesopotamian universe. Babylonians and Assyrians knew of many ways to tell the future; some simple, others complicated; some accidental and others engineered. Divination was man's fallback intellectual approach for determining what would happen in the world, and collected omens of many types juxtapose long-accumulated signs, events or occurrences from the past with their likely outcome in the living present. We are beyond grateful to have inherited thousands of lines of cuneiform omens, the tablets neatly written out and numbered sequentially into highly practical divination reference manuals, each omen beginning with the crucial word 'If'.

This raises an oddly beguiling point: ancient Mesopotamian librarians responsible for cuneiform literature liked to consider, as one catch-all category, *omens* ('*If* such-and-such a thing happens . . .'); *law codes* ('*If* someone does such-and-such a wicked thing . . .'); and *medical texts* ('*If* a person suffers from such-and-such a condition . . .'). The result was referred to by cuneiform cognoscenti as *The IFs*. It is much as we might talk of 'Ifs and Buts'.

One-liner omens existed to cover not only building your tomb, but, as we will see in the following chapter, seeing your ghost.

Omens About Building a Tomb

The most extensive compilation of useful, everyday-type omens is called *If a City*, because the first line of its Tablet I begins with this thought-provoking statement: *If a city is located on a height, living in that city could be unpleasant.* Ghost matters come up in *If a City* Tablet XVI, and are exclusively preoccupied with the calendrical date. Thirteen omens cover constructing a grave within each given month of the year out of *thirteen* (including intercalation).

If a man builds a tomb in month:	Predicted consequence:
I	that man will not grow old
II	that man will die in his prime
III	his . . . will die: his house will be dispersed
IV	evil will be released from the man's body
V	evil/death will be regular in the man's house
VI	pilfering woman will remove the (household) *lamassu* (lucky) figure/end of days
VII	that man will not be buried in that tomb
VIII	the man's son will disperse his father's house
IX	he will see profit; someone will carry off his property
X	he will escape from hardship
XI	his god will build his house
XII	whatever he strives for, that man will achieve / he will become upset
XII/2	Ishtar's wrath will be released from him

If a City *Tablet XVI.*

Lines 16–45, thereafter, focus on the *day of the week*:

If a man builds a tomb in any month of the year on day:	Predicted consequence:
1	that man's days will be short/long
2	he will die in his prime
3	his son will die
4	there will be an order of a prominent person against him
5	he will not be buried; he will not return from a journey he takes
6	there will be divine terror/divine mercy for the man
7	the hand of a god will affect that man
8	the punishment of his god will be released from him
9	his adversary will be overcome/will overcome him
10	he will fall in an unknown place
11	he will not be buried inside it
12	Ishtar will harass him in his prime
13	a son will rebel against his father
14	the man will grow old
15	he will become ill with dropsy and will not be buried
16	that man will be put to death
17	he will be devastated in his prime

If a man builds a tomb in any month of the year on day:	Predicted consequence:
18	illness will seize him; that man will not be healthy
19	losses will be established for the man
20	lost brother / divine wrath; he will rebel
21	that man will rebel against his brother
22	the king will arrest that man
23	his prayer will be agreeable to the god
24	in his family a prominent man will harass him evilly / his family will change
25	he will not be healthy; that man will be devastated
26	his days will be long
27	an evil attendant spirit will approach the man
28	his wife will rebel against him
29	his days will be long; he will be buried in the tomb he built
30	that man will become poor

If a City *Tablet XVI*.

The drift of these omens, when you read them over thoughtfully, is really quite off-putting: a plan to build a tomb only looked good for *four out of thirteen* months and *three out of thirty* days, awkward when hoping for a propitious moment or if pushed for time. In fact, the whole matter is quite mysterious. If everyone believed that it was madness to build a family vault eight out of twelve months of the year, not to mention all but three days, the omens themselves would be redundant: the dictum need only be: if you are planning on excavating the cellar, do it only on the twenty-third, twenty-sixth or twenty-ninth of IV, XI, XII or XII/2. And everybody would be doing the same thing. The schemat, accordingly, can hardly be an inflexibly rigid framework. To this crucial point we will return.

May His Ghosts Drink Pure Water!

Only seldom do private cuneiform tomb inscriptions of any kind come to light to match that of a Nimrud queen. One complete example, which was found with a broken duplicate, dates to perhaps the eighteenth-century bc and is from southern Mesopotamia. The wording of this inscription reflects the writer's understandable apprehension about the future that would be meaningful to the future Babylonian to whom the appeal is made, and even today it is curiously affecting:

> *If ever,*
> *A long time from now,*
> *Far into future time,*
> *In the days to come,*
> *Anyone should find this tomb,*
> *May he not clear it away;*
> *May he restore it;*
> *May that man, who finds this,*
> *Not despise it;*
> *Rather he should say as follows:*
>   *'This tomb,*
>   *I shall certainly restore it.'*
> *May the favour he did*
> *be requited to him!*

Above, may his omens
Be propitious!
Below,
May his ghosts
Drink pure water!

This object was set up within the tomb, underground, rather than standing outside like a modern tombstone. It is unknown whether graves in Mesopotamian cemeteries had any kind of marker equivalent to our gravestones. We certainly do not find cuneiform *Here lies . . .* inscriptions that preserve a person's name. Domestic urban burials, though, unless in clearly delineated circumstances, could be lost to sight and would probably often be vulnerable to disturbance or disruption by later digging and building operations. This anxiety was compounded by permanent worry about the tranquil post-mortem existence of one's own family ghosts. A roughly contemporary tomb inscription of the same genre prefers bullying in preference to the soft, fellow-Babylonian style, threatening dire consequences to anyone who interferes with his grave:

[Whoever] opens this grave
and does not repair it for a long time,
May Anum, Enlil, and Ea destroy his seed!
May the Anunna (Netherworld) gods,
Below [. . .]

It seems only poetic justice that much of this over-aggressive warning has broken away. Safeguarding family tombs was important for many reasons, but ghosts with a sense of grievance might take umbrage at neglect.

5

Living with Ghosts

For night's swift dragons cut the clouds full fast
And yonder shines Aurora's harbinger;
At whose approach, ghosts, wandering here and
    there,
Troop home to churchyards: damned spirits all,
That in crossways and floods have burial
Already to their wormy beds are gone
                            A Midsummer Night's Dream,
                                            Act 3, Scene 2

Normal Life

Ghosts were just part of normal life in the Land-between-the-Rivers. As claimed at the beginning of this book, the picture presented by their cuneiform writings is that the Mesopotamian population did more than merely believe in them. Ghosts were taken entirely for granted as part of human life within the surrounding world. On top of that, Mesopotamian ghosts were, I think, to a considerable extent tolerated and even treated with sympathy, for many ghosts were literally familiar, and ghostly encounters did not necessarily add up to much. The grievance and resentment that characterised the worst kind of ghost, however, could easily develop into outright malice and the need for vengeance with unpleasant consequences for the victim. Only when things really got out of hand was it necessary to take steps. In extreme circumstances there were qualified professionals who had seen everything before and knew what to do.

Who Became a Ghost?

At any given moment, therefore, an *eṭemmu*-ghost could appear
to a Babylonian or Assyrian individual, busy about their daily
lives, thinking about altogether different things. What lent an
essential 'normality' to the matter was the understanding that
those who came back from the Netherworld *had their reason.*
There were two basic grounds for understandable restlessness in
a revenant: *ghost rights*, disregard of which always led to unhappy
or resentful ghosts, and *circumstances of death,* covering
unwished-for or sticky endings, which always left ghosts with an
unresolved problem. Troublesome spectral visitors thus constitute
two groups.

Mesopotamian spirits of the dead, confined to their
Netherworld, expected certain services from their living relatives
to sweeten their lot, for sustenance down below was, at least
officially, very basic. As we have seen, this traditional arrangement
was a well-established and deep-seated matter, and breakdowns
in the system brought about complaint in the shady person. The
fact that ghosts had their rights, tantamount to a contract, represents a peculiarly Babylonian system. Treating ancestors with
ritual and respect is central in the history of the world's ghost
systems, but the intense responsibility-bearing concentration
lavished on the matter in ancient Mesopotamia stands out as
another national first-ghost characteristic.

Troubled ghosts at the wrong end of premature, violent or
unresolved death, however, have close counterparts in the world
beyond Mesopotamia, near and far and thereafter. Any such
ghost harbours permanent resentment or jealousy and its behaviour towards the living, needful as it is of 'closure', is propelled
by a perpetual and insatiable sense of 'unfinished business' while
doomed for eternal time to walk the night. This state of affairs
seems to have driven troubled ghosts, who like to return to the
scene of the crime, ever since.

For the Mesopotamian in his ghost world, the crucial difference between *ghost rights* and *cause of death* is that something could be done only about the former.

A Ghost Magic Tablet

Now we are aware of this situation, let us jump right in with classic Mesopotamian ghost-trouble procedure. The clay document with this text in cuneiform is from the city of Assur, capital in the eighth century bc, and it sets the scene admirably. What had begun as unwelcome visitations and turned into persecution had ended up as a chronic problem with distinct medical symptoms:

> *If a ghost afflicts a man and lingers in his body and cannot be loosed: as the sun goes down you make an offering to Shamash; you call upon the ghosts of family and kin; you purify the place.*
>
> *In the morning you set up a reed altar before Shamash and put on it twelve small loaves and . . . bread. You pour out dates and flour. You set up a juniper censer. You set out some silver from a silversmith for Shamash. You make a funerary offering to the family ghosts. You raise up the . . . in your hand and before Shamash you recite as follows: '. . .' and you have him say as follows:*

In the background is one very restless and unsettled spectral personality who has been supposed to be safely down in the Netherworld. The victim has unsuccessfully tried certain tricks to get rid of the ghost as his suffering increases, and to compound his difficulties the ghost's identity is unknown. The sufferer therefore appeals to the sun god Shamash, in charge of justice, for the complaint is couched as if pleading before a magistrate, while, on top of that, during the night, Shamash is centrally placed with regard to administration of ghostly matters and knows all entrances and exits. The justice the sufferer seeks is liberation from his unwanted trouble. This dangerous ghost, moreover, malevolent enough in itself, is thought to have been *set on* his victim, raising the question of who in the background was behind such villainy. Shamash is 'technically' responsible for the ghost's escaping the Netherworld but hardly for inflicting it on an innocent person who should, in Mesopotamian terms, have been protected all along by his own personal deity.

The family ghosts here, well treated and in good shape down below, are clearly understood to be keeping an eye on things in the world above and can be recruited by their relatives as allies. Shamash's attention was usually preoccupied elsewhere in the world and he has to be attracted by a purification process with incense and offerings of bread, dates and flour. A handful of scrap silver as a heavenly bribe also helps. The main incantation details first the sufferer's quite grievous complaints and requests that the offerings made, with cool water, satisfy this ghost, who is understood to lack the attentions that all ghosts deserve, good and bad, even if he has other grounds for resentment:

> *Shamash, I cried out to you, listen to me!*
> *In your presence, let me live life to the full!*
> *A ghost smites me again and again; a ghost is making me ill;*
>   *a ghost afflicts me.*
> *A ghost continually pursues me; a ghost cannot be loosed*
>   *from my body.*
> *All my flesh hurts me, the muscles of my limbs are paralysed.*
> *They are constantly standing at my head. They constantly . . .*
>   *my . . . They hold hardship ready for me.*
> *A ghost was set on me so as to consume me. May he be*
>   *dispelled from my body and let me give him bread as a*
>   *funeral offering to eat, let me give him water as a funerary*
>   *offering to drink. Let me make a display for him.*
> *The ghost who was set on me so as to consume me, may he*
>   *be loosed from my body, may he be expelled and may he*

eat good things, may he drink good things, may he eat
small loaves, may he drink cold water . . .

Then comes the nub of the incantation, the roll-call of ghosts
who might have a plausible grievance, since the first step in driving
out the victim's ghost is to establish its identity and what might
have prompted its appearance. This enquiry, was, in fact, the
major responsibility for the diviner or exorcist, and dictated his
line of approach. This passage, with its characteristic ghost-list
form, is a direct descendant of the far older Sumerian Utu incantation quoted in the preceding chapter. As if to emphasise the
complications that faced him, the sufferer's symptoms might
equally be due to one or other demons, so their names are tacked
too, just in case:

Whether you be a strange ghost whose name nobody knows,
or a roving ghost,
or a roaming ghost,
or the ghost of someone who was abandoned in the steppe,
or the ghost of someone who drowned in water,
or a ghost of someone who drowned in a river,
or the ghost of someone who drowned in a well,
or the ghost of someone who died of hunger,
or a ghost of someone who died of thirst,
or the ghost of someone who died in a fire,
or the ghost of someone who died of a chill,
or the ghost of someone who died through a crime against a
  god,
or the ghost of someone who died through a crime against
  the king,
or the ghost of someone who was thrown in a dike or irriga-
  tion ditch,
or the ghost of someone who died being pursued,
or a . . . ghost or a murderous ghost,
or a ghost who has no one to pour water for him,

or a ghost who has no one to care for him . . .
Whether you be an evil ghost,
or an evil gallû-*demon,*
or an evil god,
or an evil rābiṣu-*demon,*
or Any Evil whatever, that has a name,
You shall not come near my body again. You are expelled and
    driven out.
Shamash!
May he be conjured away by you, may he be conjured away
    by Ea and Asalluḫi,
May he be conjured away by the great gods of Heaven and
    Underworld, not to approach my body again.

The long spell is recited three times and sealed with a water libation. The exorcist-scribe responsible for the composition then remarks that if the ghost 'cannot be dispelled' the recitation must be repeated another three times, followed by water-pouring out of a dog-skull. This suggests that some visible indication that the ghost had been dispelled was to be looked for, such as the liberated individual's standing up with a shout of joy, knowing himself cured, or perhaps something less spectacular was awaited:

He should speak this, three times.
He pours out a libation of water and then prostrates himself.
If the ghost who afflicts him cannot be dispelled you have
    him do it again three times.
The third time you have the patient lift up water in the skull
    of a dog before Shamash, and then he says as follows:
    'The ghost who afflicts me and cannot be dispelled from
    my body:
    I pour out a libation of water to him from the skull of a
    dog.'
He should pour out that water libation and that ghost will be
    kept away.

The list of usual suspects included in this magic spell reflects the two basic categories of ghosts mentioned above, and can be fleshed out with the help of similar contemporary spells, including the descriptions of ghosts in Tablet IV of the multi-tablet basic incantation work entitled *Evil Demons*. The end product is an insurance-company type of full-coverage ghost list.

Possible Ghosts to be Encountered

GROUP I: INDIVIDUALS UNHAPPY OR RESENTFUL
1. A ghost who rises up from the Netherworld

This sounds like a ghost who just came up and no one knows why.

2. A ghost who has no grave
3. An unburied ghost

Dying without a grave, accidentally or otherwise, was a terrible fate. It was a weapon in warfare and judgement, for no quietus was attainable. Hammurapi of Babylon, in the eighteenth century bc, threatens that the soldiers of any other king who does not follow his laws should be thrown on the plain in heaps and his troops denied burial. Other laws show that executed criminals were similarly treated.

4. A ghost who has no one to care for him
5. A ghost who has no one to take charge of him
6. A ghost who has no one to make a funerary offering
7. A ghost who gets no scrap of offering
8. A ghost who has no one to pour out a water libation
9. A ghost who gets no libation of water
10. A ghost who has no one to call him by name
11. A forgotten ghost

The explicit emphasis here as to post-mortem entitlements of the dead encapsulates the very serious social responsibility that fell to their living descendants. Details of what this involved follow.

12. The ghost of a relative
13. The ghost of a stranger

Within the complex of ghostly intercourse, individuals in ancient Mesopotamia differentiated on a deep level between family ghosts and those of strangers, as exactly as contrasted here. Familiar ghosts were those of the family itself, in the broadest sense, including cousins, second cousins, in-laws and out-laws. It is very probable that tribal allegiance underpinned this reality on an even broader level, for the ancient Semitic population of Babylonia assuredly retained such affiliation even though it surfaces infrequently in their documents. The distinction between familiar and unfamiliar ghosts is brought out very clearly in the many omens that predict the consequence of seeing a ghost. That familiar ghosts were seen to exist and interact with the living so intimately is, as discussed, a direct consequence of the twin subjects of housing and burial practice.

14. A persecuting ghost
15. A roaming ghost
16. A roving ghost

The contrast between delinquent ghosts 'roving', and 'roaming' could well be diagnostically significant, for a roving ghost, for example, might cause chronic pain in the cranium and temples; roaring in the ears; dryness of palate; numbness and the sensation of paralysis; continuous breast pain; shortness of breath and hair standing on end; attack by chills and numbness in the limbs; a crushing sensation in the chest; constant depression; raging hunger with inability to eat, and finally, vomiting day and night. It is probable in such diagnoses that no patient suffered all these symptoms together.

17. A runaway ghost
18. A ghost of an evil man
19. A murderous ghost

The last two types of individual, evil and murderous, are altogether bad news when alive, and those from whose ghosts the worst was to be expected. The range of ghostly personalities reflected in cuneiform writings matches those of the living, for living persons they once all were; some, therefore, are sad and ineffective, others needy, stubborn and wilful; while certain ghosts were mean, nasty, spiteful, dangerous or downright lethal. A Babylonian scribe once reflected that the ghost is the spitting image (*andunanu*) of the dead person, encapsulating a deep truth.

20. A ghost of a woman who died a virgin
21. A ghost of a boy not yet at puberty
22. A ghost of a man who died unmarried
23. A ghost of a hierodule sick of body
24. A ghost of a woman who died in childbirth
25. A ghost of a woman who died suckling her child
26. A ghost of a weeping woman who died suckling her child
27. A ghost of a wetnurse
28. A ghost of a wailing woman

The restless end of this sad group of women is a timeless theme.

Childbirth in antiquity was, as need hardly be stressed, hazardous, and the specialist she-demon Lamashtu, daughter of Anu (met briefly in Chapter 3), was always cruising, on the lookout for Mesopotamian women in travail or those with a new baby. Amulets and a magical ritual cycle with incantations were available to deter her dread attentions and safeguard women at their most vulnerable time, from which the following description comes:

Night after night, daybreak after daybreak,
   regularly does she return to a woman whose entrance-ways
are blocked.
It is every day that Daughter-of-Anu counts the pregnant women,
always following those about to give birth.
She counts their months, marking their days on the wall.
On those about to give birth she casts a spell:
   'Bring me your sons that I may give suck!
   In the mouths of your daughters let me give the breast!'

The ghosts of those who died in childbirth were inconsolable forever, and history and literature have been beset with them ever since.

GROUP 2: INDIVIDUALS WHO MET STICKY ENDS
1.   Someone who was killed in battle
2.   Someone who was killed with a weapon

War dead meant ghosts in great number. A seventh-century astronomical report from King Ashurbanipal's royal library at Nineveh predicts that the cemetery (lit. 'lying-place') of heroes (fallen in war) will enlarge; stodgily explained by the ancient commentator as referring to 'many deaths'.

Dead soldiers left behind after battles, both one's own and those of the enemy, must have always represented brewing trouble for those back home responsible for combating ghosts. Already in the mid-third millennium bc the struggles between the Sumerian cities of Umma and Lagash over the desirable No-Man's Land that lay between them ended up with burial mounds heaped over the corpses, sometimes for enemy high-ups, later for many fallen soldiers. It has been suggested that the close geographical proximity of the cities at war in the third millennium indicated fear of ghosts in the covering up of heaped bodies, among other possible reasons. The fighters were all fellow Sumerians, after all, with one shared language and most things in common. Later,

Assyrians, with a political eye to the influentially frightful, wreaked awful vengeance on their enemies, doubtless jumping up and down and shouting 'Kill! Kill!' before heaping up severed heads, skulls or unburied corpses, impaling enemies on poles, hanging their flayed skins over city walls, burning bodies, and hanging heads on trees around defeated enemy cities. Reign by reign the accounts become increasingly blood-chilling, culminating in the celebrated Chapter 1 achievements of Ashurbanipal, and one cannot help but wonder what soldiers imagined they might face later on when those tortured, wandering ghosts marshalled themselves. Perhaps such massive military events with lingering consequences of this kind led to recitation or ritual by specialist personnel in the Assyrian army, to settle the dead in bulk.

3. Someone whose body was cast into the fields
4. Someone abandoned in the steppe
5. Someone who died in the steppe
6. Someone lying in a ditch

These cases are, practically speaking, non-peaceful versions of types 2–3 above. The final case above rather suggests a calamitous end to a weekend's serious drinking.

7. Someone not covered with dust

Probably meaning lost and without a grave.

8. Someone who was drenched by a storm
9. Someone who was submerged in the steppe by the storm god
10. Someone who perished in a marsh

The marshes were above all in the deep south, a landscape where an outsider could easily become lost for good.

11. Someone who perished on a river bank
12. Someone made to collapse on a river bank
13. Someone drowned in water
14. Someone who died in water
15. Someone who drowned in the river
16. Someone who drowned while crossing the river

'I raised my head,' remarked Gilgamesh at Uruk to the sun god Shamash, 'on the rampart. My gaze fell on a corpse drifting down the river; afloat on the water. I, too, shall become like that; just so shall I be!'

This moment of literary meditation shows that there was nothing unusual in seeing a Mesopotamian body floating downstream; indeed, over and above victims of drowning, it is not improbable that slipping a dead body into the river could be a practical alternative to burial.

17. Someone who drowned in a well

Accidents in wells might not have been so uncommon. The myth of the god Erra refers to a well 200 foot deep, falling into which, no one could survive, and an Old Babylonian letter mentions two workers who fell into a local well, one breaking his clavicle; certain omens, too, predict that an individual will drown in a river or a well. Slipping someone stunned by a blow head-first down a well after dark is a neat way to murder them, of course.

18. Someone who drowned in a ship
19. Someone who died of hunger
20. Someone who died of hunger in prison
21. Someone who died of thirst
22. Someone who died of thirst in prison

There were prisons, known as *bīt ṣibitti* or *bīt kišerti*, in which prisoners were sometimes chained hand and foot. The common expression for regaining freedom was 'to see the light'. That their unfortunate inmates might languish to the point of expiring with neither bread nor water gives one a suggestive glimpse of their nature.

23. Someone who died of a sin against a god
24. Someone who died of an offence against the king

A sin against a god or the king: transgressions of this kind are exhaustively covered in the ancient magical series called *Šurpu*, 'Burning', in which spells and procedures are given to dispel them.

25. Someone who burnt to death in a fire
26. Someone who slipped from a date palm
27. Someone who fell off a roof
28. Someone who was struck by a mooring pole and died
29. Someone who was dead from the prick of a pin

The dictum was that someone burnt to death who could not be buried would find no rest thereafter: see Chapter 8. Normal, or partly freakish kinds of accidents are followed by animal cases.

30. Someone who was killed by a lion
31. Someone who was mauled by a dog
32. Someone who was killed by being gored by an ox

Texts often speak of events like this; dogs caused rabies, and responsibility for dangerous ox behaviour was covered by legislation.

33. Someone who died of leprosy
34. Someone who died of sunstroke

The word here either means 'sunstroke' or chill. Study of fever and sunstroke in medical and other texts does not include examples of fatality. Perhaps this also refers to someone who perished in the open desert.

For Babylonian men and women, accordingly, ghosts were an unpredictable reality. Everyone knew that ghosts must be unhappy: those responsible could list all the reasons. Omens, spells and rituals were available who could help the experienced diviner or exorcist in assessing his case as well as dealing with it. Crucial for understanding just what was portended were the facts concerning the sighting or sightings. It is here that the ghost omens come into play.

Omens: Seeing and Hearing a Ghost

Tablets XIX and XXI of the compilation *If a City* have a good deal to say about ghosts, with extensive coverage of what might be expected by a person who actually sees, or hears, one. The omens explicitly distinguish very carefully between a ghost, an *eṭemmu*, and a dead man, *mītu*, the distinction being between a *familiar* ghost, that is, a family member or acquaintance, and a completely *unfamiliar* ghost from somewhere outside.

It is clear, on reflection, that ghosts, even of grandparents or other close relatives, could not always be identified, and probably no one at all would remember further back than grandparents. Perhaps they relied on the human feeling that a visiting ghost was not inimical towards them but somehow part of the clan. *Who actually are you?* was a pressing question addressed to what was probably a family ghost, but possibly not:

> *Spell. You, dead person who keeps appearing to me, whether*
> *father or mother, whether brother or sister, whether family or*
> *clan . . .*   CT 23 15–22

It is easy to imagine that deceased members of extended or extending families who had long inhabited the same place would not only feel close to their descendants but also tied to the rooms and passages where they had spent so much of their lives. What, then, do the omens predict for the family ghost-spotter?

Familiar Ghost Omens

- *If a ghost in a man's house makes an appearance: dispersal of the house*
- *If a ghost in a man's house constantly causes fear: dispersal of the house*
- *If a ghost in a man's house constantly cries out [variant: constantly cries out at the gate]: dispersal of the house*
- *If a ghost in a man's house cries out and one who can hear hears it: overthrow of the house: the man will die and mourning [follow]*
- *If a ghost in a man's house constantly causes terror: end of days*
- *If a ghost in a man's house moans above the bed: relocation of bed and house*
- *If a ghost in a man's house moans below the bed: relocation of bed and house*

(from *If a City*, Tablet XIX)

Each of these seven ghosts is already in the house, family ghosts who have come up from below and are intermittently or openly 'residing' in their former premises. Some have obviously already been seen more than once.

In four cases the ghost makes sounds. Seeing a ghost is one thing, but to the Babylonian, hearing a ghost was always something else, for it seems that any sound they might come out with would be dangerous. The automatic fear generated by hearing a ghost, I imagine, interprets the sound as clamour by the dead for the living to come and join them. Only in the fourth of these omens is the death of the house-owner predicted, and that is when the ghostly cries are heard by 'one who can hear'. This means an individual *who can hear such things*, as if the ghostly pitch could be like that of a dog whistle or a hard-to-discern bass rumble that most persons would not notice; it does not mean simply a person who is not deaf.

- *If a ghost in a man's house constantly cries out during the evening watch that man will not grow old*
- *If a ghost in a man's house constantly cries out during the midnight watch: attaining a wish [variant: end of days]*
- *If a ghost in a man's house constantly cries out during the daylight watch that man will experience a god's mercy*
- *If a ghost in a man's house constantly cries out at midday hardship will afflict the owner of the house*
- *If a ghost in a man's house constantly cries out at midday brightness a mortally sick person will die in the man's house*
- *If a ghost in a man's house constantly cries out in the evening: for a high-born, end of days; for a poor man, he will experience reconciliation with the gods*
- *If a ghost in a man's house constantly cries out in the morning, divine anger against the man will be dispelled*
- *If a ghost in a man's house rumbles: Hand-of-Lugalbanda; that house will experience hardship*
- *If a ghost in a man's house constantly cries out very much: Hand-of-the-Anunnaki; he will experience trouble*
                               (from *If a City*, Tablet XIX)

To the specialist the time of the experience is thus highly diagnostic, and nine possibilities are covered. Interestingly, Mesopotamian ghosts are perfectly visible in a daylight hour sighting as well as in the – to us conventional – dead of night. The second omen in this section includes the contradictory options of *attaining a wish* or *end of days*. This does not mean that the diviners could not make up their minds, but reflects how the scholars who compiled the omen manual from the older tablets at their disposal included disparate textual traditions in a space-saving way. Your Babylonian would, if asked, *either* acknowledge that some people believe one thing and others another, *or*, if pressed, would suggest that a simple omen does not always predict a simple outcome, for diverse factors at a given moment could have their effect. *Hand-of-Lugalbanda* and *Hand-of-the-Anunnaki* are two terms from a Mesopotamian attributive system of medical diagnosis in which the 'hand' responsible for the patient's condition can be that of a god, a demon or even a *ghost*.

- *If a ghost in a man's house enters the ear of the owner of the house: dispersal of the house*
- *If a ghost in a man's house enters the ear of the mistress of the house mourning will fall on that man's house*
- *If a ghost in a man's house enters the ear of a son of the house his father will die*
- *If a ghost in a man's house enters the ear of a daughter of the house her mother will die*

(from *If a City*, Tablet XIX)

These four very focused omens deal with a family ghost's entering a person's ear, always something to be afeared of. Serious diseases and medical conditions were attributed to the worst kind of ghosts, who, bent on evil, entered the porches of the ear of a sleeping victim, giving rise to the diagnosis of *Hand-of-a-Ghost*. There were established procedures to combat this, of course.

- *If in a man's house ghosts growl; Hand-of-the-Anunnaki gods; that house will experience evil*
- *If in a man's house ghosts weep; Hand-of-Shamash; that house will experience disease*
- *If in a man's house ghosts cry out; Hand-of-Shamash; that house will be dispersed*

(from *If a City*, Tablet XIX)

These three omens speak of voluble ghosts, plural. Perhaps they all share the same grievance against the family. Shamash, the sun god, normally benevolent, is behind it all, too, overlapping with the 'set on' reference in the incantation above. Two other omens, in contrast, document ominous ghosts who enter the house from outside. It sounds as if they are unlikely to belong to the family.

- *If a ghost enters a man's house the owner of the house will die*
- *If a ghost enters a man's house and constantly cries out, the mistress of the house will die*

(from *If a City*, Tablet XIX)

Unfamiliar Ghost Omens

The omen handbook also documents face-to-face encounters with a dead man, *mītu*. This dead man is seen in the house, but it is hardly possible that the word refers to a recently deceased but still unburied family member. The very deep-seated ancient Semitic compulsion to bury the dead as quickly as possible applied likewise among the Babylonians, so a corpse in anyone's house would never be there for long. These dead men, as already mentioned, must be ghosts seen in the house whose identity is unknown or unrecognisable.

- *If a dead man in a man's house like a living one is seen, that man will die: dispersal of the house*
- *If a dead man in a man's house like a living one is constantly seen . . .*
- *If a dead man in a man's house like a living one constantly causes fear: dispersal of the house*
- *If a dead man in a man's house like a living one constantly cries out towards the house at the gate: dispersal of the house*

(from *If a City*, Tablet XXI)

The phrase 'like a living one' probably means the spectre must be clothed, and so, for a minute, could be thought to be a living – but unfamiliar – person. The succeeding omens, as well as dwelling morbidly on the consequences for the household, include close details of such a dead man's clothing and even his ring:

- *If in a man's house a son of the house sees a dead man, his brother will die*
- *If in a man's house a daughter of the house sees a dead man, his sister will die*
- *If in a man's house the owner of the house sees a dead man, his son will die*
- *If in a man's house the mistress of the house sees a dead man, the owner of the house will die*
- *If in a man's house the steward of the house sees a dead man, whatever he owns will be lost*
- *If in a man's house the housekeeper of the house sees a dead man, whatever he owns will be lost*
- *If in a man's house his brother sees a dead man, whatever he owns will be lost*
- *If in a man's house his grandfather sees a dead man, that man . . .*
- *If in a man's house the owner of the house sees a dead man adorned with a ring . . .*
- *If in a man's house the owner of the house sees a dead man wrapped in cloths: uprising, claims . . .*
- *If in a man's house the owner of the house sees a dead man and there is a smell: no attaining of . . .*

and, finally, the omen that seems to reflect fear of premature burial, as indicated in Chapter 3:

- *If a dead man in his grave comes back to life with people nearby, that city . . .*

(from *If a City*, Tablet XXI)

How did these Ghost Omens Function?

Most ghosts, probably, were of the local and family type, but what must have been especially frightening was the idea that a dangerous ghost might be unconnected with anyone at all in one's personal world – a killer bent on random street murder – or a ghost fastened on his or her victim through mistaken identity. When the Mesopotamian ghost literature available to us is taken at face value as answering human need in stressful circumstances – rather than docketed as a byway corner of man's curious history – the drawing-up of ghost lists and their behaviour had more than a technical use. *Whether you are* a such-and-such ghost worked most effectively if the listening ghost, smugly immune and anonymous in the rafters, suddenly hears his identity declaimed and realises he is under the searchlight. In practice the effective exorcist is likely to have questioned his patient along the lines of: *Has anybody in your family gone missing?* or, *Did any of your aunts, or great aunts, die in childbirth?* or, *à la* Scotland Yard, *Can you think of anything else you can tell me that might be helpful?* A gentle coaxing of that kind might bring out an unmade connection or a realisation of 'who it must be' that would be halfway to a cure.

Undeniably, a sighting did not usually add up to good news.

In fact, almost all of these cases, notwithstanding that the ghosts might be familiar, are reckoned to bode ill. The implications to the modern ghost investigator bred on later, fear-laden literature require clarification. Ghosts that have appeared over the last two hundred years or more to titillate in stories, books and films, clanking in chains, almost inevitably herald bad news or imminent personal disaster. It would be a grave misjudgement to take these faraway Mesopotamian scenarios as comparable in this way, implying an unswerving, backdated historical rule that *ghosts mean bad news*. The crucial point behind the Mesopotamian welter of ominous predictions is that they were compiled to enable and facilitate solution: they lead to avoidance, prevention or deflection of misfortune through ritual. There is no flirting here with spine-chilling, ineluctable Hollywood fate; this is a practical handbook to deal with a real and common problem among human beings. Underneath is the idea that ghosts who came back often wanted the living to return with them. You ignored ghost omens, in other words, at your peril!

Ghost Omens in Use

How did this authoritative ghost-visit and tomb-building omen assemblage come into being to account for a whole calendar year, and how were the omens really used? The mass of predictions cannot be arbitrary inventions, for how would they ever come to obtain the status of authority or dogma? Odd associations between, say, a frightening ghostly visit paired with a contemporary disaster – such as could occur in any family – would always survive in people's memory. Documentation of such matters was meat and drink to diviners, who were always looking for associated phenomena where underlying cause and effect could be perceived, indicating that a repeat outcome was always possible. Ghost records, alongside the other very different omen compilations, would begin to accumulate and extend themselves. The fully finished system would not only encapsulate coincidences or strange events over the recallable history of the wider social community, but surely also be the result of protracted 'door to door' data collection, literally proactively interviewing old people with long memories, for the overarching plan was to establish some entry for each month and each day of the month.

If we are instructed that a person who starts tomb-construction on the fifteenth of any month of the year will not only become ill with dropsy but, in the end, will not even get buried themselves, it is a fairly safe bet that *no one ever did start such a construction.* For that matter, if everyone who lived in a city on a hill was fated to find life chronically unpleasant, *no one would live in such a city*. We are compelled, accordingly, to interpret these one-line omens not so much as fixed cause-and-effect rulings, but as a *set of warnings*. If someone encountered a ghost under particular conditions there should always be an omen that clarified the potential corresponding danger that could be looked up and, all being well, averted. When a *pater familias* undertook to construct a hospitable tomb for his extended family, the possible consequences (in view of what had happened in the past) had to be considered in consultation with those who knew, and pious, preventative or protective steps taken, as the case may be. Avoiding bad omens and burying the dead with or without flattering ostentation did not, however, guarantee domestic tranquillity. Ghosts who needed or wanted to come back, came back, notwithstanding.

Whenever an omen clearly predicted misfortune or evil, it was necessary to act. Customised cuneiform rituals called *namburbû* ('its release') provided the right procedure to dispel a particular predicted danger. Really serious threats enshrined in the omen tradition, once identified, could always be deflected in that way, but for some unexplained reason by no means every individual omen had a matching ritual waiting in the wings. Ritual instructions were usually carried out by an *āšipu*-exorcist, or his apprentice, acting for the affected person.

Just How Unpleasant Can Ghosts Really Be?

The ghostly visits itemised one by one in *If a City* omens are a useful index in our investigations, but as flat one-liners they hardly bring such episodes to life. It is easy, reading them through, to forget that each entry embodied real fear, apprehension, horror, nightmare, sweat – hot and cold – and panic in the breasts of their poor victims all that time ago. We are fortunate that one magical spell in the incantation series *Evil Demons* brings all this much more vividly to life, for it describes in ninety-nine lines of text exactly what it was like to be visited by an unknown, unidentified ghost of the roaming, malicious hooligan type. I translate the whole cuneiform thing unapologetically in full. It is a little black book of ghosts; they are all there. The unique ghost-hunter's document.

In lines 5 and 7 and 23–4 these ghosts *spy* on people; in lines 25–63, in contrast, they are right inside the house, *right in the sick-room* of someone already ill, with a range of torments and vindictive actions (including pulling faces and sticking out tongues!) designed to hasten the sufferer's end; in the hope that they will give up their own ghost and follow their torturers to the Netherworld. Lines 85–99 complement our established roll-call of revenants who came to a sticky end with one or two new cases, and confirm the classic disturbed cases for whom there is no comforting family in the background. Certain lines within the spell could technically apply to any of a group of evil demons, but I think the whole of this wonderful passage is concerned with ghosts. There are several blocks of closely related lines, and the very structured content clearly derives from a different background tradition from texts that we have already looked at. The qualification 'So-and-So' indicates that this text was for recitation, where the name of the sufferer (and that of his father) would be inserted. This shows that a ghost is certainly the problem and represents a detailed, persistent attempt to foil its every mean trick. The opening words, 'I adjure', are followed by some broken lines, but we can tell that the exorcist is speaking this long but irresistible list out loud:

> *Whether you are one who constantly clambers over mud walls . . .*
> 5 *who are the owl (?), the Watcher, who has evil at his disposal*
> *who . . . whose god . . .*
> *who are* bennu, *the Watcher of the night*
> *who constantly scratch like a wolf*
> *who constantly flash like lightning*

10 *who constantly flicker like a flame,*
who constantly . . . like fire
who constantly shine like daylight
who constantly shine like a star
who are constantly obscure like a black spot

15 *who overwhelm constantly like an* **alû**-*demon*
who constantly pick on victims like a **lilû**-*demon*
who constantly enter houses
who constantly pass over thresholds
who constantly clamber over roofs

20 *who constantly stroll about house foundations*
who are constantly present in holes
who constantly seek a fine young man or fine young
woman in the street
who are the Watcher at noon
who are the Watcher of what people say

25 *who constantly stand at the head of a sick person*
who constantly sit before the head of a sick person
who constantly walk before the head of a sick person
who eat with him when he eats
who drink with him when he drinks

30 *who constantly frighten the sick person, So-and-So*
who constantly scare the sick person, So-and-So
who constantly terrify the sick person. So-and-So
who scare the sick person, So-and-So
who constantly create obstacles before a sick person
who constantly wrinkle the nose before a sick person

35 *who bare the teeth before a sick person*
who constantly sit before a sick person
who constantly grind your teeth before a sick person
who constantly put out your tongues before a sick
person
who constantly open your mouths before a sick person

40 *who constantly pretend to be lame before a sick person*
who butt like an ox before a sick person

who display might like a wild ox before a sick person
who are massive like a wild pig before a sick person
who bark like a dog before a sick person
45 *who constantly moan like a badger (?) before a sick person*
who roar like a lion before an invalid
who constantly slither like a snake before a sick person
who constantly slither like a viper before a sick person
who constantly slither like an adder before a sick person
50 *who constantly slither like a chameleon (?) before a sick*
person
who constantly slither like worms before a sick person
who constantly slither like a lizard before a sick person
who are always dark like pulled-out hair before a sick
person
who are always a dark billy-goat before a sick person
55 *who are always dark like a she-goat before a sick person*
who are always black like a kid before a sick person
who are always dense like a lamb before a sick person
who are always . . . like a fox before a sick person
who always fly like a wasp before a sick person
60 *who always mingle like a cord before a sick person (?)*
who cover yourselves like a naked man before a sick person
who are ever black like bitumen before a sick person
who are white like gypsum before a sick person
who constantly walk in the street
65 *who constantly sit in the streets*
who constantly recline in the squares
who constantly pick on the city of an evening
who constantly prowl in the city of an evening
who constantly seek out the city of an evening
70 *who constantly clamber over walls*
who constantly spread yourself in toilets
who constantly squat in the foundations
who constantly frequent houses
who constantly leap over ditches

75   *who constantly hide in crevices*
     who are exposed in the river
     who are slaughtered in the river
     who are divided at the river
     who are constantly doused in the river
80   *who prowl in the river when in flood*
     who prowl in a river
     who constantly walk in forests
     who constantly sneak about in forests
     who tread paths
85   *who have no guide in the steppe*
     who have been killed in battle
     who have been smitten with a weapon
     who have been smitten with a might weapon
     who have been slaughtered with a dagger
90   *who have been killed with a mooring pole*
     who have been threshed with spikes
     who have been impaled on poles
     who have perished during destruction
     who have neither father nor mother
95   *who have neither brother nor sister*
     who have no family, kith or kin
     who have neither son nor daughter
     who have no heir to libate water
     who have been laid to rest among peers

Evil Demons Tablet 11 Section 2

Probably there were others, too . . .

Responsibilities to the Dead

The Mesopotamian dead, then, were entitled to due care and attention on an enduring basis. Responsibility for discharging these obligations rested on the oldest son in the family, often resident in the family house, or some substitute if need be; in this context, the individual was known as the 'caretaker'. Tradition had it, as we will see, that the Netherworld regimen was not all that it might be, and one cannot help but see these family offerings as supplements, rather like home cooking delivered to people who are struggling to recover in a ward on hospital meals. That the ghosts had clear rights in this regard is explicit and there were three distinct obligations that had to be met:

1. Funerary offerings, *kispu*.
2. Water-pouring, *naq mê*. Ideally, this was cold water, and clean too. Delivery downwards was facilitated by a pipe.
3. Pronouncing their name aloud, *šuma zakāru*. This was a good way to ensure that dead individuals were not forgotten, and is to be understood both literally and metaphorically. Most fathers unashamedly preferred sons, and medical texts concerned with the unfulfilled desire for a child refer to it by the same word, *šumu*, 'a name', clearly illustrating the awareness of family continuum, backwards into the past, forwards into the future (as we have seen in Chapter 3). Girls, I'm afraid, were never in the first rank for expectant Mesopotamian fathers.

This recitation typically accompanied the *kispu* offering:

You, the ghosts of my family, creators of all of us,
of my father, my mother, my grandmother,
my brother, my sister, of my family,
kith and kin, who all sleep in the Netherworld,
I have made the offering to you,
I have treated you with respect, heaped praise on you,
*   honoured you.*
Today do you stand before Shamash and Gilgamesh;
Judge my judgement, help with my decision!

The link with deceased ancestors as family creators is very direct. It is clear that there was a certain quid-pro-quo element involved; in this spell, dead family members are supposed to intercede on the speaker's behalf with Shamash the sun god, lauded administrator of justice Above and Below; acting, in this case, as sometimes occurs with Gilgamesh, as judicial denizen of the depths. The text goes on to request also the ghostly family's protection against evil and troublesome forces as well. Such an inscription enlarges our understanding of the diaphanous milieu in which family ghosts operated, since, on the one hand, the dead were in some sense literally accessible beneath their feet, buried even on the premises; and, on the other, far below in the Big Underworld, interacting with or avoiding very powerful forces of which we today have knowledge from the literary Netherworld texts. Nobody who repeated the words of this recitation believed that Shamash or Gilgamesh actually lived in their family cellar, nor did they believe – had anyone held a gun to their head – that their water pipe went all the way down to the Netherworld. We encounter here an example of the very human capacity to combine parallel beliefs, complimentary or contradictory as they may be, whose function is shared and whose reality is supported by ritual, without apparent difficulty. Passages in cuneiform leave us in no doubt that sliding into interrupted or erratic offering service was a fatal mistake *vis-à-vis* the equanimity of the dead, to the point that they would likely make an appearance in the house, where, not meeting with satisfaction, they would become clamorous and troublesome.

Family ghosts of those buried below who decided to make an appearance were considered to 'live' on or within domestic premises for the duration, or at the very least have free access to it; but, like Victorian children, they were to be unseen and unheard. This view of things probably reflects multiple-generation family residence in one spot quite as much as burial within the house and the obligations it bestowed on the living. Family ghosts, when they did choose to make an appearance, did not always meet with fear or hostility if they were not too much of a nuisance: not infrequently they were regarded with sympathy. A sudden manifestation, of course, would make anybody jump, but it seems that, for a Babylonian, just seeing a family ghost at first was a little like finding a mouse in the kitchen – a bit of a fright, a sense of irritation and the knowledge that something would have to be done about it. Encounter with a ghost, however, always had its implications, often varying far beyond simple fright to extreme ominous danger and physical or psychological sickness.

A Gentle Answer . . .

Consider, finally, the following item of homely but revealing advice:

> If somebody in bed sees a dead person, he should say,
> 'I have mentioned your name with the ghosts, I have mentioned your name with the funerary offerings.'

With these words, the speaker shows us that he can distinguish for certain a ghost that is part of his family and one that is not. This *dead person* is a definite outsider. It exemplifies the transparent 'ours or theirs' view that underpins ghost texts. It also shows that a dissatisfied ghost from an uncaring household on the loose can try and adopt a new family, rather like cats do in London. The outside ghost is befriended and treated like the others: trouble is avoided all round.

6

Ghost Magic 1: Words and Deeds

The leperous distilment; whose effect
Hold such an enmity with blood of man
That swift as quicksilver it courses through
The natural gates and alleys of the body

Hamlet, Act 1, Scene 5

Discomfort and trouble caused to Mesopotamians by ghosts took both external and internal forms. Seeing or hearing one, as we have seen, was redolent with possible danger, and the physical and psychological effects of being watched, followed and crowded in on were chronically distressing and unsettling. The more dangerous ghosts, bent on possession, could intrude right into a person's life in a way that a modern defence lawyer would describe as stalking. The most fearful could literally invade a person's body, often by the ear; or form a strangely intimate alliance with their victim, unsolicited and unwanted for certain, but likened in the incantations to marriage, and requiring a mock divorce to regain freedom, so that a limpet ghost could be prized off, sent away or deflected to a new partner. A ghost on the inside could wreak a great deal of damage.

Since this matter was so much part of daily life it is under-standable that much activity was devoted to dealing with those Mesopotamian ghosts who decided to look in on those who remained 'upstairs'. We are lucky that the ghost omen literature is complemented by many pertinent writings in cuneiform: inscribed amulets, incantations and rituals to keep them at bay or wheedle or bully the ghostly tormentors into leaving living persons alone. Amulets, varied prophylactic objects worn about the body or hung up somewhere visible, had been a deep-seated fixture among human beings since remote prehistory, and that system, too, shows no diminishment of popularity in the world of modern times. Amulets both uninscribed and inscribed were always a vital component of the Mesopotamian exorcist's repertoire.

Uninscribed Anti-Ghost Amulets

The simplest ghost amulets consisted of certain plants or naturally occurring substances sewn up in little bags, worn around the neck or hidden under clothing. Elementary devices of this kind were prescribed for clients who had seen a ghost in a dream, for example. Such an experience was no doubt especially unsettling for what Jeeves called the 'psychology of the individual', since the dreamer could neither run away nor prevent recurrence and the likely implications were obvious. This is a typical plant-amulet for wearing against unknown visitants:

> *If a person often sees dead people in his dreams you stitch up kasû, atā'išu, 'dog's-tongue' and a soiled rag in the hide of a dead cow with a dormouse tendon and put it around his neck.*
>
> K 2175+ iv 13–14

Materials in the Exorcist's Bag for amuletic use against dream-ghosts included seeds of many plants and trees (most of which we cannot yet precisely identify), strong-smelling materials such as fish oil, sulphur, naphtha and certain minerals, or, more elaborately, a human finger bone in a soiled rag, dust from a human skull in oil, hair of an ape or dust off a lion's skin. Sometimes, we learn, the materials could be mixed in cedar oil and stitched up, or the practitioner could rub him with the resulting lump first and then wrap. A completely different approach advocated juniper (with or without a sprinkle of aromatics) rubbed on the soles of the troubled dreamer's feet before they touch the ground in the morning.

Inscribed Anti-Ghost Amulets

Amulets with carefully inscribed words of significance and power were available to combat evil in all its forms, and many examples addressed ghosts in particular. Such amulets had to be written, of course, by a qualified person, a trained scribe with the requisite knowledge of traditional materials, and were much more than a step up from simple amulets without words. Prevention being preferable to cure, the sensible approach was to keep ghosts off in the first place.

Cheap and Cheerful

Two modest clay amulets from the fourth century bc represent the simplest – and cheapest – resource of written type procurable from a professional. Both are nineteenth-century-ad archaeological finds from the ancient Babylonian city of Sippar and they not only represent what was obviously a simple 'everyday' amuletic expedient but were probably also written by the same hand. They are almond-shaped beads of clay, about one inch long, inscribed in cuneiform and bored through lengthways for a string. There are no others known. Each carries the same Akkadian message written in Sumerian shorthand. Considering that only nine cuneiform signs are used, it is surprisingly informative for us:

> *Spell of God Asalluḫi:*
> *Ghost! Do not keep coming in!*

Asalluḫi is an inside name for Marduk, chief god of the Babylonian state pantheon, and master of everything that required the application of magic. Putting his name as 'owner' on a ghost-banishing spell was the most effective possible move. Many full-length and more literary Babylonian spells proclaim to demons that their written content is a spell of such-and-such a god, but with these small amuletic inscriptions the fact that it *is a spell from Marduk* is, uniquely, half of the whole utterance. The second line embodies the essence, addressing the ghost head-on in direct speech, 'Ghost!' and telling it straight, 'Do not keep coming in!' The reiterative 'keep-doing' Babylonian verb form conveys that this is no ghost who might have been half-glimpsed once or twice; it is one that *keeps on appearing* in the house. In this way the amulet reveals its own case history: here is a ghost that is really beginning to get on someone's nerves. In fact, it tells us more.

Amulet-writers with their handbook of time-hardened spells, much like cylinder-seal-cutters with their hardstones, congregated in the markets or in the neighbourhood of the main temples and could always provide what was needed at a variety of prices. These paired clay amulets are as pared down as possible, and could be made and written on the spot. Significantly, no client's name is included, which suggests that such amulets were, in fact, produced in advance, dried and stored until needed, to be handed over with a reassuring 'Wear this round your neck and the thing will go away.'

It is easy to imagine that such an amulet would provide comfort and fortify the victim in case of further sightings.

Old-Style Sumerian

Close attention should be paid to the following four exotic and unfamiliar ghost words:

zizig nu' edaš saggiš luabdaš.

Together they make up an enduringly popular ghost-repelling amulet spell, whispered over two entire millennia of time and important enough to be included in a large reference magic work of the first millennium bc, most of which was already ancient by then. In addition to versions on amulets and tablets, the same spell is sometimes written on private cylinder seals used to seal documents for personal security against possible ghosts. The language is a bizarre kind of Sumerian that would have got poor marks in school, but I think was deliberately made to sound as well as look archaic; it probably means something like,

Among living things,
Do ye not come up!
Raise thy head,
Ye corpse!

Magical Sevens

A second group of closely related ghost spells also turns up on stone amulets and clay tablets. The oldest known example dates to sometime before 2000 bc; it is written in very spidery script on a tablet now in Penn University Museum, Philadelphia.

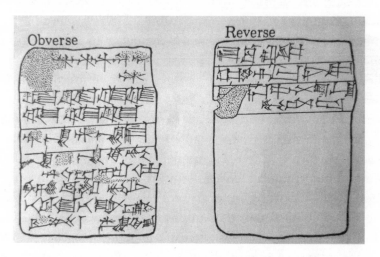

CBS 8235, Penn Museum. Line drawing by the author.

The first two cuneiform signs, god and ghost, are each repeated sevenfold, a well-known magical device found far beyond the borders of Mesopotamia. Certain sophisticated amulets of this type write literally 'god, seven of it, ghost, seven of it' instead of literally repeating the signs seven times.

> *God god god god god god god*
> *Ghost ghost ghost ghost ghost ghost ghost*
> *Lord An, Enlil,*
> *Brother Enki and Utu, father of the city of evil*
> *Who has a great offering-bowl;*
> *Dead one, ghost, dying one, corpse or*
> *Corpse in the Netherworld:*
> *Enki, in the House of the Netherworld*
> *Spoke out:*
> *'The ghostly wanderer will stand aside for the sufferer'*

The First Mumbo-Jumbo

The next spell occurs in varying forms on tablets as well as stone amulets; one tablet example labels the incantation helpfully, and unambiguously, as 'a spell against a divine dead man who has died'. Part of the magic comes from a stanza of four lines neither ancient Sumerian nor Akkadian, but almost certainly in the barbaric language of Elam, spoken over the border in ancient Iran. This is strongly suggested by the -*laḫ* ending that characterises each word. Given the amulets' long distribution over time – nearly two thousand years – and the range of archaeological sites where they have been discovered, it is not surprising that the words come down to us in different forms. They are magic, after all. I commend to you these special ghost words just as they appear in four of the amulets:

Am1	*si-en-ti-la-aḫ*	*nu-me-la-aḫ*	*nu-ud-la-aḫ*	*si-id-la-aḫ*
Am2	*zi-ib-ši-la-aḫ*	*nu-me-la-aḫ*	*ši-ti-la-aḫ*	*gú-úḫ-la-aḫ*
Am3	*zi-ib-šhi-la-aḫ*	*nu-me-la-aḫ*	*ḫa-ti-la-aḫ*	*gú-úḫ-la-aḫ*
Am4	*zi-in-zi-la-aḫ*	*zi-hi-la-aḫ*	*ḫu-úḫ-la-aḫ*	*ḫu-uḫ-ti-la-aḫ*

You can pronounce these anti-ghost words unabashedly as they are spelled: *sentilaḫ*, *zinzilaḫ* and so on: the *-laḫ* bit probably sounds something like a guttural *-lach*. The patient reader who inspects this data carefully will see that the four words as found in the four amulet versions are sometimes identical, sometimes similar and in places quite different. This we can account for, since these very ancient utterances correspond to the mumbo-jumbo or *abracadabra* of our world; magic words that many know but none comprehend, for their origin and true significance are lost in the time mists. The allure of foreign, exotic and un-intelligible words like these bits of Elamite would be irresistible to folk magicians everywhere.

Those spell-casters who repeated these ghost words in Nineveh or Babylon knew them off by ear and off by heart with, almost certainly, no understanding at all of what they meant. After long-term repetition and wide-flung transmission the consonants vary, but the words underneath nevertheless come through. I think they must represent the *earliest recorded example of mumbo-jumbo* in the history of magic.

Where Did The Ghost Words Come From?

It is ironic that in this first historical case we are able to deduce where these exotic words did come from. In 1983 Wilfred Lambert pointed out that a dog warden at the city of Drehem in southern Iraq called Zimzilaḫ – a name that can hardly be dissociated from the *zinzilaḫ* of the spell – received a dead donkey on day four of month seven in the year 2042 bc. Judging by his resound-ingly un-Mesopotamian name, this individual had to be an Elamite, and the small cuneiform tablet in which he makes an appearance is but part of a complex administrative system that prevailed at the end of the third millennium bc. Small tablets recording one or two daily deliveries such as this example existed, and have been found, in multitudes. At the end of a given month, the content of related small documents was entered into large, heavy, multi-columned cuneiform tablets of a pettifogging, small-minded, book-keeping nature that would quicken the pulse of any of today's Inland Revenue brigade: our early Sumerian administrators represent, practically speaking, their linear ancestors.

We can imagine just such a Sumerian record of about 2000 bc, with wages for a group of four or five immigrant Elamite dog-handlers on the temple staff payroll, coming to light centuries later, during building or canal digging, or just lying about on the surface of an old tell. In a landscape full of waiting archaeology, exemplified by the land of Iraq, such things happen even today. The find, 'old' beyond dispute, passed from hand to hand, will have eventually been shown to some seasoned tablet reader, for we know that serious scribes were always on the lookout for ancient pieces of writing, the older the better. Such exotic, unintelligible names, puzzled over and theorised about, could easily be classified as, and come to function as, 'magic words', incorporated within the exorcist's repertoire as words of power stemming from an earlier time or distant culture. Transmission by secret word of mouth with copying and recopying would institute the process of distortion of the words. In the dismissive anti-ghost spell that began *zi-in-zi-la-aḫ zi-hi-la-aḫ* we have a textbook demonstration of how a cherished item of perfectly unfathomable mumbo-jumbo can originate in *realia* whose original meaning was wildly different and altogether inappropriate.

The Elamite dogs were probably Sarabi mastiffs, with the foreign expert *Zimzilaḫ* brought over to join Sumerian estate staff to look after, control and no doubt breed them. Maybe the supply of equid meat was as much for the dogs as their handlers. Mastiffs of this kind are depicted with almost photographic realism in an eighth-century-bc sculptured wall panel from an Assyrian palace at Nineveh. Handlers with reinforced rope or leather collars were as essential then as had no doubt been the case in 2000 bc.

Confronting Ghosts

A powerful amulet with its special written signs was always a good investment and might well come in time to be an heirloom, but not all ghosts were intimidated by them, or in any way deterred from indulging their own displeasing plans. Something more involved and committed was often required, especially if the troublesome ghost was all too present and showing no signs of vanishing of its own volition. It is often clear in the wording of spells that the victim of unwanted ghostly attentions had already suffered a good deal before turning to professional intervention.

In the case of the two simple clay amulets from the market, we have a ghost who *keeps on appearing*; in longer ritual texts, likewise, we are told that they have *constantly* been appearing, or are even following the victim wherever they go. This tells us that human beings in ancient Mesopotamia tended to put up with ghostly discomfort for a good deal of time before actually doing anything about it, much as today it is often only intense and persistent tooth pain that results in a dental appointment.

This throws a certain light on the ghost apparition omens of the *If a City* series considered in Chapter 5. The omens adopt the intimidatingly explicit position that the consequences of so much as *seeing a ghost* are usually fatal, suggesting that people should drop everything and run at once for professional assistance. The practical magic texts that confront and banish ghosts reflect no corresponding level of direct fear, but rather a blend of tolerance, indignation and annoyance; only in extreme cases comes the recognition that something would really have to be done about their persecutor. This demonstrates that the prescriptive and formalised *If a City* omen system represents, in other words, the law of the letter rather than the spirit, and that the omen tradition cannot have been as important or central as it presents itself to us, not least by its sheer bulk, in influ-encing people's day-to-day lives. The omens were there in the background and accessible to enquiry, and they provided a warning system. While *namburbû* literature with its customised magical procedures was on hand to avert evil implicit in a given omen, their range as we know of it is selective and far from numerous; as already mentioned, there is no prescribed ritual for each individual omen within any of the many ominous categories, as there really 'ought' to be if every prediction embodied the same level of un-ignorable threat. Sympathy, or at least tolerance, for ghosts is not far under the surface. Those spells that painstakingly list the reasons for ghosts being ghosts concede thereby that, 'in a way', they can hardly be blamed, and devices to drive ghosts away brutally are the least common.

Proceedings involving spells and incantations were usually conducted by an *āšipu*-exorcist. Those for whom ghost-banishing operations were available were undoubtedly richer than poorer, and urban rather than rustic. Can we visualise one of these long-vanished practitioners? Perhaps they were short and plump, oily in manner and hypnotic of voice, but I somehow prefer to visualise them otherwise as skinny and taciturn. There is a long Akkadian hymn to Gula, goddess of healing, which includes a description of the *āšipu* whose healing craft she directed:

> *I am a physician, I can heal*
> *I carry around all (healing) herbs, I drive away disease,*
> *I gird myself with the leather bag containing health-giving*
> *   incantations*
> *I carry around texts that bring recovery,*
> *I give cures to mankind,*
> *My pure dressing alleviates the wound*
> *My soft bandage relieves diseases.*
> *At the raising of my eyes the dead come back to life,*
> *At the opening of my mouth palsy disappears . . .*

If we could have but half-an-hour's conversation with that old Gula . . .

AN ANTI-GHOST PORTFOLIO

One body of anti-ghost magic indispensable to the working *āšipu* is found on the British Museum tablet K 2175+ from the Royal Nineveh Library. Large manual tablets of this type usually arrived in the museum of the nineteenth century broken into many pieces, not through careless excavation or thoughtless transport, but as the result of the library destruction to which they had been subjected long before during the fall of Nineveh in 612 bc. Scholars have worked with dramatically shattered tablets ever since to identify pieces that belong and put readable inscriptions back together. Many have laboured over this particular ghost tablet over the last hundred and fifty years, and today this anti-ghost compilation consists of fifteen re-joined pieces and fragments. There are, no doubt, still bits to be identified or found. From this I have selected some short passages of practical anti-ghost magic.

1. *That's enough!*

If the sufferer often sees dead persons, the exorcist makes up a preparation of cedar oil, sulphur, algae, bitumen and one or two plants. With this he smears the sufferer's gate, door, bolt, both sides of his bed, his table and reed mat, and, thanks to this barrier, he will no longer see them. Next an incantation must be recited, in which two species of sharp thorn (called *baltu* and *ašāgu*) feature as symbolic defences, with a protective magic circle:

> *You, dead person who keeps being seen by me, whether father or mother, whether brother or sister, whether my kith or my kin or my relations, whether you be a buried person's ghost or an unburied person's ghost, or one who died of an offence against a god or one who died of an offence against the king, or a ghost who has no one to pour water for him; should you approach my bed, may* baltu-*thorn hold you back, may* ašāgu-*thorn hold you back, may the magic circle hold you back. You,*

like nearby clouds, may you not return, may you not return,
behind you may you not return . . .

This incantation has to be recited seven times while the exorcist
pours sweet oil over the two kinds of thorn and the circle, probably of flour, with which the bed has been surrounded. Then the
sufferer is made to recite the next incantation himself:

Ghost who keeps appearing to me, whether you be a strange
ghost, or a forgotten ghost, or a roving ghost who has no one
to care for him, whether you be a ghost who died as a result
of a sin against a god or an offence against the king or a ghost
who died when his fate was completed; do not approach, do
not come close to my bed, may the wall hold you back, may
the door turn back your breast.

    At the command of Ea, Shamash and the exorcist of the
gods, Asalluḫi, you are abjured by Heaven, you are abjured by
Earth. May it never release you, as you are abjured. May
Anzagar, who can loosen the bound, turn away your breast.

This spell uses the word *mītu*, dead person, as the generic term
for an unidentified ghost, in contrast to the omens where it is
restricted to unfamiliar ghosts.

2. *Not even one of us!*
The following, an '*Incantation against often seeing dead persons*',
is recited three times after setting out seven small loaves of roasted
grain flour. The practitioner fills an ox hoof with water drawn
from a well, a river, a ditch and groat water. Roasted grain flour
is thrown in front of it and a libation offered.

Ghost who has been set on me and pursues me day and night
and abuses me, whether a strange ghost or a forgotten ghost
or a ghost whose name is not invoked, or a ghost who has no
one to care for it, or a . . . ghost who was killed by a weapon,

or a ghost who died due to a sin against a god or an offence against the king . . . may he accept this as his portion and leave me be!

Thanks to some unnamed miscreant, the victim here is being persecuted by a non-family ghost whom he cannot identify, so a preliminary list of likely candidates is optimistically included. Exploiting a ghost at large for malicious or evil ends in this way seems to be a very refined manifestation of wickedness. The ghost is offered his customary portion, fresh water and nourishment, to which each was entitled from their own family. This does not mean that the speaker committed to continue with offerings from then on, however; it is clearly a symbolic one-off gesture. The ox hoof for libations, as well as the horn, appears in several of these passages; the soothing waters go below.

3. *Leave me be!*
In this case a small ritual is to be enacted by the river. An area of the bank is swept, and pure water sprinkled. The exorcist has come prepared with a censer to burn juniper, and this is set up. Good beer is libated. It is perhaps at this point that the spell has to be recited by the victim of ghostly persecution.

Shamash, king of Heaven and Earth, judge of Above and Below, lord of the dead, director of the living.
Shamash, the dead persons who have been set on me and are often being seen by me, whether the ghost of my father or my mother or the ghost of my brother or my sister, let them accept this from me and leave me be.

After that the exorcist pours out three libations of donkey urine from an ox hoof to the ghost who has appeared to the individual and the dead persons will be cut off. In this case a family ghost has been 'set on' by someone unnamed. The ritual is similar to what precedes, except for the recommendation of donkey urine.

Possibly this had a deep significance, but one can hardly refrain from thinking that the thirsty ghost – for ghosts were always thirsty – might take it for refreshing beer and receive a punitive shock.

4. *Not on your life!*
The following incantation has the same title as no. 2 above and is my first choice as an anti-ghost spell, with its gruesome ruin as the ghosts' stomping ground when they are out on the razzle:

> *Dead people! Why do you keep appearing to me?*
> *Whose cities are ruin heaps, who are but bones?*
> *I am not going to Kutha, the Ghostly Assembly!*
> *You, why do you always walk behind me?*
> *You are abjured by Abatu the Queen, by Ereshkigal the*
>   *Queen,*
> *By Ningeshtinanna, scribe of the gods,*
> *Whose stylus is of lapis and carnelian!*

They beckon the victim with bony finger to follow them to the Netherworld to join their ranks, to Kutha, where the divine scribe waits to complete his entry in the fateful record. The speaker defies the ghosts with terse thrusts: *Going am I not!* The city of Kutha, in southern Iraq, is where Nergal, death god, was at home, for his great temple was situated there, and that is where Ishtar gained access to the Netherworld on her own fateful journey; see Chapter 9.

There is something intriguing about this Queen Abatu, for no person today knows anything about her. Since she is a Netherworld queen, Abatu is probably the word usually written *ammatu*, meaning earth and therefore a name for the Netherworld. Her relationship with the ruling queen remains unknown, for Ereshkigal ruled imperiously over her Netherworld – as we will see – and Ningeshtinanna, she of the ultimate in luxury writing implements, was in charge of records and knew when ghosts who were supposed to be 'in' were, in fact, 'out'. Sometimes the goddess Bēlet-ṣēri had the same job:

> *In the absence of Bēlet-ṣēri, august Scribe of the*
> *   Netherworld,*
> *No foot can enter Hades,*
> *Nor any path negotiate the Netherworld*

Mere mention of these stern authorities in the background should suffice to send off any annoying visitor from below. In a further ritual from the same ghost-magic compilation, a cedarwood stylus is symbolically presented to Ningeshtinanna.

Consider for a moment the line, 'You, why do you always walk behind me?' Of all utterances in all cuneiform ghost literature this remark should strike a chord in anyone who has ever had the feeling that *something is there, somewhere behind me, watching whatever I do . . .*

The ritual takes place at dusk with a fire to hand and a well nearby. A pit is opened up towards the setting sun using a bronze spade. An ox horn is filled with ditch water mixed with roasted grain, with some other substance charred over the fire and added in. The *Dead people!* spell is recited and the liquid poured down the well, substituted for the appeasing cold-water offering that should properly be made to deceased family members; an existing well would certainly be quick and direct. As a final touch, a censer with some appropriate fumigant and a torch are passed by the victim, who should then be liberated.

5. *Cut him off for me!*
Two incantations are recommended here for the sufferer from persistent ghostly visitations. First:

> *Enki, to drive out the evildoer,*
> *Enki, to drive out the evildoer,*
> *Enki, to drive out mankind's evildoer,*

May he despatch for me the order!
May he make strike for me the order!
May he send it back where it came from!
Evil tongue stand aside!

Enki himself, in charge of exorcistic words and magic, is recruited
to protect the speaker in an old-fashioned-sounding incantation
written in Sumerian. To avoid further trouble, Shamash, who
can see all where mere mortals see nothing, is asked to step in
and 'block their path'. This is no figure of speech: it refers literally to a route or routes up from below whereby ghosts slip out
of the Netherworld. Crafty or experienced ghosts knew routes
that others didn't. With divine intervention they will be denied
such illicit access to mankind. The sufferer is to wash his hands
with soap and gypsum, and recite this second spell:

Oh Shamash, the evil ghost whom you know but I do not know,
he shall not approach me, he shall not come near me, he shall
not draw near me; block his path!

The same mixture of roasted grain in water is added to an ox
hoof, but here it has to be stirred – not shaken – before Shamash
with a blade of alfalfa-grass. Libating the result means that the
dead persons will be cut off.

6. What you will need

This short and tantalising tablet looks like a typical Assyrian
seventh-century-bc letter, but it is a taciturn inventory of what
is needed for a specific type of ghost-removal ritual. In this
instance three figurines are needed. One represents the dead
person to whom the evil ghost 'belongs'; this figurine and that
of the victim are to be united, after they are sent on their journey,
probably meaning they are buried together in the vessel. The
third figurine is curious. Perhaps that is to represent the identity
of the ghost when it is abroad, troubling other persons. Maybe

its head is cut off with the axe to end its earthly presence so that the remainder can also be sent back down where it belongs.

- *You clothe a clay figurine of the dead person with a red garment as an attachment*
- *You dress a clay figurine of the evil ghost in an everyday shift*
- *Travel provisions*
- *A copper axe*
- *Three shekels of lead*
- *Three shekels of copper*
- *Four grains of silver*
- *A figurine of the ghost made of dung, straw and donkey urine*
- *A copper cooking-vessel of seven shekels (weight)*
- *A copper lid*

7. Divorcing a dead partner

This more elaborate procedure is to tackle a much graver ghost problem, when a 'person has been chosen as partner by a dead person and the ghost afflicts him'. The exorcist who has been called in to sort things out has more to do. First, a suitable 'clay pit' is identified, or possibly opened up, to provide the clay to make the figurines. The site has to be purified by tossing flour into it. In the morning the victim has to say,

> *I shall buy enough clay-pit clay for images of* Any Evil, *and of my sorcerer and my sorceress.*

The exorcist pinches off clay to make figurines of what he calls the sorcerer and sorceress, giving them some appurtenance to hold. The two figures are dressed in everyday shifts and anointed with sweet oil. Then the exorcist sweeps the ground before Shamash and sprinkles it with pure water. A pure seat spread with a cloth must be provided for Shamash, and a reed altar.

Two other important gods are involved: Ea and Asalluḫi. All three are given food portions three times, dates and flour and other grain scattered, copper ritual vessels are set up and aromatic censers. This offering arrangement is central.

> *For the ghosts of his family you set up a seat to the left of the offering arrangement. For the (other) ghosts of his family, you set up a seat to the left of the (first) ghosts. You make funerary offerings to those ghosts of his family. You give them gifts. You exalt them, you honour them.*
>
> *Secondly, you lay out hot broth for the (second) relatives and present them with a gift. You exalt them, you honour them. You libate water for them. You make a pure sacrifice before Shamash. You bring the shoulder, caul fat and roasted meat close to the offering table. You libate beer. You put aside ribs for the ghost of his family.*

Note that seats are provided for at least some of the ghosts. At the end the sufferer is to recite a spell beginning '*Begone*, Any Evil' three times, thus dispelling that source of trouble via its likeness. Then, *You lift up the figurines . . .*: obviously the climax of the ritual, but the remainder of the text is lost. I think it probable that a sorcerer or sorceress is conceived to have played a role in fixing the troublesome ghost on the victim. The ghost in question is one of the family, the two groups of relatives the father's and mother's sides, one member of whom is at fault. The evil agency at the back, *Any Evil*, is dispelled, the sorcerer undone, and all the ghosts treated royally. The guilty one hopefully goes back down with the others and gives up its naughty behaviour.

Also Useful Against Ghosts

According to another document, when repeatedly seeing dead persons, the sufferer lies down for two nights with figurines of the persecutors made by the exorcist. Then, after sweeping and the usual offerings, this simple pronouncement is recited to Shamash three times:

> *Shamash, you are the one who makes the dead go aright,*
> > *Those Above and Below; Judge my case!*
> *Whether it be Fright, or an evil Croucher Demon, or Panic*
> > *that has terrified me in the night,*
> *This one (male) is given as my substitute! This one (female) is*
> > *given in my place!*

The figurines are made to swear by Heaven and Earth and then they are buried in the shade of a thorny bush, surrounded by flour mixed with cress. The client then enters the tavern-keeper's house and pours out beer for the three gods, Ea, Shamash and Asalluḫi. As he goes in,

> *When he touches the door and bolt he will be better.*

An incantation for the same purpose is to be recited and an amulet-stone necklace worn thereafter; the spell includes an interesting theological conceit twist at the end:

> *From today you are cut off! From today you are loosened!*
> *From today you are distant! From today you are excluded!*
> *From today you are untied! From today you are remote!*
> *From the body of So-and-So be off with you, after your fate!*

Ghosts, too, have their destiny.

Ghosts and Illness

Babylonian exorcists and doctors attributed a good range of symptoms and problems to the attentions of ghosts. Sometimes the problems were diagnosed as due to a specific kind of malevolent ghost, such as a *Pursuing Ghost*. This is the diagnosis:

If a person continually suffers from headache and roaring in his ears, his eyes are dim, he has constant pain in his neck, his arms are numb all the time and he has a sharp pain in his kidney, his insides are all churned up and he has paralysis of the feet: a Pursuing Ghost *has been constantly after him.*

The ritual takes place at a curious astrological time:

On the fifteenth day, when Sin (the moon) and Shamash (the sun) stand together, you dress that person in sackcloth. With a flint knife you scarify his temple and draw blood. You have him sit in a reed hut making him face north. You set up a juniper censer to Sin facing west. You libate cow's milk. You set up a cypress censer to Shamash facing east. You libate good beer. That person should recite as follows:

> *To my left is Sin, crescent moon of the great heavens;*
> *To my right is the father of the black-headed, Shamash the judge; gods on both sides, fathers of the great gods, who pronounce verdicts for the widespread people.*
> *An evil wind has blown upon me, a Pursuing Ghost has been constantly after me: I am truly grieved, confused and churned up, (ready for) your judgement. Save me, that I am no longer wronged!*

He should recite this seven times; then he should come out of the reed hut and change his clothing, putting on clean garments. To Sin he recites as follows:

> *Nanna, light of heaven and earth, drive out the unpleasant sickness from my body!*

He recites this three times, and then to Shamash he recites as follows:

Utu, great judge, father of the black-headed, may the evil wind, from where it has installed itself, like smoke, go up to heaven! Let me declare your praise!

If he says this three times it will no longer trouble him.

Hand-of-a-Ghost

Many medical problems were attributed to what the Babylonians described as a 'Hand', common among which is that called Hand-of-a-Ghost: šu-gedim-ma in Sumerian, in Akkadian *qāt eṭemmi*. The origin of the expression lies in the conception of disease or affliction as a touch by something external, although in general usage it is probable that the 'etymology' was forgotten and that such-and-such a *Hand* was something analogous to what we would call a 'condition'. There was a whole group of such 'hands'; others belonged to gods, goddesses or certain demons, as occur in the ghost omens. Ghost-Hand represented a catch-all term for the internal problems thought ultimately to be due to evil or dangerous ghosts. The problems involve, for example, bad headache; throbbing temples; pain in the neck; bloodshot or swollen eyes sometimes dividing the body left from right sides; ringing and roaring in the ears; paralysis and dizziness; nausea and intestinal pain; numb feeling; breathing difficulty; fever; and mental troubles. They are related problems, as we might see them.

If Ghost-Hand afflicts a person so that his temples throb, you rub on (four named) plants. You put water with tamarisk out overnight under the stars. In the morning he should drink it on an empty stomach and he will recover.

In order to remove and loosen Ghost-Hand you make him eat owl-flesh. You char the leftovers in the fire, grind it up and mix it with cedar resin. You recite over it the incantation Evil

Finger-Pointing. *Smear that on his temples and it will not come back and will no longer afflict him.*

We know this curiously social-aware *Evil Finger-Pointing* spell in Sumerian and Akkadian bilingual form, and it was popular; but it seems only tangentially relevant to the purpose for which it is prescribed in this case:

Evil finger-pointing by people,
Evil reputation among the populace,
Grievous curse of god and goddess,
Transgressing the border of the gods:
To walk about safely in the face of this,
To avert their punishment,
No god can achieve it;
Enki, king of the Apsÿ,
And his son Asalluñi
Can achieve it.
I can do it again!

Ghosts and Ears

A learned tradition among Babylonian scholars established that ghosts bent on medical malice entered the human body above all via the ear. This is not surprising, for physical access must be by one or other orifice, and human beings usually sleep with at least one ear unguarded. The most unwelcome consequence of aural penetration by a ghost was the condition known as *šinīt ṭēmi*, a kind of madness, literally 'changing of reason'. A very bad case indeed is discussed in Chapter 7 and see Chapter 14.

Roaring in the Ears

Often magical recitations are to be whispered right into the patient's ears, despatching magic words to undo ill effects. Several cases of 'roaring in the ears' are treated in this way in the compendia, the spells carefully conveyed in clear writing, sometimes with special spells for right and left ears. These spells, exactly as with the ghost amulets, can be in an Elamite-like mumbo-jumbo, with many spelling variations; one incantation actually includes the word *napir*, the Elamite word for god. It is scarcely coincidental that mumbo-jumbo with this Elamite flavour is practically restricted to anti-ghost magic.

An exception occurs with the childbirth demoness Lamashtu, no ghost, who is described as 'a female Elamite' *(elamâti)*; and two short bead amulets against her in particular are of this Elamitish type, with these strange phrases: *zurrugu zurrugu kili zurrugu*, and *kirišti libi kirišti la libi*. Addressing her in her own language rather than in Sumerian or Babylonian would bring her up short, startled: what lies behind the conventions that Elamite repels ghosts is less transparent; perhaps there was a tradition that Elamite was spoken in some eastern quarter of the Netherworld. In any case, it is unlikely that any of these barbaric utterances would have been understood by a seventh-century exorcist or ghost-whisperer. But there, no one on the planet today can translate them either.

7

Ghost Magic 2: Pictures and Conversations

Look here on this picture and on this . . .
Hamlet, Act 3, Scene 4

The getting-rid-of-ghosts magical procedure that we have looked at so far has been more or less straightforward, blending traditional spells and ritual together to repel or banish troublesome ghosts. There is a small group of such tablets that stand apart from the majority in one very important regard. They are instruction manuals for the preparation of magical figures modelled in the round for repelling or dispelling ghosts, but here the instructions are illustrated by *line drawings* in the body of the text, drawn directly into the clay surface. These diagrams provide a technical guide for the apprentice exorcist, who will need to produce one or other figurine in clay for the ritual.

While clay is the perfect medium for impressing cuneiform wedges, it is just the opposite for thin and delicate line drawings. They can only be produced by a skilled hand using a fine point, for the smooth surface of prepared writing clay exposes the slightest error most unforgivingly. Illustrated cuneiform tablets, as might be imagined, are very far from numerous, and it is fortunate for this investigation that three of the known examples belong in the anti-ghost portfolio. They are each from the first millennium bc.

Drawings Case 1

THE OLDEST VERSION

The first tablet in this section – although written in Akkadian – does not come from Mesopotamian territory at all, for it was excavated at Boghazköy, the ancient Hittite capital, in what is now modern Turkey. It was written down there sometime around 1450 bc, and it is most fortunate for us that some Hittite ghost specialist did so, for he has preserved for us an old Mesopotamian tradition that has not survived so early in the cuneiform homeland. The Hittites adopted cuneiform writing and imported learning from Mesopotamian teachers during the earlier second millennium bc, and the archaeologists at Boghazköy came upon many interesting tablets in Akkadian side by side with those in local Hittite or Hurrian language. This much-travelled ghost ritual, surviving against all odds, starts us off on a detective ghost story here that ends in a quite unexpected outcome.

The Boghazköy tablet itself includes no drawing, but it gives us a written description so detailed that the modern cuneiform scholar Daniel Schwemer could generate his own drawing in studying it. In fact, many workers have scratched their heads over the difficulties in understanding this cuneiform text. Broadly speaking, an intrusive *Evil-Panic* ghost, male, is to be provided with an alluring 'wife', the archetype specimen of Kipling's 'rag, and a bone and a hank of hair'. The exorcist's instructions begin like this:

> If a ghost afflicts a person you take a section of reed. At the node, where the leaf is, you give her a face. You fashion a yellow mouth and lips of wax. You move down a finger-width and bore a hole through from one side to the other. You insert a twig. You make the arms and forearms like a scarecrow (?). You draw on a navel and a vulva. You bore through the upper part of the section of reed. You tear off a twig and lay it through centrally. You comb out hair and wrap it round the

twig lying through. You turban her with bands, and clothe her with everyday sashes and a cloak. You gird her with a cord at the hips. You thread carnelian on a cord twined by a woman and set it round her neck. You place a silver diadem on her head.

This is the step-by-step set of drawings produced according to the ancient instructions:

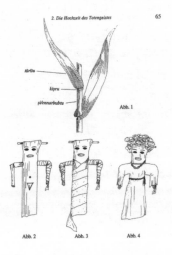

The Boghazköy 'wife' as reconstructed in Schwemer 1998: 65.

The only adjustment I would make to this drawing (and only with the benefit of the illustrated tablet that follows) is to make the arms bend *upwards* rather than downwards, assuming that the unknown Akkadian word describing the position of the arms and forearms, *šaqišaq uršē*, can be translated 'scarecrow'. Also, the 'wife' should have her diadem. They are ritually married, ghost and figurine, and off they go together. Her desirability is delineated and heightened for the watching ghost's benefit by a three-day show, during which the real wife is banished from sight and the new one installed and visibly treated as her replacement. Their conversation is even scripted:

> *For three days she (the ghost) lies on the bed with him and his wife stays away. On the left side of the bed, for the three days, he treats her like a wife. When eating bread, he brings the bread he is eating near her and addresses her as follows: 'Eat this! You are my substitute!' When he partakes of the food portion, he brings it near her and addresses her, 'It is given to you!' When he drinks beer, he brings the beer of which he is partaking and addresses her, 'Drink!'*

Disarmingly free of sexual jealousy, the liberated victim urges the ghost to enjoy his 'honeymoon' to the full. It is curious that the skinny 'wife', who is set up with all her heart could desire, is given a nickname, Tiny One (*zerzerru*).

> *On the third day he raises up water with emmer warmed in the sun. He gives her a box for a bed and a chair. You set out before her . . . winnowed groats, beer-bread, malt porridge and . . . Before Shamash you recite as follows:*

> > *'You have been provisioned. Your dowry has been handed over. Tiny One, you have everything you need. You have been given as substitute for, and in place of, So-and-so, son of So-and-so. The* Evil-Panic *ghost, or the* mukil-rēå-lemutti-*demon, which has been set on So-and-so, son of So-and-so, he is now your husband: you are given to him. You must take him out of the body of So-and-so, son of So-and-so, and go away.'*

Addressing the ghost or demon:

> *'Like a lion of Shamash, go wild over her!'*

The drainage hole by the wall has to be enlarged so that the Woman can be set in it with all her provisions with her face to the setting sun. Bowls with their contents are set down and the bed made in front of her. Then the opening is sealed up with clay. Clay mixed with cress is used to mark out fourteen lines towards the curtain tassels of the patient's bed. He then is to speak out these words:

> Any Evil *shall no longer walk behind me!* Any Evil *is no longer attached to me!*

He addresses the ghost:

> *You have been provided with food rations! You have been provisioned! You have been married off! You are her husband! You must take your wife and go away! From the body of So-and-so, son of So-and-so are you expelled, are you banished, are you removed, are you driven away! By heaven and earth are you . . . !*

Finally, the sufferer's possessions are washed and the reed torch is passed by him and the offering arrangements taken down.
Peace of mind . . .

THE LATER VERSIONS
Eight hundred years later this Bronze Age ritual was still alive and in use in the land of its origin, between the Euphrates and Tigris rivers. We have four cuneiform tablets to demonstrate this, two of the seventh century bc, one from Assur, also an Assyrian capital, the other from Sultantepe, an Assyrian town near Urfa in southern Turkey. At the end of the sixth century bc, a tablet from Babylon overlaps with this material, as does a fourth-century-bc tablet from Uruk, also in southern Iraq. The problem to be addressed is an intense form of *Ghost-Hand* following entry through the ear, with the following effect:

> *If a man has been attacked by an alteration of mind so that his personality has changed, his words contradict themselves,*

*his intelligence is affected (and) he talks excessively, in order
to restore him to his senses you put a human bone, a bone of
a male pig, and a fox bone around his neck. You fumigate him
over the fire, anoint him with fat of wild animals and he will
recover.*

What is described is the kind of madness called *šinīt ṭēmi*, 'alter-
ation of the mind', in Akkadian, when the crucial element of
balanced human intelligence called *ṭēmu* is disrupted. It is the
same term that underpins the creation of the human being in
Chapter 2. Here it is the consequence of malevolent intrusion
into a person's head by a savage ghost in order to mess with it.

The Version from Assur, Sultantepe and Uruk:
*You make a figurine for him out of reed and set its clay head
on it. You wrap it in a cloak and clothe it in an everyday shift.
You place a . . . cloth on its . . . and put a [piece of] dog skin
underneath it . . .*
   He eats the . . . and he will recover.

Figurine 1, on its piece of dog skin, is set at the head of the
patient's bed; he then takes his medicine. The heads of six species
of birds and a bat are next to be charred in the fire, and then
come instructions, incomplete (but related to what we have seen
before), to make Figurine 2:

*You make a . . . of reeds. You . . . and set a . . . on his face.
You . . . and set a . . . on his . . . You clothe it in a cloak. You
. . . and set it up at the head of his bed.*
   *You . . . and spread . . . over his ear . . . and that afflicted
person will recover.*
   *You libate . . . to him out of an ox hoof . . . You supply
him with travel provisions, and put him into a drain-hole in
the wall, turn his face to the setting sun . . .*

Both reed figures are *male*, according to the pronouns and suffixes (which are distinguished in Assyrian dialect). The infuriatingly broken and unreadable beginning of the first line probably contained Figurine 2's name:

You make . . . of reeds.

Some medicament in this case is applied to the patient's ear, the ghost's point of entry. The well-provisioned Figurine 2, echoing the married-off female doll in the earlier ritual, goes down the drain, carrying off the ghost and freeing the tormented victim. The ghost is thus simply transferred from patient to Figurine 2.

THE VERSION FROM BABYLON

After this we pick up the tradition at Babylon, thanks to one of the most interesting tablets in the whole British Museum collection, which – considering that there are about 130,000 cuneiform tablets in that unique treasure house – is saying something. Like many, it arrived in London in 1881 broken in pieces. Identifying 'joins' under such circumstances to reconstruct a cuneiform tablet from fragments is the Assyriologist's constant ambition. BM 40183+ happens to be my personal best. Eleven joining fragments have now been identified to be glued back together by expert hands.

This tablet, visible in Plate 3, includes two extraordinary drawings to guide the exorcist. The scribe left an empty space between two long passages of writing, and both figures are drawn in with remarkable skill and confidence, and are even labelled with their names.

The beginning portion of the tablet is still missing. We find the Assyrian charred-bird-heads ritual. Then follows a figurine procedure similar to what we have seen, but with the crucial addition of the figurine's name. It becomes clear that it is Figurine 2 that is described, for the making of Figurine 1 was covered in the beginning lines that are now missing in the Babylon tablet:

> *You make a clay image of Abaknana and anoint its face with red clay water. You put a . . . on its head. You take it out . . . and dress it in an everyday garment. On the seventh day you place it at the head of that sick man. You place the skin of a virgin goat in front of the sick man.*

Figurine 2 at Babylon is thus called *Abaknana*, a name otherwise unknown. Its face is anointed with red clay paste and it wears an everyday shift, with some item of headgear. On the seventh day, Figurine 2 is set up by the patient's head on the skin of a virgin goat, similar to Assyrian practice. Then, however, we read:

> *If he constantly strikes* That Woman *the sick man will find respite and recover.*

This passage introduces us obliquely to Babylon's Figurine 1, *That Woman*, whose manufacture details are lost. We are doubly fortunate that we can look on excellent likenesses of both personalities.

FIGURINE 1: *THAT WOMAN*
The cuneiform label to her left, reading downwards, says, '*That Woman*, whose likeness is of reeds.' The drawing shows a female figure in head and torso, with bent arms stretched out right and left. Her right hand projects round the left side of the tablet. Both hands are empty, but with the forefinger pointing straight out. One point is very surprising, the fact that the figure is shown full-face, looking out at us. Frontal presentation is simply not to be seen in ancient Near Eastern art; it is virtually a matter of canonical principle. She is either wearing a tight-fitting cap, or her own hair lies taut across the cranium, tied either side with a ribbon and bunched much as the hair of the *Queen of the Night* in Plate 7. Like her predecessor from ancient Turkey, she sports a studded diadem. The torso is mounted on a reed pole, possibly two reeds fixed

together, which stretches down to the lower ruling that frames the panel. It is quite remarkable how close this image is to the description (and modern drawing) of the 'wife' in the Boghazköy text.

That Figurine 1 is pole-mounted suggests in itself that it should *rotate*, which correlates with the injunction that the afflicted person should constantly 'strike' *That Woman*, for the Akkadian verb used, basically 'to hit or strike', possesses also the nuance 'to flick', or 'to flip'. I assume that once the image is installed at the head of the bed, the patient taps or flips it so that it quivers like a scarecrow in a field or spins round, thereby startling and scattering nearby ghosts on the ear-prowl. The original second-millennium female figurine was certainly used as the wife of the sufferer and married off to the ghost. Whether such an entity had also been a moving, scarecrow-like spinner in its earlier incarnation we cannot know, but it seems probable.

FIGURINE 2: ABAKNANA

The central drawing shows a seated human figure. The cuneiform label to his left, reading downward the back of the throne, tells us in cuneiform syllables that this is the 'Image of *a-ba-ak-na-na*'; the second, orientated left to right, preserves only, 'Image of *a-b[a-*'. This drawing is no mundane exorcist's model for everyday use, for Figurine 2 is portrayed as a contemporary Babylonian king. He wears the well-known cap-shaped crown of a first-millennium Babylonian ruler, which here has a clear border and delicate decoration at the back. The king's cap in fact projects rather stylishly above the ruling that marks off the illustrated panel into the text above. He is bearded and faces to the right. Some portions of his upper garment survive, enough to show that it was decorated at least around the neck or upper body, and that it had sleeves that reached to the wrist. Both arms are outstretched. Abaknana's left hand is clearly drawn, with a long, grasping thumb and long thumbnail. He holds what is evidently a four-fronded flail. His right hand encloses, about one-third of the way down, a long upright pole that rests on the ground and reaches the top of the illustrated panel. The surviving section shows five circumventing rings that are somehow attached to the object. Both flail and pole are well-known symbols of Babylonian kingship. The throne is a tall, straight-backed affair. It is topped by a fan-shaped palmette that probably originally had eight leaves with a central finial at the top. The back of the throne is ornamented with carvings and projecting fittings, indicated in the clay with marks and circles respectively. The decorated lower portion of the throne back swells out slightly, like an animal leg, and the throne feet are squat ovals, possibly hoof-shaped; both happily survive in the drawing.

At Babylon, *That Woman* acts both as fixture to scare off ghosts around the patient's bed and a wife to be married to Abaknana, standing in for the patient, a sort of marrying one's nurse principle. Both follow the earlier route down to the Netherworld. This would all make sense if *That Woman* both deterred ghostly attention as a moving prophylactic device and, simultaneously, was thought to absorb the evil into herself, like certain anti-mosquito devices. Once Abaknana accepts her and formalises the marriage by stating, as Babylonian men did, when they had to, in real life, 'She is my wife', the exorcist tells her to take her Abaknana in place of the afflicted person and be off, liberating him. After a ritual with a parched and crushed human bone and a bird with its throat cut, the figurine has to be confined, probably in some small structure. Seven days later the roof is swept and offerings made. Then the following conversation takes place:

> Exorcist to Abaknana: '*You have been made to take a wife.*'
> Abaknana in reply: '*She is my wife.*'
> Exorcist to *That Woman*: '*You may take your husband as substitute for So-and-so, son of So-and-so.*'
> Exorcist to ghost: '. . . *Go away.*'

When they are seated, the female figurine is put together with the travel provisions into a drain-hole in the wall with its face turned to the setting sun with flour and alkali thrown in. Then, as an afterthought, a useful follow-up amulet for the patient in the form of a flying insect and a locust in a leather bag is prescribed.

The description of making Abaknana (reddened face, simple everyday shift, headgear) hardly prepares the tablet reader for the full-scale regal dress reaching to the ground, ornate crown and throne, and the classic symbols of royalty that we see in the drawing. The Babylonian account has overlaid the inherited ancient ritual for ghost-banishing with the case of a king troubled with mental disturbance, no doubt thought to be due to the same cause.

WHO WAS ABAKNANA?

I suggest that the drawing on the madness tablet is no generic representation of a Babylonian king but deliberately reflects the contemporary state image of King Nabonidus, the last native king of Babylon (c. 556–539 bc). This may seem a brave claim, and it has *world stage implications* beyond the question of ghosts and ghosts alone, but evidence supports it, and the trail has to be followed now that we've started. Four points are raised for the reader's armchair consideration:

I. THE PICTURE OF KING NABONIDUS

The image in Figure 1, Plate 5, occurs on a large, oval-topped stone stela showing the standing, right-facing figure of King Nabonidus in all his regalia, watched over symbolically by the Moon, the Sun and the goddess Ishtar. We know it is he thanks to lines of writing on one side, unnoticed by the Persian vandal who obliterated the whole of the front inscription. King Nabonidus's dress and pose – not to mention the royal pole symbol – are closely similar to those of Abaknana, in Figure 2, Plate 4.

2. THE NAME ABAKNANA

This *Abaknana* is otherwise unknown, and, as presented, it is not a conventional Mesopotamian name. When we dissect *a-ba-ak-na-na* sign by sign, however, out comes meaning in Sumerian, which can then be translated in Akkadian:

In Sumerian a-ba means 'who',
in Akkadian *mannu*.

In Sumerian ak is the verb 'to do',
in Akkadian *epēšu*.

In Sumerian the spelling *-na-na* could represent the name
of the moon god, Nanna, in Akkadian Sin.

This allows us to understand Abaknana as a conventional and standard Mesopotamian type of name, Aba-ak-Nanna, 'Who has done this, O Sin?' or, translated into Akkadian, *Mannu-ipuš-Sin*.

3. NABONIDUS AND THE MOON

King Nabonidus the man was a passionate devotee of the moon god Sin, brought up that way by his mother Adda-guppi, a priestess of Sin at Harran in south-eastern Turkey, and her inculcations ultimately landed him in a great deal of trouble. The king's lifelong promotion of Sin worship culminated in conflict with the state clergy of the god Marduk at Babylon, and ultimately paved the way for the relatively straightforward takeover of the Babylonian Empire by Cyrus the Great, in 539 bc. In another stone stela, discovered at Harran, Nabonidus presented the world with his own self-view of his accession:

The great deed of Sin, of which nobody among the gods and goddesses knew, which since distant days had not befallen the land, and the people have now seen but not recorded on tablets for eternity, that you, Sin, lord of the gods and goddess residing in heaven, have come down from heaven in the time of Nabonidus, (and) I, Nabonidus, the only son who has nobody, in whose heart was no thought of kingship, the gods and goddess prayed on my behalf to Sin and he called me to kingship . . .

The 'great deed' matches entirely the thought-process conveyed by his old-fashioned Sumerian name, meaning the miraculous feat that landed him where he was, from the humblest beginnings, with the world at his feet, haloed, so to speak, with moonbeams. This name, Abaknana, could have existed, unnoticed, side by side with his throne name *Nabû-na'id* (meaning Nabu-is-praised). It was perhaps adopted by him on accession for private religious purposes, or even bestowed on him by ever-adoring mother Adda-guppi. Once king, his life's work was to supplant the Marduk cult with that of the moon god Sin. His reputation spiralled downwards beyond recall when he abandoned Babylon for a ten-year period to live at the oasis of Teima in Arabia, worshipping the Moon, with Belshazzar his son acting as Regent at home. His failure to act as proper king and take the hand of the god Marduk during the New Year Festival was unforgivable, and his consistently unorthodox and eccentric behaviour by Babylonian standards left him, in later eyes, a *mad person*. In time this kingly madness shifted away from Nabonidus, where it properly belonged, to Nebuchadnezzar, Babylon's greatest ruler (c. 605–c. 562 bc), whose own reputation at the hands of the Prophets and the Book of Daniel after his treatment of Jerusalem generated Blake's unforgettable image of madman for all time. Cyrus, king of Persia and incoming conqueror of the venerable city, left us a literary work of satire in Babylonian cuneiform that surveyed the bizarre reign and deeds of Babylonia's last ruler with an acerbic and propagandistic eye:

> *He had made the image of a deity that nobody had ever seen*
> *in this country . . . He called it by the name of Nanna . . .*
> *gabbling prayers that no one understands . . .*
>
> *As to the effigies in Marduk's own temple . . . he looks at*
> *those effigies and utters blasphemies . . .*

In this composition, the *Persian Verse Account*, the *Private Eye*
overview of Nabonidus's sacrilege actually includes the Akkadian
word for 'madness', and indicates that, in some people's eyes,
even in his own time, Nabonidus was, ever-so-slightly insane.

With this in mind the appearance of King Abaknana inside this
complex ritual for extreme mental disturbance at the hands of
intrusive ghosts might find explanation. If King Nabonidus was
widely regarded during his lifetime as a lunatic, among Marduk
believers, for example, he could easily have become a stock figure
of the mad monarch type such as George III of England or
Charles VI of France. Then again, if chronic ill health beset him,
he can hardly have escaped the attentions of the then famous
Babylonian specialists, and perhaps some major curative ritual
based on a complicated ancient ritual was developed for him,
and this began a tradition. While certain ritual cures on behalf
of a client depended on figurines, for the highest in the land a
portrait in miniature would be needed. One such survives for the
hypochondriac and ailing Assyrian king Esarhaddon (681–669
bc), carved in white stone like a superlative chess piece to represent
him in ritual, or allow him to sit immobile under the eyes of
Assur in his temple.

For many centuries, then, serious cases of mental disturbance
following hostile ghosts intruding by the ear could be combated
by an elaborate ritual with a Female Figurine and a Figurine of
the Patient, such as that which was discovered at Boghazköy from
about 1450 bc, itself certainly derived from earlier Babylonian
praxis. From our Babylon tablet, written nearly one thousand

years later, we see that, during the second half of the first millennium bc the full-blown ritual incorporated the Mad King in the
role of the Patient and was ever after associated with it.

4. ABAKNANA ALIAS *MANNU-IPUŠ-SIN*

There is one final point I can offer about the name Abaknana,
with its Akkadian equivalent *Mannu-ipuš-Sin*. Lucian, the
second-century Greek satirist, wrote in his *Necyomantia* about
one *Menippus*, who was determined to descend to Hades, and
recruited help to that end from a Chaldean at Babylon – a white-
haired cuneiform scholar with beard, expert in ghosts:

> I [Menippus] resolved to go to Babylon . . . I had been told
> that by incantations and other rites they could open the gates
> of Hades, take down any one they chose in safety, and bring
> him up again . . . When I arrived, I found a wise and wonderful
> Chaldean; he was white-haired, with a long imposing beard,
> and called Mithrobarzanes. My prayers and supplications at
> last induced him to name a price for conducting me down.
> Taking me under his charge, he . . . brought me down for twenty-
> nine successive mornings to the Euphrates, where he bathed
> me, apostrophising the rising sun in a long formula, of which
> I never caught much . . . but he appeared to be invoking spirits.
> This charm completed, he spat thrice upon my face, and I went
> home, not letting my eyes meet those of any one we passed
> . . . When he thought me sufficiently prepared, he took me at
> midnight to the Tigris, purified and rubbed me over, sanctified
> me with torches and squills and other things, muttering the
> charm aforesaid, then made a magic circle round me to protect
> me from ghosts, and finally led me home backwards just as I
> was; it was now time to arrange our voyage.

My friend Mark Geller theorised some years ago that the Greek
Menippus recorded in this narrative reflected the Babylonian
name *Mannu-ipuš*; this brilliant idea now seems substantially

123

more than probable. It looks as if this later story also preserves its echo of the troubled King Nabonidus, haunted and half-crazed, turning in desperation for rescue to his wise and learned Babylonian specialists.

Drawings Case 2

The second picture tablet at our disposal brings us face to face with *Any Evil*, a peculiarly Mesopotamian idea, and a name that will have been repeatedly stumbled upon by the Mesopotamian ghost-hunter in this book. We must clarify why that should be, and then we can inspect his one and only portrait. Much is made clear in the following well-preserved example of Assyrian ghost magic excavated at the site of Assur. The symptoms experienced by the exorcist's client might be due to a ghost, but there are also dangerous, demonic candidates (an alû-*demon or a* gallû-*demon or a* mukil-rēš-lemutti-*demon*). Or, it could be *Any Evil*:

> *You collect together dust from an abandoned town, dust from an abandoned house, dust from an abandoned temple, dust from a grave, dust from the foundations, dust from an aban-doned canal and dust from the road. You mix them with ox blood. You make a figurine of* Any Evil. *You clothe it in lion's skin. You thread a piece of carnelian and put it round his neck. You provide him with a water skin and give him travel provi-sions.*

The requisite quantities of dust, seven types, must obviously be already to hand for the practising specialist, conjuring up a graspable jar section of the apothecary's shelf. Dust, of course, is a prime component for those whose destiny is once again the Netherworld. Possibly, too, there was an additional medium, likely clay, to produce a stable figurine that could be dressed to star in a ritual before the fateful journey. What is revealing is the exorcist's analysis. Ghost attack symptoms endured by the patient, as we know, might include paralysis, convulsions, numbness, dizziness, joint-pain and the kind of mental trouble endured by Nabonidus, but the same could be attributable to one of several agents. While a malevolent ghost is clearly the most likely, we can take it that the victim had not actually seen the ghost, or not with certainty, otherwise the exorcist would have extracted that diagnostic information out of them at once. It could be any one of the three listed above or, *Any Evil*, the Akkadian *mimma lemnu.*

This *Any Evil* often rounds off lists of evil forces in incantations, and was a device to cover any diabolical entity whose name might have been overlooked and ensure that none escaped being named. It is, one might reflect, the remote ancestor of those polished clauses that one encounters today in insurance policies or book contracts, to cover 'anything else that we haven't thought of'. The constant reliance on this 'or any other evil' codicil meant, however, that in time *Any Evil* came to evolve into an entity in its own right; a rare case of an abstraction acquiring a physical body, in a very Mesopotamian way, to the extent that, in the end, its likeness could even be drawn or modelled.

The ritual lasts for three days. Nine dishes of barley gruel are set up on the roof of the sufferer's house. Water and beer with roasted grain flour is libated. Cedar wood shavings and flour encircle the installation and the whole is covered over by an unbaked fermenting-vessel, to be watched over by Shamash by day and the stars by night. The exorcist has to set up twenty-two juniper censers before Shamash and scatter emmer flour before the Gods of the Night, reciting the following over the whole period:

> *Ghost or* Any Evil, *from this day forward, you are removed, driven out, banished and defeated from the body of So-and-so, son of So-and-so! The god appointed to you, the goddess appointed to you, have removed you from the body of So-and-so, son of So-and-so!*

On the third day, in the late afternoon, an offering table is set up before Shamash. The victim lifts up the *Any Evil* figurine and addresses the sun god, stressing his benevolence towards mankind, much as found in Sumerian a millennium before:

> . . . *at your rising the world is bright. The homeless girl, the widow, the forsaken woman and the unmarried woman: at your appearance all humanity warms itself. The wild animals, living creatures, beasts of the steppe constantly bring you their lives and limbs. You decide the case of wronged man or woman; you make sure their verdicts are right.*

Then we come to the nub:

> *I, So-and-so, son of So-and-so, kneel in weariness.*
>
> *I, who through anger of god and goddess am bound by an Obligation: an* utukku*-demon, a* rābiṣu*-demon, a ghost or a* lilû*-demon have weighed out paralysis, convulsions, numbness, dizziness, joint-pain and insanity for me: every day they make me howl.*
>
> *Shamash, you are the judge: I brought you my life. I kneel for judgment in the case concerning the suffering that afflicts me. Judge my case. Give me a verdict. Until you have given my verdict in my case may you give no other verdict in any other case. After you have given a decision in my case, and after my Obligation has released me and fled my body, wherever I put my trust may the gods accept what you say. May Heaven delight in you and Earth rejoice in you!*

The figurine is placed in a jar and made to swear the standard exorcistic formula, 'By Earth are you abjured! By Heaven are you abjured! By Shamash are you abjured!' The mouth of the jar is sealed and the whole thing buried in some abandoned spot.

The ritual focuses on *Any Evil* and the ghost at the same time. The legal-sounding Obligation that he wishes to have cleared up openly by Judge Shamash in his court probably follows the victim's failure in his contract of understanding with the ghost and it is ultimately a matter of food and drink. He can have had no such contract or obligation with any of the demons. Interestingly, three other well-known illness and trouble-bringing demons are sneaked in as possible additional culprits in the sequence *utukku*-demon, *rābiṣu*-demon, ghost or *lilû*-demon. Psychologically, the evolving text allows scope for mentioning *all* likely suspects, and throwing them in at this stage looks like seizing a good opportunity to get a really clean slate. Only one character, however, goes into the pot. It must be *Any Evil*, for he has the only figurine. Part of his job, then, is to take away all and any evil, once and for all, including the ghost whom Shamash has just warned off. Overlap in wording like this in banishing texts is not uncommon, and in some sense, too, this document is a template, where demon names could be added in or removed according to circumstances. Rather than leave gaps, the scribe has written So-and-so, son of So-and-so, where the name of the client and his own father's name would be inserted in use. The name of the father is included to establish, for the benefit of those on both sides of the great divide, that this was the correct individual.

RELATED VERSIONS
Here we bring in three small tablets of later date, with this material having been identified in the British Museum during work in preparation for this book.

1 K 6073+ from Nineveh
This abnormally thin tablet is in the Babylonian handwriting so disliked in the royal Assyrian library. The scribe records that he copied out his tablet swiftly from an Assyrian tablet, for making some ritual installation. K 6073+ is, therefore, a copy made by a local scribe in Babylonia from an interesting old Assyrian exemplar, transposed into large and clear Babylonian script as he did so. This tablet must have been collected on one of Ashurbanipal's library-raiding trips somewhere in Babylonia and carried off to Nineveh

to be incorporated in the king's library, where it lay waiting until the excavations of the 1850s. This unusual and roundabout history, Assyria to Babylonia to Assyria, shows that the text was hard to locate, which can be explained because this particular incantation contains several obscure puns and esoteric writings that were probably considered to make it more than normally powerful.

2 BM 47701+

This overlapping source is the reverse of a small, single-column cuneiform tablet from Babylon written down in about 550 bc, and arriving in the British Museum on 3 March 1881. Like the Nineveh duplicate it has a one-line library tag:

> *Quickly excerpted [from] a writing board of Anu-balassu-iqbi.*

Judging by his name, Anu-balassu-iqbi was from Uruk, the highly important ancient city in southern Iraq that housed many remarkable scholars and extensive libraries, and this attribution shows that the same compilation of ghost magic was in use there too. It is this second tablet that gives us the likeness of *Any Evil.*

3 BM 40635 from Babylon

This fragmentary tablet is roughly contemporary with and similar to no. 2. Here the lower half of the reverse is uninscribed, but the surface is too damaged to show whether it might once have contained a drawing.

DIAGNOSIS AND TREATMENT CONTINUE

Continuing with the big Assur tablet and its small Babylon duplicates, we can follow the diagnosis and treatment as it proceeded, now including, as well as the pursuing ghost, the *lilû*-demon, *ardat-lilû*-demon, epilepsy or *Any Evil.*

> *You have him collect some horse urine. You mix it with flour and make a figurine of the ghost or* Any Evil. *You write its*

*name. You make it hold its mouth with its right hand and its
rear end with its left. You put a copper chain on it. You nail a
wooden peg into its mouth. You rub it with goat hair and place
it before Shamash.*

The list of possible causes is sandwiched between the ghost and
Any Evil, and it is of one or other of the two that a figurine is
now to be made. Here, flour mixed with horse urine is the medium
and the resulting medium is sufficiently clay-like to take the
writing of its name. The grade-A power spell at the end indicates
that the source of the trouble would do well to go back where
he came from without more ado, for many of the greatest gods
of Mesopotamia are to gang up on him:

May Shamash, king of justice, confound your plans!
May the sage of the gods, Marduk, cover your face!
May Ningeshtinanna, female accountant, herald and meas-
  urer, cut off your water in the underworld pipe!
May Ningishzida, chamberlain of the broad underworld, turn
  back your breast!
May Usmû, vizier of Eridu, send you away!
May Ninurta, lord of weapons, smite your neck!
May Dingirmaḫ, the great mother, curse you!
Be abjured by Heaven! Be abjured by Earth!
Be abjured by Shamash, the judge, my lord, may he send you
  away! From the body of So-and-so, son of So-and-so are
  you banished, torn out, sent away! Do not turn back
  again!
Before Shamash, my lord, you are abjured by the south wind,
  the north wind, the west wind and the east wind!
Any Evil of So-and-so, son of So-and-so, I am the exorcist of
  Eridu; I abjure you, do not look behind you!

The figurine is set inside a lidded copper vessel, its face turned
to the left. Then some structure is to be made at the head of the

victim's bed and the figurine made to enter it (as described in the Abaknana ritual). For three days the spell is recited day and night and flour scattered. On the third day at sunset the figurine is taken out to the steppe, a pit dug, and it is buried therein facing the setting sun. The spoil is replaced, flour scattered and a magic circle of roast barley marks the spot. The blood of a slaughtered dove is libated over it. Do not look behind you!

The picture of Any Evil

Anu-balassu-iqbi, or his follower at Babylon, rose to the challenge of depicting abstract *Any Evil* in a line drawing without apparent trouble. Theoretically, the proposal rivals the difficulty of drawing a *muchness*, the idea of which so confused Alice, but a good exorcist knew what the enemy looked like: the result is an anthropomorphic, lion-headed entity in a long skirt, obviously related to a variety of better-known Mesopotamian images of non-humans, good and bad. This characteristic explains why the *Any Evil* figurine in the preceding ritual passage was clad in lion skin. The corporeal incarnation of *Any Evil* encountered face to face in the Netherworld by Prince Kummaya (see Chapter 11) had two heads, we are told: one of a lion; the other word, tantalisingly, is broken away.

Drawings Case 3

Here we showcase our third illustrated case with BM 47817, also acquired from Babylon in the nineteenth century, and reaching the British Museum on 3 November 1883. It is the latest in date of the three case studies, probably written down in the fourth century bc. Half is completely missing and what does survive shows scars from an enthusiastic local excavating tool, but it is a gem notwithstanding.

This text, too, was excerpted from a longer tablet. Thanks to the scribe, Marduk-apla-iddin, son of Dābibu, we have both the first line and catch-line (the first line of the following tablet), showing that the anti-ghost recipes are ordered according to the increasing gravity of the conditions:

First line: *If a ghost seizes hold of a person and pursues him and cannot be loosed from his body*

Catch-line: *If a ghost has seized hold of a person and it persists, and cannot be loosed from his body*

Library tag: *Excerpted for study. He who fears Nabû* (god of writing) *will not carry it off by theft or deliberately from the house of Marduk-apla-iddin, son of Dābibu.*

The ritual describes making figurines of both a man and a woman. The idea, of course, is to furnish the restless ghost with a female partner who will distract him from his troublesome work among the living and carry him off. Marduk-apla-iddin's incantation to Shamash is almost completely lost, but we do have his *drawings*. They have been done with a great deal of delicacy and authority. Thanks to the artist's care we can actually see (a) the ghost and (b) the woman, as if they were walking down the street in front of us. The left-hand likeness must, accordingly, be the oldest drawing of a ghost in the history of the world.

If a ghost seizes hold of a person and pursues him and cannot be loosed, you purify the potter's pit and throw barley flour into the potter's pit. You pinch off clay and make figurines of a man and a woman. You dress the man in an everyday shift and equip him with travel provisions. You wrap the woman in four red garments and clothe her in a purple cloth. You give her a golden brooch. You equip her fully with bed, chair, mat and towel; you give her a comb and a flask.

At sunrise towards the sun you make the ritual arrangements and set up two carnelian vessels of beer. You set in place a special vessel and set up a juniper censer with juniper. You draw

> *the curtain like that of the diviner. You . . . the figurines together*
> *with their equipment and place them in position . . . and say*
> *as follows,*
>   *Shamash, lord of the broad . . .*

We only have these first five lines of the spell. Everything else in this marvellous cuneiform tablet is irretrievably lost until the very ends of the last two lines:

> *. . . together with their travel provisions to the . . .*
> *. . . Do not look behind you!*

That such a delicate pair of drawings survived the tablet's turbulent history is fortuitous, but even today it is not difficult to see what is going on. Both figures are walking to the right, apparently barefoot. The ghost is a male of some age, skinny, hair tied behind his head and with a full beard. He wears a wrap round his shoulders, which differs slightly from the shift described in the ritual. There are no other indications visible on the lower torso or the limbs to indicate further items of clothing. Significantly, the ghost is shown with his arms stretched forwards and downwards in front of him, the wrists shackled together by a rope. The drawing of this lead disappears into a long crack in the surface of the tablet and its original extent is now no longer clear, but we can be *entirely sure* that the other end was firmly held by the female.

That female strides forward with confidence and self-awareness. She is, I feel, voluptuous, dressed in a close-fitting skullcap and an ankle-length robe with an upper garment, conforming to the items of clothing described in the text. In addition, she wears a necklace, judging by the curved lines at her neck. She has a straight back and is in the prime of condition, irresistible and dominating at the same time. The specialist called in to deal with the case concluded that what this ageing, lonely ghost needed was a lover; they would supply a custom-made example to take complete control and lead him away to eternal bliss below. There is a feel of the 'living happily ever after' about the two of them, walking on through the mists of the millennia, off down to the Netherworld, but still, rather miraculously, in our sights.

8

The Descents of Inanna and Ishtar and Other Netherworld Stories

If a man were Porter of Hell Gate,
He should have old turning the key
                                        Macbeth, Act 2, Scene 3

Mesopotamian ghosts, we know, were supposed to be down in their Netherworld. We know, too, that they were not always in residence and sometimes felt prompted or impelled to return. In the background to daily life, and in the backdrop to escaped ghosts, their Netherworld lay in wait like school after a long summer holiday. We have already considered as best we can the general view of what lay ahead for everyone on the basis of archaeological discovery, but that is only one way of looking at the problem, and that sort approach is, in Assyriology, a recent development. There has also been the literature.

Underground Literature

Assyriologists, and those who have made use of cuneiform resources since Akkadian literature first reached the world outside the British Museum in the nineteenth century, have been substantially misled on the subject of the Mesopotamian Netherworld. The reason is that the first direct evidence they encountered was found among the clear and readable tablets from Nineveh, among which was the memorable and stirring narrative known today as *Ishtar's Descent*. This opened with a handful of poetic lines in Akkadian that became at once and ever after the defining characterisation of the Mesopotamian Netherworld view. In fact, its latter-day viral status is hardly artificial, for the same passage was incorporated, virtually word for word, in three separate literary Netherworld compositions:

To the House of Darkness, the Seat of Irkalla,
To the house from where no one who enters can leave
To the journey from which there is no going back
To the house whose dwellers are deprived of light
Where dust is their sustenance, clay their food;
They see no light, dwelling in darkness
They are clad, like birds, with wings as garments
On door and bolt dust gathers.

It is a description that, once read, stays perforce in the mind. But if one plays the simple game of imagining oneself an inmate in this House of Gloom, reasonable questions present themselves at once. How could any human being tolerate it? Ghosts of dead Sumerians, Akkadians, Assyrians and Babylonians will have been arriving in an endless stream since the Time before the Flood, now utterly unfathomable in number, even to a mathematician adept at counting large numbers in cuneiform sixties. A population stretching out to the remote, ill-lit horizon in every direction, gated in the dust, hunched over with their wings wrapped about them, waiting and waiting in unending blackness and despondency like depressed and inscrutable penguins. And the local regimen? Dust and clay, with extra dust, perhaps, for any young Olivers asking for *more*. It sounds, in the modern expression, like hell.

But this is not Hell in apposition to Heaven, for no forked choice between reward or punishment awaited the Mesopotamians; they arrived too early in history. The conception is like one of those *little-ease* Tower-of-London nightmares: as described, it is, for a human being, nothing more than eternal uncomfortable punishment. Such a destiny is hard for us to accept as that which Mesopotamian Man *really had in mind* as his eyes grew dim and life drew to a close, even when our own sensibilities are blunted by the frightful prospects that later religions imposed on Later Humanity. There was the one outcome, and good or bad behaviour when alive made not a whit of difference. All men died equal.

How, more importantly, can we square this fateful destination with the dedicated ghost literature in its various forms examined in the preceding chapters? Who would expect a ghost, mild-mannered or piratical as it may be, to stay a moment down in such a Netherworld if escape were possible? Which son would forget about the offerings for his departed father incarcerated below if convinced of the dryness and meagreness of the daily diet? And how could the idea of being locked in for eternity, waiting for nothing with the end of the tunnel unlighted, have gained currency as a belief system?

The answer is that *Ishtar's Descent* and the related Netherworld compositions prized by us represent *literary tradition*, which has its own content and purpose, but can in no way be taken to represent day-to-day belief, or be viewed as a model for its understanding. It is that which explains the contrast between Caitlín Barrett's *Pleasant Afterlife*, modelled out of the Mesopotamian ground from the evidence of burial practice, and the operatic enormity of the Netherworld bestowed on us by mythological literature. Real-life practice and traditional narratives about the gods represent different perspectives, if not different worlds.

The inception of the tradition that food and drink should be offered to the dead, on burial and thereafter, must be incalculably remote, a reflex of the long-inherited prehistoric idea that the dead or some part of them went somewhere and would be needful of sustenance wherever they might be. By the time we meet this idea wrapped inside cuneiform texts, it is an entrenched part of daily life, a round of unquestioned duties that devolves upon the eldest son, and his eldest son after him, and that would be carried out accordingly, although – if we are to believe the ghosts– with human-type lapses.

With Sumerian Netherworld literature, however ancient its

ideas might be, its formation, development and even canonisation occurred relatively late, even if our picture of its history and evolution from the second millennium bc is patchy. A timeless, domestic, family-based after-death tradition runs independently of sophisticated literature with its own complex of messages and purposes. It is self-evident that Mesopotamian behaviour towards the dead as reflected in archaeology is not predicated on the literary descriptions, nor is it a response to its obvious deficits. The two strands are largely self-sustaining.

While common beliefs about death and dying were undoubtedly shared across the population, urban to rustic, they endured without support from, or overlapping with, writing. The Netherworld narratives, in this respect, are the direct opposite. They are venerable and literary, and dependent for their being known exclusively on the work of the scribal schools. There they were read and copied out, partly for their own sake and partly as exercise material in mastering literary Sumerian and the writing of its grammar. Of course, individuals among the unwashed and illiterate might know of the stories in outline, or have heard them recited, or have experienced something of them, but only a very slim minority of persons went to school, learned to read and write, and went on their way educated in the classics. The likelihood is that the population at large had but the sketchiest knowledge of the Netherworld literature and its properties that loom so large to us today. Ancient scholars and other individuals may have reflected philosophically on such matters and wondered this way and that, but, if so, there is no echo of it within our grasp.

The paradigm in which death and the departure of the ghost take place in everyday life is of a ballooning, anti-vacuum nature where it is unneedful to ask ourselves whether, so to speak, Mesopotamians 'actually believed' one or other parts of the whole, or one aspect as opposed to another. If you asked a Babylonian whether the *arūtu* offering pipe, perhaps three feet in length, in his yard really reached down to the Netherworld, for example, which everyone knew at one and the same time to lie at a depth beyond imagination (100 leagues, some say), he would look at you without replying, because the question has no validity. Inherited traditions about the big experiences were registered and propagated by a part of the mind where such interrogation had no place. There was an embracing, conceptual system that was socially and psychologically functional, and the toing-and-froing with their very human ghosts was no symbolic, artificial construction in lieu of active belief, but part of life itself.

The view of the Netherworld enshrined in the literary narratives represents a particular and peculiar perspective. It concerns gods and goddesses, life and death with undertones obscure; all cuneiformists who have worked on them agree that there are old and sometimes deep strands woven into the finished literature available to us. Their importance as iconic Mesopotamian writings is unassailable, but they are no guide to what happened on the ground. In this chapter we look at the famous literature that has imposed on us so dramatic a view of the Mesopotamian Netherworld. There are four narratives here: one in Sumerian and three in Akkadian.

1. *The Descent of Inanna*

The classical composition *Inanna's Descent* goes back to the early second millennium bc and is known in this original form only in Sumerian. The ancient title was the opening line, *From Great Above to Great Below*, which establishes the starting point at once: we are to descend to the Netherworld.

La belle Inanna, Sumerian goddess among goddesses, is the central figure of the narrative. She is goddess of sex (and love, and war, and other things), and the underlying concern of the myth is the process, where the living things are, of nature; of copulation, insemination and reproduction. The eternal, cyclic changing of the seasons provides the trigger: the flourishing of new life followed by its quiescence. Inanna thus descends into the Netherworld and perishes there; she is then resurrected and ascends to the world above. This mirror to nature is interwoven with a Sumerian lament for the god Dumuzi, Inanna's lover, who was taken down to the Netherworld as a substitute for the now absent Inanna. Dumuzi is an important god of agriculture, so his presence in the Netherworld likewise ties in with the seasonal changes. The solution was that Inanna and Dumuzi would each spend half the year in the darkness below, in what we might describe as a 'job-share' arrangement. Other literary texts in Sumerian tell us that he was carried away in the Mesopotamian month named after him, Tammuz, which in our calendar is June/July. Dumuzi was thus out of the picture from midsummer to midwinter, when vegetation dies down and vanishes. Inanna's tour of duty was therefore from midwinter to midsummer, when animals do not copulate. Two literary motifs are intertwined here to create one literary composition of great power and drama, but there is another dimension, for Inanna, whose symbol is often an eight-pointed star, has an *astral* identity: she is Venus. By the time this story was committed to clay and stylus, Venus, the second brightest object in the night sky, had been attentively observed and followed by generations of Mesopotamian sky-watchers, for the planet's natural orbit is erratic compared to the stars and most of the other planets; the planet periodically disappears and reappears and stimulated speculation and interpretation. As the story begins, the goddess passes through Ganzir, the gate to the Netherworld that marks the border between Earth and Below. Since the early studies of the Sumerian composition, it has been well established how Inanna's astral cycle of rising and setting underpins, or is enveloped within, the finished *Descent* myth narrative. In a separate Inanna story, when the frisky gardener Shukaletuda first beholds the irresistible form of Inanna, risen out of the Netherworld, he describes her as a 'lone travelling divine ghost'.

8. The Descents of Inanna and Ishtar and Other Netherworld Stories

Inanna's Descent is too drawn out to give in full here, however, so I have summarised the narrative with the help of quotations. As is characteristic with Sumerian literature, repetition and development of lines builds tension; it is easy to imagine this work recited by narrator, with voices, moving figures and music.

It beginneth:
From Great Heaven to Great Below she has set her mind
From Great Heaven to Great Below the goddess has set her
    mind
From Great Heaven to Great Below Inanna has set her mind
My mistress has abandoned Heaven, abandoned Earth;
    she descends to the Netherworld
Inanna has abandoned Heaven, abandoned Earth;
    she descends to the Netherworld . . .

Inanna thereby abandoned her crucial offices of the en and the lagar priesthoods as well as all the main city temples (Uruk, Bad-Tibira, Zabalam, Adab, Nippur, Kish, Akkad; and yet more). The goddess took with her the seven 'me's' (as the Sumerians called them: there is no possible English equivalent in word or concept), which, in knowing hands, classified and administered every facet of existence, and which often crop up in Sumerian mythology. Next, and importantly for the story, we are told of the goddess's apparel:

Head: a turban (the 'pure headdress')
Forehead: a wig
Neck: small lapis lazuli beads
Breast: two matching egg-shaped beads
Body: a pala dress (the 'garment of ladyship')
Eyes: mascara (called 'Let-a-man-come, let-him come')
Breast: pectoral (called 'Come-man, come')
Hand: a golden ring

Off went Inanna, carrying her lapis-lazuli measuring rod and line, giving instructions over her shoulder to her second-in-command, the goddess Ninshubur, who was following. Once Inanna had arrived in the Netherworld, her side-kick on earth was to visit each of the listed temples, now virtual ruins without their mistress, to kick up a big fuss:

> *Make a lament for me in my ruined temples*
> *Pound the drum for me in the sanctuary*
> *Make the rounds of the gods' temples for me:*
> *Scratch at your eyes! Scratch at your nose!*
> *Scratch at your ears, the public place!*
> *Scratch at your anus, the private place!*

Dressed as a pauper Ninshubur was to go to each temple and address the resident deity with the same speech, the first example being Enlil in the Ekur:

> *Father Enlil, allow no one to subjugate your daughter in the*
>   *Netherworld*
> *Don't let your precious metal be alloyed there with the dirt*
>   *of the Netherworld*
> *Don't let your precious lapis lazuli be split there by the*
>   *mason's stone*
> *Don't let your boxwood be chopped up there with the*
>   *carpenter's timber*
> *Don't let the young lady Inanna be subjugated in the*
>   *Netherworld*

These strange lines have suggested that, perhaps, the reference is to Inanna in the form of a sculpture and that in the background is some procession through the cities of Sumer that the goddess mentions, their order indicating its route. Inanna tells her to keep in mind that Father Enki at Eridu, 'knows about the Plant of Life and the Water of Life and is the one who will restore me to life', thereby revealing to the listener that she knows perfectly well what will happen to her. The text is generous with conversations:

> When Inanna arrived at the Ganzir Palace
> She pushed aggressively at the gate to the Netherworld
> She shouted aggressively at the gate to the Netherworld:
>> 'Open up, Gatekeeper, open up!
>> Open up, Neti, open up!
>> I am all alone and I want to come in!'
> Neti, Head Netherworld-Gatekeeper, answered Inanna the
>> Pure:
>> 'Who are you?'
>> 'I am Inanna, going to the East'
>> 'If you are Inanna, and you're going East,
>> Why have you travelled to the Land-of-No-Return?
> What inclination prompted you to take the road from which
>> no traveller returns?'

Her answer was that she had come to attend the funeral rites of Gugalanna, husband of her elder sister, Ereshkigal. Neti, insecure as to procedure, consulted Ereshkigal about the 'lone girl, your sister Inanna', arrived bedecked with all her paraphernalia, aggressively demanding access. Queen Ereshkigal was very put out and instructed Neti to bolt all seven of the Netherworld Gates.

> Then let each gate of the Ganzir Palace [the Netherworld
>> Gates] be opened one by one.
>> As for her, after she enters,
>> When she has been subjugated, her clothes stripped off,
>> They are to be taken away.'

Inanna was forced to remove one item of her apparel for each gate before she was allowed through:

> '*Come on, Inanna, come through.*'
> *And when Inanna entered,*
> *When she entered the first gate,*
> *The turban, the Pure Headdress, was removed from her*
>   *head.*
>   '*What is going on here?*'
>   '*Be calm, Inanna. The me's of the Netherworld are being*
>   *fulfilled.*
>   *Inanna, you must not open your mouth against the sacred*
>   *customs of the Netherworld!*'

This gate-by-gate denudation of the goddess, in accordance with 'sacred customs' about which she knew nothing, proceeded as instructed. Once through Gate 7, completely naked, the goddess had to sit on her sister's throne after the latter had pointedly vacated it.

> *The Anunnaki, the seven Judges, rendered their decision*
>   *against her.*
> *They looked at her with the look of death,*
> *They spoke to her with the speech of anger,*
> *The shouted at her with the shout of guilt,*
> *The afflicted woman was turned into a corpse*
> *And the corpse was hung on a hook.*

Such was the fate of Goddess Inanna. Three days later, Ninshubur, back at home, carried out her mistress's instructions. She met with angry rejections wherever she went; this one is typical:

> *In his rage Father Enlil answered Ninshubur:*
>   '*My daughter craved Great Heaven and Great Below also.*
>   *Inanna craved Great Heaven and Great Below also.*
>   *The me's of the Netherworld are me's which are not to be*
>   *coveted,*
>   *For whoever gets them must remain in the Netherworld.*

144

> *Whoever, having gained that place, could want to come*
> *back up again?'*

In the end Father Enki answered the wearied Ninshubur. Using dirt from under his fingernails, he created the kurgarra and the galaturra, handing the former the Plant of Life and the latter the Water of Life. They were to go down to the Netherworld and 'flit about the gates like flies and slip in through the door pivots as if they were ghosts themselves'. There they would find the naked, pregnant Ereshkigal, wracked with pain in belly and back. They should act sympathetically, but be ruthless in bargaining:

> *'Just say to her: "Give us that corpse that is hanging on*
> *that hook"'*
> *She will say:*
> *'That is the corpse of your mistress'*
> *You say to her:*
> *'Whether it is that of our king or that of our mistress, give*
> *it to us anyway'*
> *Then they will give you that corpse that was hanging on the*
> *hook.*
> *At that, one of you sprinkle it with the Plant of Life and the*
> *other with Water of Life.*
> *Thus will Inanna arise.*

Everything unfolded as Enki had predicted. 'Take your mistress . . .' said Ereshkigal, conceding, to the galaturra and the kurgarra. However, just as Inanna was going up the Anunnaki, the Divine Judges, grabbed her, declaring:

> *'Who has ever gone up out of the Netherworld?*
> *Who has ever gone up out of the Netherworld alive?*
> *If Inanna wants to go out of the Netherworld*
> *Let her provide a substitute for herself.'*

This bargain proposal is the nub of the story, and very ominous for Dumuzi. Inanna is watched by a convoy of demons at every step on her journey back up and her hunt for Dumuzi. These demons, big and small, needing neither food nor drink, indeed they,

Eat no grain offering
Drink no libation
Accept no sweet gifts
Never enjoy the pleasure of love-making
Never have sweet children to kiss
Rather do they tear the wife away from her husband in love-
  making
Snatch children from their father's knee
Kidnap the bride from her marriage chamber

They try to take Ninshubur as her mistress's substitute, but Inanna protects her life-saver, the recruiter of Enki's help. City by city they demand the resident god to take Inanna's place, but she refuses each until they all arrive at the great Apple Tree that grows in the plain of Kulaba, where they find Dumuzi the Shepherd, magnificently dressed, seated on a magnificent throne. The demons seize him by his thighs, and,

The seven of them poured the milk out of his churns
The seven of them shook their heads like [. . .]
The shepherd played his flute and pipe no longer before her.

Inanna was roused to use identical wording to compensate for her own painful treatment:

She looked at him with the look of death
She spoke to him with the speech of anger
She shouted at him with the shout of guilt
  (saying) 'As for him, take him away!'

The wailing Dumuzi implored sun god Utu, his brother-in-law, to change his hand and foot into those of a reptile so that he could escape the demons. At this point the well-preserved manuscript becomes fragmentary. Utu pulls off the reptile changes and Dumuzi escapes at first, but the demons end in capturing him. We next hear Ereshkigal speaking very firmly to Dumuzi in person, and, as we would put it, copying in the absent Inanna:

> 'You: *one-half of the year*; your sister: *one-half of the year!*
> *On the day* you *designate: on that day* you go up.
> *On the day that* your sister *designates* she goes up.'
> *And thus it was that Inanna the Pure handed Dumuzi over as*
>   *her substitute.*
> *Sweet is the praise of Inanna the Pure!*

2. *The Descent of Ishtar*

The *Descent of Ishtar* is written in Akkadian and comes to us in seventh-century tablets from the libraries of Assyrian Nineveh and Assur. It is a *distillation* of the older and much longer Sumerian *Inanna's Descent*. Unusually, the two interrelated versions are not translated one from the other, or combined to make a bilingual version. When they are compared, the *Descent of Ishtar* skimps on detail and requires filling out or knowledge of the original to make sense of what happens. Broadly speaking, Assyrian Ishtar, like Sumerian Inanna before her, braved her sister Ereshkigal, all-powerful subterranean queen, and went down to the Netherworld to rescue her dead lover Dumuzi.

The *Descent of Ishtar* opens with the description already quoted that, brochure-like, appears also almost word for word in Nergal and Ereshkigal below, and Gilgamesh Tablet VII.

Introduction

> To the Underworld, Land-of-No-Return,
> Ishtar, daughter of Sin, set her mind,
> Did the daughter of Sin indeed set her mind.
> To the House of Darkness, the Seat of Irkalla,
> To the house from where no one who enters can leave
> To the journey from which there is no going back
> To the house whose dwellers are deprived of light
> Where dust is their sustenance, clay their food;
> They see no light, dwelling in darkness
> They are clad, like birds, with wings as garments
> On door and bolt dust gathers.

The crucial point, of course, is what happened next.

> When Ishtar reached the gate to the Underworld
> She addressed speech to the Gatekeeper:
>
> 'Gatekeeper!' she said, 'open your gate for me!
> Indeed, open your gate for me so I can come in!
> If you don't open the gate I will be unable to come in.
> I will break down the door and I will smash the bolt!
> I will break down the doorframes and knock over the door
> panes
> I will smash the hinges and rip off the knob!
> I will make the dead rise up so they consume the living;
> The dead will outnumber the living!'

Ereshkigal is livid in the face when she hears from her Gatekeeper who it is that waits at the gate, for the presence of her living sister inside her deep, dark kingdom threatens structure and stability both Above and Below. Ishtar is carrying her skipping-rope with which she can whip things up even in front of the great god Ea. The queen decides there and then to kill Ishtar. First, she must get her in her power.

> 'Go, Gatekeeper. Open your gate for her.
> Treat her according to the age-old rules.'
> The Gatekeeper went and opened his gate for her.
> 'Come in, My Lady, that Kutha can rejoice over you,
> That the palace of the Underworld can delight over you!'

> He let her through the first gate, and loosened and took off
> the great tiara on her head.

> 'Why, Gatekeeper, did you take off the great tiara on my
> head?'
> 'Come in, My Lady; thus are the rules of the Mistress of the
> Netherworld . . .'

This, however, is only Gate 1 of seven. As with her predecessor, the process is solemnly repeated, whereby Ishtar is successively deprived of her earrings, necklace, breast pins, birth-stone girdle, bracelets and anklets and, finally, her shift; again she is naked and diminished when ushered into the presence of her sister queen. Ereshkigal instructs her vizier, Namtar, to send all manner of diseases, sixty in number (including eye, arm, foot, heart and head disease), against Ishtar to stifle her life. The consequences in the familiar world above are dire, for all sexual connection in the animal and human kingdoms is thereby terminated. Under these circumstances the god Ea, to whom appeal had been made, created a strangely ambiguous and seductive being, a *zikru*, called Aṣuṣu-namir – an *assinnu*, otherwise known to function within Ishtar's cult circle – to beguile Ereshkigal with his considerable charms into giving him whatever he requested. In this case the demand was perspicaciously for the skin bag hanging on the wall containing the Water of Life with which Ishtar could be revivified. She sees this as a 'request of me that should not have been made', and curses and reviles Aṣuṣu-namir. Namtar is sent to bring in the Anunnaki Judges and he sprinkles Ishtar with the essential Waters of Life.

At length Ishtar is able to proceed back through Gates 7 to 1, her articles of apparel returned to her one by one each. Dumuzi, the 'lover of her youth', is to pay the penalty and be her substitute.

> *'You shall not rob me of my only brother*
> *On the day when Dumuzi comes back up*
> *The lapis lazuli pipe and carnelian ring coming with him,*
> *And male and female mourners come up with him,*
> *So shall the dead come up and smell the smoke offering.'*

This concluding passage refers to the annual ritual in Assyria known as *taklimtu*, in which a statue of Dumuzi was bathed and anointed, then to lie in state. This took place in Nineveh, and it seems likely that the *Descent of Ishtar* was recited or performed as part of that festival.

The Netherworld at Kutha

Although the *Ishtar's Descent* tablets were written in seventh-century-bc Assyria, we learn from the Gatekeeper's ironic address to Ishtar, 'Come in, My Lady, that Kutha can rejoice over you', that the entrance to the Underworld was at the important *Babylonian* site of Kutha. This lay to the south, modern Tell Ibrahim, about twenty-five miles north-east of Babylon. The location indicates that the narrative took its first-millennium form in a southern Mesopotamia context, and was specifically associated with the cult of Nergal, god of death. The site of Kutha has not been seriously investigated, but a full-scale excavation today would no doubt produce startling discoveries, for that is where Nergal was at home. Here was his great temple Emeslam, founded long before by the Sumerian King Shulgi at the turn of the second millennium bc, and many surviving cuneiform texts refer to the city in a funereal context. As the magic incantation already quoted in Chapter 6 memorably declares,

8. The Descents of Inanna and Ishtar and Other Netherworld Stories

I will not go to Kutha, the ghosts' assembly point!

We can imagine an imposing Gate to the Netherworld structure within Nergal's Babylonian temple complex, separate from the cella where sat the god's great cult statue. It does not take a great deal more imagination to visualise some appropriate installation leading to an ancient subterranean structure, manned and protected by priests and temple personnel, with a flourishing cult centre attached, healers and practitioners to hand, and vendors with amulets and talismans for sale. In Chapter 10, Part 2, a possible northern Assyrian equivalent at Tarbiṣu and an existing Underworld-installation of this type are considered.

For first-millennium readers and listeners, we can be sure, Queen Ereshkigal's Netherworld was certainly 'down there', beneath their feet. If we try to visualise the seven-gate path all the way down from Above to Below that she literally followed, the descent must have meandered on a gentle gradient with leisurely curves:

Author's half-serious sketch map of Ishtar's passage de rite, redrawn by James Fraser.

3. *Nergal and Ereshkigal*

The story of Nergal and Ereshkigal is also known to us only in Akkadian. One version of the story comes on first-millennium-bc tablets from the sites of Assyrian Sultantepe (in modern Turkey) and Babylonian Uruk (in southern Iraq); between them they preserve a good proportion of the roughly seven hundred and fifty original lines of text. There is, however, an older and shorter version of the story which only takes up about ninety lines, found on a cuneiform tablet excavated at Amarna in *Egypt*, a rare example of Mesopotamian literature so far from the cuneiform heartland. Tablets from Amarna were strange-looking, of unusual clay with untidy or informal cuneiform signs, and in the nineteenth century doubts circulated that they were genuine, let alone truly harvested from Egyptian soil. Genuine they certainly proved to be, however, written mostly in Akkadian with a few local features thrown in, the bulk of them royal correspondence – the Amarna letters – that threw new light on the countries under Egyptian hegemony and their relations with Egyptian authority in the fourteenth century bc.

A small number of tablets were not letters, but lexical and dictionary texts or mythological stories. The two important literary compositions are *Nergal and Ereshkigal*, set in the Netherworld, and *Adapa and the South Wind*. The former today is partly in the British Museum, partly in the Vorderasiatisches Museum, Berlin, for its post-'excavation' history was adventurous. Both works are written in a confident hand unlike the relaxed 'Syro-Hittite' cuneiform style of most of the Amarna correspondence, similar to the letters sent to Amarna from Babylon itself and exemplifying their Mesopotamian origin. These works of imported Mesopotamian learning provide a glimpse of an on-site cuneiform teaching and training, reflecting the Pharaoh's need for competent cuneiform scribes on his staff to work in international governance, for Akkadian written in cuneiform was by then the lingua

franca of the surrounding world. The teaching function of the
Nergal and Ereshkigal tablet is explicit in the simplicity of
the spelling signs used and the pruned-down feel of the narrative. Practical tablet work also reveals itself in black and red
ink marks on the clay surface to aid in reading or line counting;
this is a home Egyptian practice, natural on papyri, transferred
to clay.

The Amarna story plunges right in. Ereshkigal is Queen of
the Netherworld, in post and unable to get away, but clearly *au
fait* with what's in the air:

> When the gods organised a banquet
> They sent a messenger
> To their sister Ereshkigal:
>   'We cannot go down to you
>   And you cannot come up to us.
>   So, send someone to collect your share of the food!'
> Ereshkigal sent Namtar, her vizier.
> Namtar went up to high Heaven.
> When Namtar entered the gods stood up,
> [. . .] and pronounced a blessing on Namtar,
> their older sister's messenger.

Alone of the gods, Nergal refuses to do honour to Envoy Namtar,
a real slap in the face. When Namtar delivers Ereshkigal's food
portion, she is highly offended at the insult and tells him to go
back up and bring her the culprit for execution. Namtar goes
back up to Heaven to find Nergal, who, meanwhile, has disguised
himself. It seems then that the supreme god Ea gives Nergal a
throne for Ereshkigal. Nergal is still afraid that the Netherworld
queen will kill him, so when he descends, he takes with him two
sets of seven of his adjutant disease-bringing demons to see him
through the, this time, fourteen manned gates. Fortified by their
presence, Nergal declares:

> '*Gatekeeper, Gatekeeper, open your gate!*
> *Loosen the bolts so I can come in.*
> *I have been despatched*
>   *to your Mistress, Ereshkigal!*'

Despite his disguise Nergal is recognised by the loyal Namtar, who of course reports to his mistress, who has him welcome Nergal. The demons are left standing at the gates as Nergal enters the court of Ereshkigal. He, however, grabs her by the hair in order to kill her on the spot, but disaster is averted when she offers him her hand to rule the Netherworld by her side. He accepts. The story at Amarna is thus fairly straightforward, and transparently is composed to explain how Nergal ended up in the Netherworld as Ereshkigal's husband and joint ruler.

The first-millennium versions, written down about seven hundred years later, present the same broad plot line, although what actually takes place is a good deal more complicated. Again, there are holes in the narratives. Kakka the messenger gets safely through seven gates and invites Ereshkigal to send her own messenger to collect her portion:

> '*Anu, your father, sent me to you,*
> *Saying, 'You can't come up,*
> *You don't come up to us in your year,*
> *and there is no going down for us.*
> *In our month we don't go down to you,*
> *So let your messenger come . . .*'

All honour her messenger except Nergal, and Ereshkigal orders Namtar to fetch Nergal down, for she has a plan to go up herself. Nergal passes through the gates to kneel before the queen as Anu's ambassador. He cannot resist the devastating beauty of Ereshkigal and they make love together for seven consecutive (days and) nights. After all that Nergal decides to go back to Heaven; but when he gets there Ea sprinkles him with water with disastrous consequences. Ereshkigal, meanwhile, washing herself, learns suddenly that he has departed. Namtar is despatched to Heaven to plead the queen's case:

> 'Ever since I was a child and a daughter
> I did not know the play of maidens,
> I did not know the romping of girls;
> That god, whom you sent to us, had intercourse with me, let
>   him lie with me again;
> Send that god to us that he may be my lover and spend nights
>   with me
> I am unclean, I am impure, I cannot render judgements of the
>   great gods, the great gods who dwell in Irkalla!
> If you do not send that god,
> According to the ordinances of Irkalla and the great
>   Netherworld
> I shall raise up the dead and they will consume the living!
> I shall make the dead more numerous than the living!'

Namtar delivers this Ishtar-like, hard-to-ignore message. The story ends in a flurry of dramatic activity: Nergal *hangs* the seven keepers of the Netherworld gates, grabs Ereshkigal, and they *make love* for another seven (days and) nights. At that point Anu, who has been keeping an eye on all this, appoints Nergal as ruler of the Netherworld by Ereshkigal's side.

4. Ningishzida Escapes the Netherworld

In 1990 Wilfred Lambert translated a partially preserved and difficult Old Babylonian tablet in Akkadian from the city of Ur, with a different Underworld narrative. The tablet originated in a schoolroom and is probably an advanced curricular extract derived from a fuller composition. The hero, or at least the principal, is the god Ningishzida, son of the god Ningirida. The narrative as it comes to us is murky, reminiscent of the

Verse that is supposed to be Evidence beginning 'They told me you had been to her' in *Alice*. Ningishzida, son of Ningirida, has been taken to the Netherworld, but we do not know why. There he is judged before the Anunna gods, and the constable-like *gallû*-demon, like his colleagues dealing with Inanna, escorts him, down we must assume, to Ereshkigal. Ningirida intercedes skilfully with this officious individual, offering enough silver to make a *life-sized statue of his son in his place*, and instructs him how to persuade Ereshkigal to agree. At his release Ningishzida is moved, inexplicably, to weep red tears. Perhaps an aetiology is concealed therein, but there is no more of the text to be had. A great deal here is unexplained; most importantly, it seems to me, why Ereshkigal should swap the young god she was after for an effigy. No doubt there were other stories set in the Netherworld, where dramatic scenery and intense drama were guaranteed.

Revisiting Chapter 3's Dead Ur-Namma

To conclude this chapter, with the Inanna/Ishtar narratives in mind, another look is called for at the arrival of the king of Ur in the Netherworld in Chapter 3. Ur-Namma knows well, we are told, about the poor quality of the food and drink there. Despite being recently deceased he is portrayed as a much larger-than-life character. At the arrival of the Big Man, all in the Netherworld experienced paroxyms of pleasure, for there were hand-outs all round, lashings of food and drink, bribes left, right and centre, and he himself was appointed straight in at the top table; next minute, indeed, he was Chief Justice at the side of Gilgamesh himself.

Ur-Namma reminds me, in this composition, of Al Capone. The Netherworld is exactly the opposite of that depicted in the official versions, to such an extent that I wonder if the whole composition is not a reaction against the primary features of the literary Netherworld picture as received: the getting in; the conditions; the diet; the works. I submit, therefore, that the Sumerian composition *Urnamma A* is not a royal, tear-stricken hagiography, but a satire against the tyrannic understanding of the Netherworld imposed from the standpoint of Inanna of Uruk.

It will have been observed that those in these stories who move freely up and down between the *Great Above* and the *Great Below* without lasting consequences are fully paid-up, blue-blood divinities. It is not for nothing that we know the Netherworld as the *Land-of-No-Return*. In the following chapter, however, we follow in the underworld exploits of two remarkable characters of whom such an assumption cannot be so safely made.

9

Gilgamesh, Enkidu
and the Netherworld

O Hero, what a Hero hadst thou been
If half thy outward graces had been placed
About thy thoughts and counsels of thy heart!
                    Much Ado About Nothing,
                              Act 4, Scene 1

We further continue our explorations below in the company of
two truly iconic Mesopotamian personalities, Gilgamesh and his
friend Enkidu, as recounted in the Sumerian composition entitled
Gilgamesh, Enkidu and the Netherworld. Between about 2000
and 1600 bc, Sumerian-speaking schoolboys everywhere read
through this composition, copied out extracts and discussed the
grammar. It was about three hundred and fifty lines long, and
benefited from a star-studded cast and fast-moving events that
undoubtedly held their youthful interest. The same narrative was
later translated into Akkadian and tacked on the end of the
famous *Epic of Gilgamesh* as Tablet XII, as we will see.

Part 1: The Sumerian Narrative

The opening Sumerian lines set the scene poetically at the very
dawn of time:

In those days, in those distant days,
In those nights, in those far-off nights,
In those years, in those distant years,
In primeval days when . . .

Important things happened. Heaven and Earth were separated. Mankind appeared. An, chief god, took Heaven; Enlil (god no. 2) took Earth, and,

As for the Netherworld, it was given to Ereshkigal as a dowry

The moment this happened Enki, no. 3 (whom they refer to here, as in other stories, as '*Father* Enki') embarked on a boat to travel alone over the waters to visit the Netherworld. There were mysterious attempts during the voyage to sink his boat with stones large and small, so his passage was stormy, and it has remained so for all the Assyriologists who have ever read this text since, for no one today seems to understand why Enki went there. It can hardly be contested, when you read the text, that Enki went there as her husband to cohabit with his wife Ereshkigal.

In the way of classical Sumerian writing, the prologue words of this composition come to be repeated three times, but despite that we hear no more about this journey thereafter, or its consequences, for the remainder of the text. I think that entitles us to read between the lines of cuneiform and make sense of it. I assume that in this composition the god Enki and the goddess Ereshkigal, in the luxury of her dowry domain, engendered a child, who plays an important role in the drama that follows.

During the frightening storm that beset Enki, one single tree planted on the bank of the River Euphrates (species ḫalub, or boxwood), had become uprooted. A woman, described only at first as 'revered on account of An's word', and 'revered on account of Enlil's word', rescued the tree and took it to 'Inanna's splendid orchard', where she planted and watered it, using her foot rather than her hand. We discover in this roundabout way that this woman was the goddess Inanna herself. The scene then moves in to the Sumerian city of Uruk where her orchard was situated. Inanna appreciates her growing tree and hankers after a magnificent chair and a bed to be carved from its wood. With the intervening years, however, as its trunk grew thick, obstacles to her plan appeared. A spell-defying serpent lay coiled among the tree's roots; the *Anzû*-eagle and its young nested in its branches and a dread Succubus (Kiskilla in Sumerian) dwelt within the trunk. The presence of these intruders made Inanna very miserable; and that she would ever get her longed-for furniture seemed increasingly unlikely. Reiterating the whole thirty-nine introductory lines, she asked her brother Utu for help:

> *When Utu was coming out of his bed chamber*
> *His sister, holy Inanna,*
> *Said to Utu, the valiant warrior,*
>   *'Brother of mine, in those remote days . . .'*

but he was just not interested. The next morning Inanna tried another idea:

> *When Utu was coming out of his bed chamber*
> *His sister, holy Inanna,*
> *Said to Gilgamesh, the warrior,*
>   *'Brother of mine, in those remote days . . .'*

and the reader – or the listener – is presented with the whole ḫalub-tree history for the third time. It is thus that we first encounter Gilgamesh.

Sometime king of Uruk and taller far than a tall man, Gilgamesh is the archetype hero of life and literature; valiant and unconquerable, his adventures are celebrated ever after in a variety of Sumerian compositions and, especially, the famous *Epic of Gilgamesh* in Akkadian. When we meet him in *Gilgamesh, Enkidu and the Netherworld*, however, he is at the outset of his career, his characteristic heroic qualities placed at the disposal of irresistible Inanna. Gilgamesh lives in Uruk, but there is nothing at the beginning of the story to make us anticipate that he would later be king. He lives in a house like everyone else; he is, too, an orphan, for neither his father nor mother is mentioned, while the carpenter's wife and daughter, he says, have become for him as his own mother and sister. On top of that he is gang leader, *primus inter pares* perhaps, already charismatic, but no high-born or privileged individual. The Sumerian word translated 'gang' here is also used for 'troop', and conveys exactly the right meaning: it is not without significance that all the gang members are, like him, fatherless and thus easily led by a dominant individual who even subjects them intermittently to physical pain. A young Marlon Brando, perhaps.

Gilgamesh was to go down in Mesopotamian history not only as a great king in the Alexander-the-Great mould, with associated stories appearing long after his demise, but also as one of semi-divine origin. Two-thirds of Gilgamesh was divine, we are later told, one-third human. The two-thirds component was from his mother, the goddess Ninsun, the one-third merely mortal; the *pater* remains a trifle *incertum*, although it suited Gilgamesh on his way to power in the city and the country to give out that his father was actually Lugalbanda, king of Uruk.

At this early stage, however, we are left uninformed about his origins. Inanna addresses him, as she does Utu, as her 'brother' when she wants his help, although only Utu was her real (and twin) brother. There is no independent indication that Inanna and Gilgamesh were literally brother and sister. Were it so the latter would be completely a god and not part a man, but while it is true that Gilgamesh's name came to be included in certain specialised lists of gods, here Inanna is manipulating him into helping her rather than implying a blood relationship, 'brother' being more like 'cousin' in Shakespeare.

> *Her brother, warrior Gilgamesh, supported her in that affair.*
> *He wrapped a special cloth of fifty minas weight around*
> *his hips*
> *Making those fifty minas look like thirty shekels.*
> *He grasped in his hand his campaign axe of bronze*
> *Of seven talents and seven minas*

He smote that spell-defying serpent within its roots;
From its branches he drove the Anzû-eagle and its young to
*   the mountain;*
From its trunk he made the Succubus who had made its home
*   there*
flee to the wildness.
*   As for the tree, he pulled it out by the roots and ripped off*
*   its branches.*
*   The sons of his city who had gone up with him*
Cut up the branches and tied them into bundles
Setting them down at the foothill of the mountain.
*   He gave wood to Holy Inanna for her chair*
He gave wood for her bed
For himself he had the roots made into his ekema (or pukku)
*   ball*
And its branches into his ellag (or mekkû) stick.

This ball-and-stick apparatus had evidently been at the back of
Gilgamesh's mind all along, for they were essential for a particular game that he relished:

Really wanting ball and puck, he played puck in the street,
He who is always boastful lauds himself in the street.
As for the young men of his city, who always desired ball
*   play,*
While he was riding on the hips of a gang of the sons of
*   widows*
They lamented, 'Oh my neck! Oh, my back!'
If one had a mother, she would bring food for her son
If one had a sister, she would pour water for her brother.

There has been a good deal of discussion among Assyriologists
about what the ekema/*pukku* and ellag/*mekkû* actually were, and
what was the game. The usual conclusion has been that they
were, respectively, a puck (unrelated!) and a stick for a kind of

human polo, where riders mount their peers rather than quadrupeds. We are told that, as darkness fell, Gilgamesh marked the spot where the ekema had last fallen, and then 'carried his ekema before him and brought it to his house'. This detail, diagnostically speaking, is highly suggestive. It means that when the game was continued at first light, the ekema had to be accurately replaced on the same spot so that play could follow from where it left off. This feature rules out that the underlying game was of the hockey or polo type, with a goal into which the ekema had to be knocked. On the contrary, it suggests that hitting the ekema with one's ellag was the essential feature of the game in itself, thereby delineating conquered territory, amid the rough horse-play. Something new about this game can now be suggested.

There is a traditional street game of very wide historical and geographical distribution known generically as *Tipcat*, with abundant local names such as *Gillidanda*. Players require a *gilli*, a small, oval-shaped piece of wood tapered at both ends, between 2.5 and 5 cm thick; and a *danda*, a wooden stick, perhaps 1 metre long. The *gilli* is placed on, say, a stone, and a player strikes one of its pointed ends sharply with the *danda* so that it flies up into the air. He then thwacks the *gilli* as hard as he can before it falls. There are many varieties of play, such as trying to drive the *gilli* furthest, or catching the *gilli* to take over the *danda*, with competitive variations between individuals or even teams. It is, above all, a *dangerous street game*, and – as witnessed by the writer in Sri Lanka on one occasion – is played with hair-raising disregard of, say, windows or passers-by. This rough-housing quality clearly applies in the Gilgamesh game, much intensified by the players having to carry one another in competition or pursuit, and it went on all day. It seems not unlikely that the game played on the streets of third-millennium Uruk was of the *Tipcat* family.

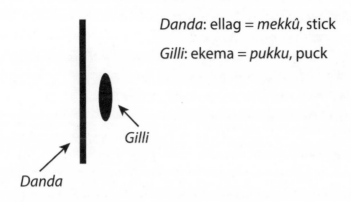

Danda: ellag = *mekkû*, stick

Gilli: ekema = *pukku*, puck

*Schematic identification of the equipment
for the game so enjoyed by Gilgamesh, drawn by James Fraser.*

The next day, however, about to resume play, Gilgamesh had rebellion on his hands. The widows were full of remonstrations on behalf of their battered sons, the young maidens likewise with regard to their brothers or sweethearts. Then something crucial happened:

> *His puck and stick fell down to the bottom of the*
>   *Netherworld*
> *He stretched out his hand but he couldn't reach it.*
> *At the Ganzir gate, in front of the Netherworld, he sat down.*
> *Gilgamesh wept, he was sobbing:*
>   *'Oh my ekema puck! Oh my ellag stick!*
>   *Oh puck, whose pleasures I had not fully enjoyed!*
>   *Oh game, in which I had not lost interest!*
>   *If only, right now, my ekema puck were still there for me*
>   *in the carpenter's house!*
>   *If only, right now, my ellag stick were still there for me*
>   *in the carpenter's house!*
>   *If only they were there for me with the carpenter's wife,*
>   *who is like the mother who bore me!*

> *If only they were there for me with the carpenter's*
> *daughter,*
> *who is like my little sister!*
> *My ekema puck has fallen down into the Netherworld:*
> *who will bring it up for me?*
> *My ellag stick has fallen down to Ganzir:*
> *who will bring it up for me?'*

Enkidu, his servant, answered him . . .

At this dramatic point we encounter the famous Enkidu: the two principal actors in all of Mesopotamian drama are now on stage!

Note that Enkidu here is Gilgamesh's servant. He is much disturbed at Gilgamesh's distress about his puck and stick:

> *'My master! You weep so much! Why are you so heartsick?*
> *Today I will bring up your ekema up from the Netherworld!*
> *I will bring up your ellag from Ganzir!'*

Gilgamesh's batman offers there and then to go and retrieve them, thereby raising an interesting question. *Why* should Enkidu be completely undeterred or uninhibited about going down into the Netherworld? Far and few between are those Mesopotamian individuals who ventured to go from Above to Below, and the alacrity with which Enkidu volunteers requires consideration.

The puck and stick are supposed to have fallen into the Netherworld due to the ongoing brouhaha of protest made by the womenfolk. This glossed-over account strikes me as mechanically unconvincing. Are we to believe that Gilgamesh started like a guilty thing when they began yelling and the instruments of contest just tumbled from his hands? Might it not rather be that Gilgamesh took the opportunity under cover of the dispute to drop the equipment deliberately down into the Netherworld, knowing that if he made a big enough fuss Enkidu would

166

immediately come to the rescue? This would mean that Gilgamesh planned to despatch his trusty lieutenant into the Netherworld for reasons of his own, manoeuvring the matter brilliantly.

It is telling, from this point of view, that for the remainder of *Gilgamesh, Enkidu and the Netherworld* we hear nothing more at all about the lost game equipment, nor do we even discover whether Gilgamesh got them back in the end. This leads me to suspect that the entire puck-and-stick episode is a plot device, and that Enkidu was, practically speaking, tricked by Gilgamesh into making the descent. Tricks are a classical feature in mythological narrative and this, I think, is a choice example.

Gilgamesh, notwithstanding, seemed well up himself on the hazards to be anticipated, and imposed clear advice on Enkidu as to how the Netherworld visitor can avoid drawing attention to himself, explaining the protocol required on coming face to face with a dead relative:

> *Do not dress in your cleanest garment*
> *they will know you are a stranger,*
> *Do not anoint yourself with sweet oil from a flask*
> *Lest they will gather round you because of the aroma,*
> *Do not hurl a throwstick in the Netherworld;*
> *Lest those struck by a throwstick will gather around you,*
> *Or take a* manu-*staff in your hand*
> *Lest the* udug-*demons will tremble on your account,*
> *Do not wear sandals on your feet!*
> *Do not shout in the Netherworld!*
> *Do not kiss the wife you loved!*
> *Do not beat the wife you hated!*
> *Do not kiss the son you loved!*
> *Do not beat the son you hated!*
> *Otherwise the complaints will hold you in the Netherworld!*

In particular, he warned, such behaviour will rouse the attention of Queen Ereshkigal, to be found lying practically uncovered in a state of perpetual mourning, her nails 'like a bronze pick-axe', while she 'pulls out her leek-like hair': not, one understands, a queen to be irritated.

There is, we may observe, no other indication that Enkidu had either a dead wife or a dead son, as Gilgamesh surely knew, so part at least of his master's advice is generic, as if quoting from rules put up on a notice board, unless it might be that he is really speaking of *himself* here, as we will see. Enkidu on his part, true to form, flouted all these instructions one by one in the same order. There was a great disturbance of the peace and by unanimous response the intruder was to be prevented from leaving:

> *Namtar did not hold him, Asag did not hold him,*
> *the Netherworld held him there!*
> *The divine udug-demon, Nergal the merciless*
> *did not hold him, the Netherworld held him!*
> *He did not fall in battle on the field of manhood,*
> *the Netherworld held him!*

Gilgamesh, pacing above meanwhile, grew increasingly nervous. He went for help to Enlil in his temple Ekur, arguing that Enkidu shouldn't be detained in the Netherworld because he had neither been taken by one of Nergal's fateful staff nor had he died in battle: it wasn't a 'normal' mortality case. There was no response. The same happened at Ur, when he turned to Sin, still weeping for his friend. *Father Enki* at Eridu, however, responded, with a proposal for the sun god Utu, who knew all the ins and outs of the Netherworld as he passed through it every night. There was no need for the troublemaker to make his own way back through the Ganzir Gate:

> *'Utu, open a chink in the Netherworld, and then*
> *Send his (Gilgamesh's) servant up to him from the*
> *Netherworld!'*

He, Utu, opened a chink (ab-làl) *in the Netherworld*
By means of his gust of wind (si-si-ig) *he sent his*
    (Gilgamesh's)
servant up to him from the Netherworld

This inventive air lift proved successful.

The two fell on each other's necks:
They embraced each other and they kissed
They exhausted one another with questions:

Gilg.   *You saw the Netherworld regulations:*
        If only you would tell me about it, my friend!
        If only you would tell me about it!
Enk.   *If I am to tell you about the Netherworld regulations*
        Sit you down, then, and weep!
Gilg.   *I sit down then, and will weep.*

Notice that there is no, 'Here, Gilgamesh, your precious stick and puck!' What does follow is a back-and-forth question-and-answer session in which Gilgamesh, impatient and insatiable for hard information about the fate of the dead, literally interrogates Enkidu. His servant is reluctant to divulge what he had seen, for he had witnessed pathetic scenes that he knew would reduce his master to tears. The questionnaire that emerges thus provokes our earliest view of dead Mesopotamians in the Mesopotamian Netherworld. The pattern runs,

Gilg.   *Did you see the man who . . .*
Enk.   *I saw him.*
Gilg.   *How does he fare?*
Enk.   *He . . .*

The Sumerian and later Akkadian translations are not necessarily identical, and the earlier version is sometimes wordier. Enkidu starts his report with *sex* in the Netherworld-to-come; he was evidently long familiar with his master's interest in, and success rate with, young women:

Enk. *When you touched your penis, it brought joy to your heart.*
Gilg. *Where is that penis? Can one 'go' there?*
Enk. *The penis is like a rotten beam, grubs devour it.*
Gilg. *Where is the vulva? I want to 'go' there.*
Enk. *The vulva is like a crack in the ground; it is filled with dust.*
Gilg. *'Woe!' said the master, and sat down in the dust.*

Gilgamesh is here called, by the way, en (literally 'master'), which defines his relationship with Enkidu, his šubur ('servant'). The same word en is later said of Gilgamesh as Lord of the city of Uruk or Kullab, when it means ruler, but Gilgamesh at this stage is not, as far as we can tell, yet in line for the throne.

This Netherworld *mise-en-scène*, as visualised during the second millennium bc, is by any judgement a remarkable human document. The ghostly residents are separated into type cases, the whole remarkable for the curious sense of realism about it all. The much longer itemisation of ghosts that fills out the magic texts (Chapter 5) reflects the same rational tradition, overlaid by the need to cover all possible cases. Here, each case is drawn out in the question-and-answer format. Considered in detail is the number of sons a man leaves behind him, from one to seven:

Gilg. *Did you see the man who had 1 son?*
Enk. *He complains about a peg fixed in his wall*

continuing,

2 sons: he sits on two bricks consuming a loaf
3 sons: he drinks water from his saddle-bag
4 sons: he rejoices like a person with a four-donkey
team
5 sons: like a nimble scribe he has easy access to the
palace
6 sons: he is as happy as a working ploughman
7 sons: he sits on a throne among junior gods, privy
to discussions

The implications here are quite clear; the family and its name must endure: the theme that lies under the *Incantation to Shamash* in Chapter 3. On top of that, filial offerings expected by a departed father will have more chance of continuing uninterruptedly with many sons, and really top-rate productivity reaps top-rate reward. The point is explicit in what follows: that 'the man with no heir eats bread that is like a fired brick', a poetic elaboration of the default Netherworld diet of clay, while, with Confucius, the man who 'failed to respect his parents' words cries, "Oh my body! Oh, my limbs!" and is always thirsty'. Revealingly, too, the person overtaken by the curse of his mother and father is deprived of an heir, and so his ghost will have to roam around ever after.

A woman who had never given birth ends up brutally cast aside like a cracked pot and no man takes pleasure in her; while the young man who never unpinned his wife's lap cloth will be forever platting a reed rope and weeping bitterly over the task, and the young woman who never unpinned her husband's lap cloth will struggle in tears making a reed mat; rope and mat are newly marital penis and vagina never put to good use.

Enki's report also covers individuals who had come to a sticky end, corresponding to the register of troubled ghosts in the banishing spells. The man eaten by a lion, for example, still cries bitterly, 'Oh my hand! Oh my foot!' while he who fell from a roof finds that they cannot repair his bones. He who lost his life in a flood, 'twitches like an ox while lice consume him'. A leper's ghost remains an outcast as in life: deprived of food and drink, he eats uprooted plants, drinks bitter water and lives outside the city, the centre of it all, 'downtown' where most ghosts congregate, as opposed to the loneliness of some empty, peripheral leper region. There are also accident cases, such as a man struck by a loom stake or a mooring pole, or the man who was burnt to death. According to Enkidu, 'his ghost does not dwell in the Netherworld; his smoke rose up to the sky'. The Akkadian *šamû* here can mean anglicé, heaven as opposed to earth, Heaven as the abode of gods, or sky as in the great canopy above our heads. Translating this as 'his smoke went up to heaven', as can be found in some publications, is misleading; this is *not* an anticipation of the later idea that Heaven with a capital H and all its associations is one possible destination for the deceased. The image reflects oblivion, as in such phrases as, 'May we together with our property ascend to heaven like smoke if we break the treaty.' The gruesome fate of being burnt to death condemns the ghost to eternal wandering.

The ghostly parents of a man fallen in battle mourn him forever and his wife weeps bitterly. One broken line refers specifically to 'the man whose corpse lies in the steppe', and when Gilgamesh asks, 'Did you see the ghost of a man for whom no one makes offerings?' he is told, 'He eats bits and pieces of collected leftover bread thrown away in the street.' Other couplets touch on personal theology, for the ghost of a man who 'deprecated his god's name' has bitter bread and water, while one who 'died because of his god' lies, obscurely, on the 'gods' couch structure'. A more extreme stance on this comes from an Old Babylonian Sumerian proverb from Ur written out on a school tablet:

A man who does not value his god will be thrown out in the desert; his body will not be buried, and his heir will not supply his ghost with drinking water through the libation pipe.

One telling line from the Akkadian version in the *Gilgamesh Epic*, of no use to the ghost specialist, conveys a different truth:

'The man who died a natural death lies drinking clean water on a bed of the gods.'

We can see from variant lines or independent material that this composition was still in flux in the city schools of the second millennium bc, meaning that scribes could import rather local ideas or incorporate much older traditions. A copy from the city of Ur, for example, has Gilgamesh adding questions that concern water, always top of the list for the Netherworld population:

'Did you see the man who, on taking an oath, insulted his god?
At the Libation Place *at the top of the Netherworld, even drinking water, he is always thirsty.'*

The *Libation Place* at the top of the Netherworld cannot pass without comment.

If this is the water that is regularly offered to the dead by those left behind, it rather gives the impression that all such offering water was conceived to arrive at the same spot, requiring ladles and politeness. Sweet water from the cosmic deep, of course, would be infinitely preferable when available. Amazingly, within this epic conversation, really old political conflicts can also resurface:

'Did you see the citizen of Girsu who carries water for his father and mother?
Facing each man there are one thousand Amorites; his ghost cannot push them off with his hands or repel them with his chest. At the Libation Place *at the top of the Netherworld the Amorite takes first place.'*

Sumerian Girsu, modern Telloh, the Sumerian city in southern Iraq, flourished in the third millennium bc, declining like Ur itself at the turn of the second millennium bc in the face of invading Amorites. These lines, probably composed when this conflict was recent, echo never-to-be-forgotten slaughter and the persistence of resentment and hostility between the ghosts of the Sumerians, who really ought to have first crack at the water, and the Amorites, who outnumbered and outnumber them completely. Behind this must lie blocking of water supplies as a form of war, for which the Amorites, dead or alive, were never forgiven, and now their ghosts are still making trouble. These few extra lines illustrate evolution and accretion in process in the content of the narrative.

Finally, we turn to questions from Gilgamesh that are revealing about *him personally*.

> *'Did you see my small stillborn who never knew their own*
>   *name?*
> *They take pleasure in syrup and ghee at tables of gold and*
>   *silver'*

The pronoun 'my' (-mu in Sumerian) certainly leaps out at the reader, since it is news to us that Gilgamesh by this point had more than once almost been a father himself. The last exchange between Gilgamesh and Enkidu in the version from Ur is the most revealing of all. Unlike most of the questions and answers, this material is only found in the Sumerian narrative and was not taken over into Akkadian:

Gilg.   *Did you see the place where my father and mother*
        sit?
Enk.   *I saw it*
Gilg.   *How do they fare?*
Enk.   *They both drink water from the place of a massacre,*
        filthy water.

With this revealing exchange, the climax of the whole back-and-forth enquiry about Netherworld conditions in general, Gilgamesh thus discloses what has really been his concern all along:

What has happened to my parents?

As I read it, the whole of the preceding rigmarole with the sports equipment, the manipulation of Enkidu, Enkidu's trip down below, and the flow of questions and answers was all designed to supply the orphaned hero from Uruk with the answer to that one pressing question. This confirms not only that Gilgamesh was an orphan, but also that the way in which his parents had died, or had been buried, left him unable to come to terms with it. His unsatisfied mourning could only be settled by Enkidu's eyewitness report as to their present condition in the Netherworld. The answer was not at all satisfactory, and perhaps what Gilgamesh had feared all along: it certainly prompted him to action. Ignorant as we are about Gilgamesh's dead premature offspring, we must wonder, too, about their mother, and what happened to her. Perhaps she died in childbirth. Somewhere, on some tablet or other, there should be an account of Gilgamesh's tragic early years and these fateful bereavements. Such a story might have touched on how Gilgamesh had first met Enkidu, too, as we will see.

As we now clearly appreciate, Gilgamesh's parents were just mortals. The goddess mother Ninsun favoured by the Uruk Public Relations Office would never be subjected to, or put up for a moment with, foul drinking water in a dangerous place crammed with the detritus of the human dead. Ninsun wouldn't even *be* in the Netherworld. It is clear that Gilgamesh's parents at the commencement of his personal story were just a man and wife, living in a house, and that his start in life was, accordingly, unexceptional.

In response to what he learned from Enkidu, Gilgamesh institutes funeral rites for his parents there and then, establishing

what was appropriate for the good Mesopotamian with regard
to respectful behaviour to the lamented dead:

> *He sent them back to [Uruk],*
> *He sent them back to their city;*
> *Gear and tools, hatchet and spear he stashed in the store,*
> *Celebrating joyfully in his palace.*
> *The young men and women of Uruk, the old men and*
> *   women of Kullab, looked upon those statues and rejoiced.*
> *As Utu came out of his bed chamber Gilgamesh raised his*
> *   head in pride,*
> *Instructing them:*
> *   'Father mine and mother mine, do you drink clear*
> *   water!'*
> *The day was not half over [. . .] they were [. . .]*

> *Gilgamesh performed mourning rites.*
> *For nine days he performed mourning rites*
> *The young men and women of Uruk, the old men and*
> *   women of Kulaba wept.*
> *Just as he had said,*
> *He drove the Girsu citizens to the edge.*
> *   'Father mine and mother mine, do you drink clear*
> *   water!'*

Gilgamesh, note, suddenly has a *palace*, and his mortal mother
is already being overlaid by her divine rival, so that the same
passage can end with this standard refrain as the last word:

> *Warrior Gilgamesh,* son of Ninsun, *praising you is sweet!*

The psychological consequence in Gilgamesh's life of the end of
mourning is noted in another tablet that carries this story, from
the city of Meturan:

It was so depressing, it was so distressing
That the lord started searching for life:
He set his mind to the land of the living.

Whereas his preoccupations had hitherto been morbid and inward-looking, all that was now settled. The hero was off on his adventures.

Part 2: *The Sumerian Narrative in Babylonian Dress*

The Sumerian story of *Gilgamesh, Enkidu and the Netherworld* formed a finished and independent narrative in its own right. There were other free-standing narratives in Sumerian in the second millennium bc that covered outstanding episodes in the hero's life, such as *Gilgamesh and Agga*, or *The Death of Gilgamesh* quoted in Chapter 3. Only part of this material survived down into the first millennium to be incorporated in the Akkadian *Gilgamesh Epic* – choice among the literature that once bewitched the audiences of ancient Mesopotamia, and still a rollicking good story today. The mature celebration of the hero stretches over eleven separate tablets, recording his friendship with Enkidu and restless search for immortality, culminating in the story of the Flood, the building of the lifeboat Ark, and the rescuing of life on the planet. For the first time we learn about Enkidu, his primitive nature, their meeting, their adventures together, Enkidu's eventual death and its effect on Gilgamesh. Two long sections of the *Gilgamesh Epic* concern Enkidu in the Netherworld, the first (Tablet VIII) on the basis of ominous dreams, the second (Tablet XII) his visit below.

Gilgamesh Tablet VIII: Enkidu's Dreams

Two dreams are experienced by Enkidu. In the first he learns he is to die, in punishment for the adventurers' earlier joint transgressions. In the second dream, unsurprisingly, he beholds the Angel of Death:

There was a man, darkened his visage,
His face like that of an anzû-eagle;
His hands were lion-paws, his claws eagle-talons,
He seized hold of my hair and was too strong for me;
When I smote him he leapt back like a skipping-rope;
When he smote me he scuttled me like a raft.

When Enkidu called for Gilgamesh in the dream to rescue him, the latter was *afraid*. And that was that. The dread Angel,

. . . smote me, he turned me into a dove;
He bound my arms like the wings of a bird,
Leading me captive to the House of Darkness, the seat of
*   Irkalla,*
To the house which those who enter cannot leave,
On the journey whose way cannot be retraced,
To the house whose residents are deprived of light,
Where dust is their sustenance, clay their food.
They are clad like birds in coats of feathers
And they cannot see light but sit in the dark.
On the door and bolt the dust lies thick
Over the House of Dust deathly silence is poured.

Here the Akkadian Gilgamesh version of the famous lines. For the Mesopotamian poets who wrote or transmitted the old stories about the Great Below, these lines could never be improved upon, and that they appear virtually word for word in *Ishtar's Descent* and *Nergal and Ereshkigal* was not narrative laziness or lack of imagination on their part: there was no point in attempting a rewrite. Enkidu himself saw the dead kings in the House of Dust during this dream:

I looked, and there were the crowns, gathered together;
There sat the kings who had worn those crowns, who had
*   ruled Mesopotamia since days of old,*

Shamash, god of Justice and Chief Ghost-Arbitrator Code of Hammurabi (ca. 1792–1750 BC) Depicted on a pillar of diorite inscribed with laws.

Ghost amulet of clay no. 1 BM 59322 (below); Ghost amulet of clay no. 2 BM 54990 (bottom).

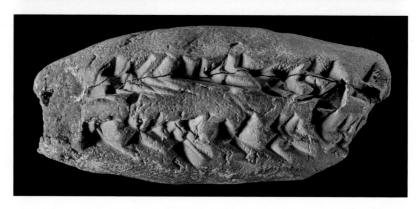

Ghost-banisher amulet in obsidian (volcanic glass), a costly material that had to be imported to Mesopotamia. The ornate writing is consciously archaising to enhance the authority of the spell.

Zimzilaḫ the dog warden (lines 3–4). A 1575 (obverse); Robert Hull Fleming Museum, Vermont. Photograph Chris Dissinger.

K 2175+; indispensable manual of anti-ghost magic.

The illustrated tablet *par excellence*. BM 40183 + 40333 + 40352 + 40377 + 40443 + 40444 + five unnumbered fragments.

The drawing of 'That Woman'.

Abaknana, a king on a throne.

Stela of Nabonidus, king of Babylon. His dress and regalia match those of Abaknana. BM 90387.

The *Persian Verse Account of Nabonidus* Cyrus's ruthless satire against the last native king of Babylon.

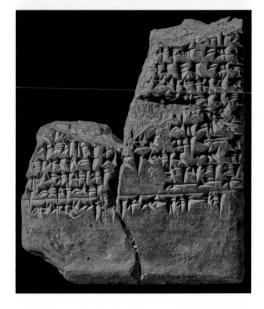

The magic tablet K 6073+ Reverse showing the colophon line at the end.

Any Evil as drawn on
BM 47701+ at Babylon.
After Anu-balassu-iqbi
of Uruk.

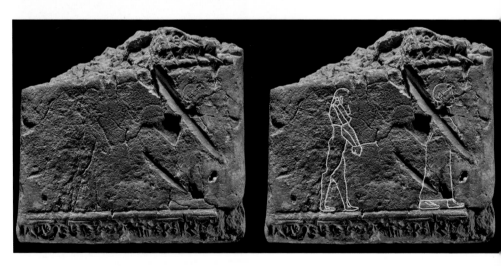

The world's first depiction of a ghost! Tablet drawing in clay, reverse of
BM 47831. White line tracing by Chris Cobb and James Fraser.

The *Queen of the Night*, the famous Old Babylonian terracotta depicting, almost certainly, the goddess Inanna. It was produced in about the eighteenth-century BC, about the period when *Inanna's Descent* was written down, and originally painted in colours; it probably hung as a wall plaque. The goddess, voluptuous and fascinating, faces us unabashed, and the creeping, feathery effect of the Netherworld ambience is already perceptible at her feet and ankles. This, coupled with her unmistakable nudity, makes it clear in my view that she must be our Inanna, although there has been endless argy-bargy about her identification by others. BM 2003, 0718.1.

Necromancy Manual 1. The Assyrian talking-ghost tablet from Nineveh. K 2779.

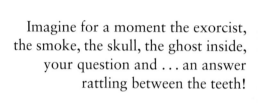

Imagine for a moment the exorcist, the smoke, the skull, the ghost inside, your question and ... an answer rattling between the teeth!

Necromancy Manual 2. The ghost-interrogating tablet from Babylon. BM 36703 obverse.

Who had served roast meat at the tables of Anu and Enlil,
Who had served loaves, who had poured out cold water from
  skins . . .

All the dead kings of Mesopotamia reaching back to the time before the Flood sat together in a special royal enclosure, distinct from lesser mortals, no longer needing their former regalia on a daily basis but with their status and distinction perpetually acknowledged! We can make a good stab at identifying those once-crowned heads ourselves, for their names, relative chronological order and lengths of reign, were carefully documented for us by ancient scholars in their *Cuneiform King Lists*. In addition, there was a clutch of attendant clergy: *en*-priests, *lagar*-priests, purification priests, *lumaḫḫu*-priests and the *gudapsû*-priests needed for the most important gods. There, too, were Etana, a human adventurer who had succeeded in going up to Heaven and was now Vizier, and the livestock god Shakkan. Most importantly,

There sat the Queen of the Netherworld, Ereshkigal,
Before her crouched Belet-ṣēri, Netherworld Scribe,
Holding the tablet and reading it out before her . . .

Power underpinned by exact record-keeping. No one could escape the system. The queen looked up when she saw Enkidu; her remarks are unfortunately only partly preserved on the tablet, but the autocratic – and perhaps slightly socially disadvantaged for the moment – tone comes across:

'Who has brought this person here?
. . . made ready,
. . . tomb'

All Enkidu's vaunted strength left him after that dream. Soon after, he fell mortally sick, lingered in agony for twelve days and then expired.

Gilgamesh Tablet XII: Enkidu Descends

Later, long after the demise of Enkidu and Gilgamesh's subsequent adventures had been accounted for, a twelfth tablet chapter
in Akkadian was added to cover an earlier visit to the Netherworld
by Enkidu, who is again described as Gilgamesh's servant. This
extra episode was translated directly into Akkadian out of the
end section of Sumerian *Gilgamesh, Enkidu and the Netherworld*,
beginning at the point when Gilgamesh was bewailing the fact
that he had not left the *pukku* and *mekku* safely in the carpenter's workshop. Thereafter the Akkadian follows the Sumerian
throughout. Both versions survive today, and they mostly overlap
exactly as with a conventional bilingual text, although no conventional interlinear combination was ever produced on a single
tablet. Despite the closeness of the translation there are certain
subtle differences presented by the Akkadian, some of which are
of considerable interest to us.

The air lift

The Sumerian sees Utu opening a chink (ab-làl) in the Netherworld,
and 'by means of his gust of wind (si-si-ig) he sent his servant
up to him (Gilgamesh) from the Netherworld'. The word sissig
means, primarily, gust of wind, or breeze, and, in this context, it
means the one energetic, big, divine puff with which Utu blows
Enkidu upwards just in time. Enkidu, who had been striding about
the Netherworld troublesomely, appears to have retained his
normal, corporeal form. But let us consider the Akkadian version.

> *'Shamash, perhaps you can open a chink* (takkapu) *in the
> Netherworld;*
> *You can bring the shade* (utukku) *of Enkidu up to him
> (Gilgamesh) from the Netherworld like a phantom* (zaqīqu)!'

These important lines are more than just a translation of the
Sumerian, for they explain both Enkidu's form – an *utukku* – and

what it looked like – a *zaqīqu*. Akkadian *zaqīqu* is the straight-forward dictionary equivalent of Sumerian sissig, meaning phantom, ghost, nothingness and foolishness as well as wind or breeze; it is said, for example, of dreams thought to waft up from below. It is important for the ghost-hunter to acknowledge that Enkidu in the Netherworld was not *dead* because, when he regained the world above, he and Gilgamesh embraced and wept on each other's neck, conversing at length. We know, equally, that Enkidu cannot have retained his normal physical, rugby-forward presence in the Underworld, for had he done so Gilgamesh's advice on how to pass unnoticed among ethereal ghosts would have been redundant.

Enkidu's Nature

The implications of the air lift tell us a good deal about Enkidu.

- On entering the Netherworld, Enkidu was somehow freed of his bodily form just as a dead arrival would be freed of his corpse.
- Enkidu was an *utukku*, ethereal and phantom-like, not an *eṭemmu*-ghost like all about him.
- For Enkidu appearing as an *utukku* was evidently both temporary and reversible.
- Enkidu was unrecognisable as an intruder by the surrounding *eṭemmu*-ghosts and would therefore readily pass for an *eṭemmu* himself.
- It is only clear-cut mortals who have an *eṭemmu*-ghost.
- The Akkadian words *utukku* and *eṭemmu* are written in Sumerian with two large and complex cuneiform signs that can be easy to confuse (see the explanation right at the end of this book).
- In the Sumerian signs, the *eṭemmu* is made up of one-third female divinity and the *utukku* two-thirds female divinity (see the explanation right at the end of this book).

- In this case, where Enkidu's Netherworld identity is so significant, the Akkadian editor spelled the telling word *utukku* syllable by syllable, just to make sure we notice: *ú-tuk-ku*.

This suggests, compellingly, that one or other of Enkidu's parents was divine, which imposes a new factor to our understanding of the *Gilgamesh Epic*. It would mean that he shared a deep and crucial quality with Gilgamesh, who himself as we have seen in the finished epic was two-thirds a god (from his mother Ninsun), and one-third mortal, and this probably explains the intimate attraction and bond between the two that underpins much of the narrative. In the end neither Gilgamesh nor Enkidu proved to be immortal, but they were equally hybrids.

To continue where this naturally leads, the simplest explanation to me is that the Sumerian god Enki was Enkidu's father. This explains the reiterated epithet *Father Enki* in the Sumerian Netherworld story, and is the reason it recurs of him later in other literary works, especially as we have already concluded that Enki went down to the Netherworld to claim – and bed – his bride. That passage, then, refers to the portion of Sumerian mythology that tells us that Enki is Enkidu's father, and the point when he was called Father. To the Mesopotamian this would be nothing startling, for his very name Enki-du means 'Enki-creator', and the increasingly common style of writing it, already known in the second millennium bc, employs the telling Sumerian sign dù, 'to create', to express the final syllable of Enkidu's name.

Later, as with Gilgamesh himself, Enkidu's parenthood issue was addressed. In the first-millennium epic he is created from scratch – a wild grass-eater running with the herd – as a foil for the rampaging Gilgamesh, the affair squeezed into appropriate cliché starring the mother goddess Aruru and war-god Ninurta:

When Aruru heard this,
She fashioned Anu's idea in her heart
Aruru washed her hands
She took a pinch of clay, she threw it down in the wild.
In the wild she created Enkidu, the hero,
An offspring of silence, knit strong by Ninurta . . .

Gilgamesh I 99–104

Perhaps, too, it was Enkidu's iconic name from deep mythology that established the pattern for the standard type of Mesopotamian personal name, being the first recorded example of the essential 'God Name + verb' type that remained popular ever after: Enki-the-creator, just as Ashurbanipal is 'Assur, creator of a son'.

The udug or *utukku* is invariably malevolent and antipathetic to mankind. Enkidu, however, is no evil demon. He is a strange and primitive character in Tablet XII, and we must conclude that Enkidu looks like a man but is, in some measure, still closer on the inside to the creatures of the Wild Wood. It is noteworthy in this regard that two of the most important Netherworld gods are described as udugs. One is Nergal, well known in this chapter, later consort of Queen Ereshkigal; he is described as a 'divine udug'. Then messenger Namtar, equally a Netherworld luminary, is described in a spell against migraine as 'the great udug-demon of the grave, the Land-of-No-Return'. These are inimical and dangerous gods, but they are distinct from udug demons in that their behaviour is not wilful, spiteful and unpredictable. Theologically, they have their jobs to do, and they are above vengeful or personal malice. Both gods, of course, were blue-blooded deities of unmixed heritage: Namtar was the son of Enlil and Ereshkigal, while Nergal, his half-brother and arriving later, was the son of Enlil and Ninlil. It is interesting therefore that they had 'udug quality' in common with Enkidu, which in itself was different from, or above, malevolent demonry.

We do not learn of Gilgamesh's own demise from the Akkadian epic, although there is the separate earlier account in Sumerian, *The Death of Gilgamesh*, discussed in Chapter 3. Here we must note that the dead Gilgamesh, once in the Netherworld and whatever his complex make-up, is described as an *eṭemmu*-ghost and not an *utukku*. That explains why he could not go down to the Netherworld himself to rescue his game equipment, and why, once in the Netherworld after his own demise and promoted from mortal king to Netherworld judge, Gilgamesh was a prime *eṭemmu* among *eṭemmus*, like his blood parents, and not an *utukku*.

The *eṭemmu*-ghost, once below, was supposed to stay there. The great mass of unstoppable *utukku* demonic elements that troubled the human race, however, came *up* freely from the Netherworld and were reluctantly sent back *to* the Netherworld by the magic powers of exorcists, where they regrouped, recharged their batteries and received instructions for new forays like fighter-pilot units. There was, accordingly, uninhibited traffic.

As we will see in this next chapter with Prince Kummaya, there was a Chief-*Utukku* in the Netherworld, with a companion Chief-*Eṭemmu*. The two presumably orchestrated the bustling, malevolent demon and ghost activity that came up from below to trouble the living, and answered for it to the Netherworld ruler, Nergal.

10

Part 1: An Assyrian Prince in the Netherworld

The prince of darkness is a gentleman
$$\textit{King Lear, Act 3, Scene 4}$$

No living human being, we have been told, was empowered to enter the Mesopotamian Netherworld, and were they to think of it, there would be no coming back for sure. It is this that makes our final Netherworld composition, *The Underworld Vision of an Assyrian Prince*, so remarkable. This literary creation from Assyrian intellectual circles is less widely known than the classic Netherworld narratives we have just sampled, and it has come down in a single clay manuscript that, at the beginning of the story, is unfortunately full of breaks and holes. It was excavated at the Assyrian capital of Assur among cuneiform documents belonging to an incantation priest of the seventh century bc. The composition has been variously considered as an item of propaganda, a religious text that anticipates Jewish revelation literature, and the first example of the genre of science fiction. In my view the narrative is, in fact, a moralistic human study of opportunistic exploitation and corruption by the powerful and its consequences for the guilty, set into a context with a very specific function.

There is another point. Readers who care for ghosts, and even purchase books to read about them, are often looking for ghost stories. What follows in this chapter is admittedly unconventional in form and hard to classify, but it would be a dispirited sceptic who would deny that it is, in some measure, a corking good Mesopotamian ghost story of a sort.

We will need two unapologetic parts to this chapter. The central portion of this document, communicated as a vison-by-night, describes a visit to the Netherworld by the one human being who experienced it; that is to say, a real ancient Assyrian, once living and breathing. In this respect it is crucially separate from the interrelated Netherworld narratives that concern gods, each the distillation of mythological – and anonymous – traditions. This human being, Kummaya by name, is, accordingly, the sole individual in the Mesopotamian record who *went* to the Netherworld, the Land-of-no-Return, *and came back* (even if the whole matter was only a dream). For that Guiness-Book reason alone he would merit our serious attention, but it is his own words, intense and realistic, that make this composition so extraordinary. Kummaya is a royal prince, son of an Assyrian king. Once we have read his Netherworld ghost story we will confront, as cushioned stay-at-home detectives, two important questions: who is Kummaya and who the king? Quite a three-pipe problem.

The narrative consists of three sections, which we can consider as Prologue, Dream-with-Vision and twin Epilogues. The Prologue reads as if narrated by an observer who witnessed the events for himself. We are in Nineveh, the 'lordly city', but do not at first understand that Kummaya is a prince of the realm.

The Prologue

Our prince, powerfully placed and profitably connected, is on a relentlessly downward path. This is due to a sorry career of indulgence, exploitation and corruption ending in guilt, with the man responsible desperate, by the end, for escape. Nothing, as we might think, changes. For his own purposes Kummaya has been able to hobnob with state diviners who specialised in interpreting animal entrails, while he is also placed to redirect important officials from their normal trustworthy tasks. They were put to supervising his own estate, for he had been accruing immeasurable wealth:

. . . responsibility for . . . the house of the inspectors of visceral omens, and he took counsel with them . . . eyes . . . from the clever book-keepers and him who protects their lord's secrets.

From the sections they counted out his . . . like well water by the bucket, day and night; he heaped his treasuries with regal jewellery.

And, in what seems to have been a heinous misdeed:

He opened the . . . for the Scribe's son
. . . he stood at his post and . . . the treasure chamber.

The populace, remarkably, retained sympathy for him, and thought that he was the victim of evil that was not his real destiny. We are told, however, that his intrinsically good nature failed to fortify him into resisting exploitation and corruption:

He no longer consulted with his inner self, but forgot the radiance (expected of him); . . . of his heart which was clothed in fear; he acted wickedly, even while his heart strove to do good.

At some point a passing inhabitant of the city of Assur was actually moved to rebuke the high-born for his behaviour, but Kummaya was undeterred. One especially telling image alludes to his disregard of how the great kings of Assyria – in whose footsteps he should be following – had behaved:

At that time . . . in the darkness, turning a pig upside-down, the city . . . a former king . . .

Eventually, abandoned by his female companions, the weeping Kummaya could not sleep. He strode about the city, resentful of citizens whom he saw having good times with their families, and wilfully destructive of property. And there were sumptuous Chicago-style banquets paid for by light-fingered tax operations, so eventually the people began to mutter and vociferate in protest.

Perhaps it was the sight of that dead pig carried hung from a pole through the streets that made Kummaya anticipate his own demise: unclean, overfed and bloated, exposed to all and sundry, it was the symbolic factor that prompted or consolidated his urge for expiation. It may have been a dawning realisation of his own, but the need to bring his chaotic career to a halt had also been felt in the palace, for the Shepherd, as they refer to the reigning Assyrian king, was evidently behind the need for intervention. Kummaya was summoned to the palace so that his deeds and situation could be discussed, and his punishment or treatment be decided on with the help of court counsellors and the top brass. Everything is to be confessed and purged away, with his own *Descent to the Netherworld* the startling, unusual and danger-filled remedy. That meant going into the right temple, and thence, to the Netherworld itself.

Access to the subterranean mysteries was to be accomplished through dreams and a vision-by-night. The documentation of events leading up to this point is covered in detail, but when it comes to Kummaya's sight of the Netherworld we are treated to little hard information. There is none of the standard Mesopotamian business of gates, darkness and wandering spectres. We cannot follow Kummaya down, step by step, matching the mounting tension of the classical accounts. *The Underworld Vision of an Assyrian Prince* owes practically nothing to the earlier dominant writings that lie in the background, but seems to spring fully formed out of a quite different world.

Temple Visit, Dreams and Vision

The words next translated mostly represent those of Kummaya himself, although sometimes the pronouns or verbs slip back from first person to the third person of the beginning narrator. This change is highlighted here by italics since it has significance.

THE VISIT

> On that day Kummaya, son of . . . went into the temple; he
> was determined on going down to the Netherworld . . . the
> middle of . . . of the whole world . . . and he set up a censer
> of juniper, whispering . . . but thereby he made light of the
> gods' words and angered the god's heart, although continuing
> to utter blessings.

Kummaya thus entered this temple on a particular date, the choice
determined by a court omen specialist, and he stayed there
overnight. This temple is not named but it was surely that of
Nergal, king of the Netherworld, founded by King Sennacherib
and later extended by Ashurbanipal. This was located at the city
of Tarbiṣu (modern Sherif Khan), which is only about five kilo-
metres north of Nineveh. The Assyrian cult of Nergal was centred
there, matching that in the famous Nergal temple Emeslam at
Kutha to the south in Babylonia (discussed in Chapter 8),
although its name is unknown.

Kummaya's first move was to burn juniper over coals, normal
in temple ritual, and to recite particular prayers that, we learn,
were not only unsuccessful but seemed to cause irritation. He
put his case first to the Netherworld goddess Allatu, whom he
likens to a 'lost orphan girl', probably in deference to some
familiar story about her, implying that he feels himself to be a
lost orphan too. Allatu, however, is insulted and outraged,
rejecting his proposal disdainfully; he can only enter the
Netherworld on the day of his destined death and that is that.
The core of her anger seems to be his presumption in proposing
entrance to the Netherworld as a living individual, which, as we
know, was forbidden.

The effect of this was to provoke the first of his two dreams
in the middle of that night. Queen Ereshkigal, under whom Allatu
served, was fully aware of his symbolic offering, and is at first
prepared to grant his wish, which is to penetrate the Netherworld
and achieve his release:

> *Ereshkigal appeared in a dream in the middle of that night and*
> *said to him,*
>   *'I take note of the offering made by you. Let me hear your*
> *prayers that I may fulfil your desire. But, without the command*
> *of my great divinity, the bowl has fallen; I shall not answer*
> *you. Why do you forsake Shamash, my favourite brother?'*

The reference here to the bowl and its falling is to a hallowed
form of divination with which the sun god Shamash, Ereshkigal's
brother, is traditionally associated. It is Shamash, she implies,
who should have taken on Kummaya's case from the beginning:
a properly conducted question-and-answer ritual would bring
release. Kummaya wakes up with a bump in inconsolable grief:

> *Kummaya awoke, keened like a dove, and . . . weeping,*
>   *'. . . let me . . . my ground, my ground',*
> *and reviled the dream over and over.*

Thereafter Kummaya prays again to Ereshkigal and to Nergal,
her spouse, who by now is seemingly within earshot. This time,
the prince is direct in his approach, promising to make more
than good the deficit owed to the exploited people, trying another
pure offering and promising to 'rotate the pig':

> *Once again, he lifted his hands and prayed to Ereshkigal, his*
> *tears flowing before Nergal, king of the broad Underworld, her*
> *husband:*
>   *'Let my . . . be substitutes for you; the widespread peoples*
> *will . . .; they will . . . one . . . they will make the very silos*
> *buckle . . . Accept (this) tamarisk, let it . . . I will turn the pig*
> *upside-down and you will disclose to me the secret plan; do*
> *not decree that I should . . .'*

With some hesitation I suggest that this expression corresponds
to our 'to turn over a new leaf', and derives directly from the

moment when Kummaya had seen a dead pig being carried upside-down from a pole and was struck by its implications, the symbolic sight generating a new turn of speech. And, we hear Kummaya say to Ereshkigal, 'you will disclose for me the secret plan'. This tantalising phrase has several possible interpretations. One is that Kummaya was fully aware that a great secret had been ruinously divulged as a result of his behaviour, as is obliquely referred to above in the text; the other is that the secret concerns his own personal future.

> *Kummaya lay down and saw a night vision. In his dream,*
> *I was captive in the House of Death. I beheld his terrifying*
> *splendour . . .*

Kummaya lay down then, says the narrator, to experience a full-blown 'night vision'. This section, in contrast to the preceding content, is recounted in the *first person*. We are told virtually nothing of where he is or what he could see of his surroundings, for he merely says, 'I was captive in the House of Death', his own voice reflecting his own thoughts, since this Hollywood expression is not a known term for the Netherworld itself, or, indeed, for a temple. This, we do well to remember, is a man undergoing an unparalleled psychic experience, stepping unconventionally into a startling new world that, ironically, is more familiar to us today from cuneiform literature than for him, for we already know the gods and demons he was now to meet face to face.

THE VISION-BY-NIGHT
The first section of Kummaya's night vision describes for us a full-scale parade of the top-rank Netherworld gods and demons. What is interesting is that the half-crazed visitor was able to name almost all of these surely terrifying figures one by one as if preparing for interrogation afterwards, describing their appearance and sometimes their pose. (Numbers have been added, with a few tourist notes by me along the way.)

1. I saw Namtar, messenger of the Netherworld, organiser of visceral omens; a man stood in front of him, whose head hair he seized in his left hand, wielding a dagger in his right . . .

2. Namtartu, his wife, had the head of a cherub; hands and feet being human.

The crucial husband and wife team, Nergal's intelligence unit, already familiar to us in the day-to-day running of the Netherworld. Namtar, however, is not usually involved with the business of omen warnings left for the experts in reading animal guts, and the mention of this probably reflects that Kummaya's consorting with entrail diviners involved misuse and abuse of divination for personal gain, and that Nergal knew all about it. The pose in which the Mesopotamian Nergal is described, victoriously smiting an enemy – held by the hair – with his weapon, is not in any way Assyrian. On the contrary, it is a hallmark deity stance in *Egyptian* iconography.

3. Death had the head of a dragon; his hands being human, his feet . . .

Death, as an entity is sometimes directly addressed in literary texts and spells; this dread figure, the Mesopotamian Angel of Death, was ready to be despatched with a doom-laden message when the moment came. The dragon is the classic fearful creature shown on the walls of Nebuchadnezzar's Processional Way at Babylon. The partial description of Death given by Kummaya contradicts the philosophical reflection in Gilgamesh Tablet X that 'one cannot draw the likeness of Death'.

4. Evil Genie, or *šēdu*, had head and hands of a human; crowned with a tiara; eagle's (?) feet. With his left foot he was trampling on a crocodile.

The standard Assyrian *šēdu*-genie is a human-headed winged bull of giant and statuesque appearance of the type familiar to all visitors to the British Museum. In magic and religious texts we encounter both good and evil *šēdu*-figures; the Netherworld figure here is no bull, however. If we understand this figure as anthropomorphic, he is to be seen as the representative head of the whole genus of evil *šēdus* (from the human and not the collegiate point of view), who despatches his hordes upwards. Again, we identify an Egyptian dimension, given the figure's stance on a crocodile. Crocodiles were familiar to the cuneiform world but they just do not feature in statues, whereas to the Egyptologist the major god Horus, bird-headed rather than -footed though he is, is often found on crocodile-back. Horus, however, is no enemy to mankind.

5. Alluḫappu-demon had a lion's head, his four hands and feet being human.
6. Upholder-of-Evil-demon had the head of a bird; his wings were outstretched wings and he flew hither and yon. His hands and feet were human.

Both *alluḫappu*, which means 'net', and Upholder-of-Evil demons regularly cause trouble to living human beings and are very familiar to the Mesopotamian exorcist from incantations and rituals. These two, who are on duty here together, cannot just be 'everyday' demons that might be encountered anywhere, but are surely Head Demons who run their respective domains, although again there is no evidence for such a hierarchy other-wise.

7. Humuṭ-tabal, Ferryman of the Netherworld, had an *anzû*-eagle head; his four hands and feet . . .

The fateful Ferryman who sees people across their last stretch of water, the Babylonian equivalent of Charon and the Styx: his name means, 'Hurry-up-and-carry-off!' Witches could be entrusted to him for shipping off below.

8.   Ghost (*eṭemmu*) had an ox's head; his four hands and feet being of a human.
9.   Evil Spirit (*utukku*) had a lion's head; his hands and feet being those of an *anzû*-eagle.

Here again, these composite figures with, I hope by now, ultra-familiar names, cannot just be token Netherworld specimens, but must be Head Ghost and Head Utukku respectively, with, therefore, administrative responsibilities for their countless cohorts. Evil comes up from the Netherworld.

10.   Shulak was a lion, rearing up all the time on his hind legs.

This demon Shulak, or his familiar envoys, was given to lurking in bathrooms and lavatories. In the palaces at Nineveh a clay lion-man figure, their benevolent (to-man) counterpart, would be buried in such places to repel them.

11.   Oath (*mamītu*) had a goat's head, his hands and feet being human.

The personified oath incorporated power, for oaths in business agreements or loyalty treaties were taken very seriously by Mesopotamians, and, as everybody knew, the evil resulting from broken or betrayed commitments ran on and would result in lasting misfortune; this frightful *mamītu* entity was the embodiment of the whole social matter.

12.   Nedu, the Porter of the Netherworld, had a lion's head and human hands and his feet were those of a bird.

The importance of gates and their keepers when going in and out of the Netherworld is explicit in the traditional accounts. Nedu is the Akkadianised version of his Sumerian predecessor Neti's name in the *Descent of Inanna*.

13.   *Any Evil* had two heads; one was the head of a lion; the second was the head of a [. . .]

This description of *Any Evil* has been taken up in Chapter 7; two-headed demons are in any case not commonplace in Mesopotamia, and our old friend *Any Evil* normally has but one.

14.   **Muḫra** had three feet, the two front ones were those of a bird; the rear one was that of a bull. He had fearsomeness and luminous splendour.

It has been suggested that **Muḫra** means, 'Face-both-Ways!' If so, he will be Nedu's lookout for trespassers from either murky direction, and, being tripedal, able to swivel promptly.

So far we have fourteen listed entities. Then, Kummaya continues,

For two gods I did not know the names – one had the head, hands and feet of an **anzû**-*eagle; in his left hand [. . .]*

The other had a man's head, he was crowned with a tiara, carried in his right hand a mace, in his left hand, before him, [. . .]

In all, fifteen (actually sixteen, ed.) *gods were present. I saw them and prayed to them.*

> *There was a man, his body black as pitch, his face resembling*
> *that of the* anzû-*eagle; he was clad in red armour, in his left*
> *hand he carried a bow, in his right hand he clasped a dagger,*
> *while he trampled on a snake with his left foot.*

This bird-headed being, above all, beckons to the Egyptologist
in all of us, for no individual in Mesopotamian religious or
magical iconography is ever depicted with a black face (despite
the Sumerians' traditional self-reference as the Black-Headed),
but this striking case unmistakably recalls Osiris, especially given
that snake-trampling is also an Egyptian, rather than Mesopotamian motif. All together the half-crazed Kummaya encountered
some seventeen larger-than-life embodiments of the very great
powers, downright evil or at the very least unpredictable, that
affect the world of men, living and dead. Three of the figures at
home in the Assyrian Netherworld, as described by him, seem
to embody qualities of, or draw upon, contemporary and neighbouring gods of ancient Egypt.

At the end of this inhibiting tour of inspection, Kummaya
ends up prostrated in prayer, his eyes lowered. When next he
looks up, we sense a change in location. Nergal, King of the
Netherworld, is seated on his throne with attendants, illuminated
by lightning, waiting for him. This could only be taking place
within the heart of the Netherworld itself; there has been an
uncharted, imperceptible, dreamlike shift in ground.

> *When* I *raised my eyes says Kummaya (there was) warrior Nergal*
> *seated on his royal throne, his head covered by the royal crown;*
> *with both hands he grasped fury-filled maces, each with two*
> *. . . heads . . . were heaped up; . . . at his sides; lightning flashed;*
> *the great Anunnaki gods knelt to his right and left. The*
> *Netherworld was full of terror, and a great silence lay before*
> *the noble youth . . . . He took me by my forelock and pulled*
> *me close before him.*
> *When I looked at him my very innards convulsed; his furious*

numinosity swept over me. I kissed the feet of his great divinity and stayed kneeling. Then I stood up while he gazed at me, shaking his head:

He raised his voice, screaming furiously against me like a raging storm, and brandished the sceptre, befitting his divinity, terrifying like a viper, to kill me.

Ishum, his vizier, the intercessor who saves lives and loves truth, said as follows:

'Do not kill this man, O king of the broad Netherworld!
Let him go, so that peoples of all lands will hear about your glorification!'

He made the heart of the all-powerful and almighty one, who binds evil, calm as pure well water.
Nergal said this to Kummaya:

'Why did you insult my beloved wife, Queen of the Netherworld? By her high command, which can never be revoked, may Bibbu, Slaughterer of the Netherworld, turn you over to the Porter, Lugalsula, that he may let you out of the gate of Ishtar and Aya.
Do not forget: do not neglect me, that I should not pass a verdict of annihilation on you. Otherwise, at the command of Shamash, let distress, deeds of violence and rebellion combined blow you over so that, through their oppressive clamour, sleep will never come to you.'

Intercession by Ishum prevented the worst, and Kummaya is, as it feels to the modern reader, let off. Perhaps the Netherworld king's scrutiny allowed him to perceive the same innate goodness in him that the Assyrian populace knew of. Nergal, in the vein of Hamlet's father's ghost, continues with this remarkable speech:

'This [corpse], which has been buried in the Netherworld, is
of the Proud Shepherd who carried out all the wishes of my
father, Assur, king of the gods. The king who from east to west
made all the lands appear as mere booty, who ruled everything;

For whom Assur, when he took up the office of high priest,
ordained that he should build the holy Akitu-house in the coun-
tryside, surrounded by abundant gardens that resemble Mount
Lebanon [. . .] for ever and ever;

Whose body the gods Yabru, Ḫumban and Naprushu look
after, whose progeny they keep healthy and whose army and
camp they rescue, so that no chariot should come anywhere
near him in battle;

He is your progenitor, eminent, knowledgeable in affairs, of
wide intelligence, broad of understanding and discernment,
who sought the plan of the earth's bond;

As for one who closed ear to his speech, sampled the taboo,
trampled on the sacred; the luminous splendour of his terrifying
majesty will overwhelm you into a puff of smoke.

Let this speech be set like a thorn in your heart; go forth up
to the world above until I have to think of you again,' he said
to me.

With that threat ringing in his ears Kummaya came to himself.

FIRST EPILOGUE
At first Prince Kummaya continues speaking, but the text soon
reverts to the third-person voice of the narrator, as is clear from
the changing verbs, here italicised:

I woke up, *and like a man who has lost blood, or wanders
alone in a reed thicket, or who is overtaken by a runner so that
his heart beats fast, or like a young offspring of a boar who
has his mate, and whose insides inflate so that wind is given
out from his mouth and his rear,* he having become inflamed
with lamenting; *calling out 'Woe my heart!'*

He shot *into the road like an arrow and scooped up dust
from street and city square into his mouth, setting up a constant
and fearful shriek, 'Woe is me!'*

He was crying out, *'Why have you decreed this for me?'* and
*through his pain the valour of Nergal and Ereshkigal who had
come to the aid of the prince was lauded before the Assyrian
population.*

How extraordinary is this! The body of a dead Assyrian king
lies in state in the Netherworld after burial, and is now seen by
his own son. What with the Egyptian-type divinities we have
already encountered, it is hard to avoid the idea of a mummy-
like sarcophagus lying in the gloom, especially since we know
royal Assyrian bodies were buried in airtight stone coffins, as in
the Assyrian mausoleum at Nimrud (Chapter 3), but there is no
home Mesopotamian parallel to this post-mortem description.
This august corpse is called Proud Shepherd, echoing the phrase
earlier of the reigning king. Opinions vary as to the identity of
this fearful dead king, and, therefore, his living successor, as we
will see.

There is another strange point. The safekeeping of this exalted
cadaver is entrusted to a trio of conspicuously non-Mesopota-
mian gods: Yabru, Ḥumban and Naprushu. They originate in
Elam, like certain anti-ghost spells, over the eastern border in
what is today Iran. According to Nergal's statement, this crack
unit of divine bodyguards was entrusted with three exceptionally
weighty state responsibilities:

1. Looking after the body of the dead king.
2. Looking after that king's progeny in life.
3. Protecting the living king in warfare.

This programme, crucial for Assyria's deep well-being, has been
mysteriously delegated to what were, in essence, three outsiders.
This triumvirate of Elamite names is not limited to Kummaya's

vision; they are already embedded, for example, in a long anti-sorcery magical spell together with a couple of fellow Elamite deities from the Elamite capital of Susa, later the objective of Ashurbanipal's Elamite War in Chapter 1:

> *In the city of Susa may Inshushinak and Laḫuratil release*
> *(that evil magic)!*
> *May Jañru, Ḫumban and Naprushu release (that evil magic),*
> *those very great gods!*

Theologically and politically, the three gods at the time of composition must have been considered completely trustworthy, even if the background to that is unknown.

This first epilogue describes the effect of Kummaya's vision, and brings his own story to a meaningful conclusion. He passes out through the Gate of Ishtar and Aya, as sanctioned by Nergal, the only glimpse we have of access or egress to the Netherworld in the text. The frantic depiction of his distress is eloquent, but what really puts this writing into the realm of poetry is Kummaya's running back and forth in the city, scooping dust in to his mouth, recalling the unforgettable Netherworld wording, '*Where dust is their sustenance, clay their food.*' This is the only line in the document that alludes to the classic literature in the background; Kummaya, flinching from the impact of the divine figures before him, ought to have seen ghosts in the Netherworld, everywhere, doing just that. Then comes the well-established literary idea (favoured also by the Hebrew prophets) that a human being, released from peril thanks to a benevolent god, must devote his time thereafter to telling everybody what happened. Kummaya is out of control, repentant and, as it were, out on probation, and the population of Nineveh are in on all of it.

SECOND EPILOGUE

The whole operatic composition winds up, however, in quite a different vein:

And that scribe, too, who had previously accepted bribes and who occupied his father's post, with the wise understanding that Ea had bestowed on him, he took the expressions of praise to heart, and said to himself,

'That the effects of the agreement may not come near me or affect me, let me always carry out my responsibilities as Nergal has ordered!'

and he went to the palace and repeated it, saying,

'Let this be my expiation!'

10

Part 2: Who was the Prince?

. . . of a free and open nature,
That thinks men honest that but seem to be so,
And will as tenderly be led by th' nose
As asses are

Othello, Act 1, Scene 3

The princely *Underworld Vision* narrative ends with an unexpected twist, as we have seen, and from which we now step further. Attention at the conclusion is diverted altogether away from Kummaya, narrator and spokesman, the only man in the history of the cuneiform world who went down to the Netherworld and survived to tell the tale. The literary climax to the work, on the contrary, is provided by the public declaration and self-cleansing of what is called *that Scribe*, the miscreant tablet-writer who is mentioned, crucially, in the earlier part of the narrative, and whose personal history is, as far as he has now shown, *the point of the whole composition*.

This 'son of the Scribe', we can see, cashes in very efficiently on Kummaya's painful experience. Somehow, he gains enlightenment and freedom thereby from responsibility for his own actions, this the very man who had 'previously accepted bribes, who occupied the post of his father'. Through the wisdom bestowed on him by the clever god Ea, he repents of his misdeeds and promises to avoid trouble by obeying the words of Nergal henceforth. His purpose is articulated in that final line: 'Let this be *my* expiation!' By the conclusion we are led to believe that the scribe is fully whitewashed. In the light of this we understand for certain that Kummaya, Royal Prince and

Netherworld Adventurer and the dodgy scribe are two distinct individuals. Who, then, are they, and what is going on? We take them in reverse order, scribe and prince, considering in each case what we can of the 'psychology of the individual'.

The Scribe: Urad-Gula, Son of Adad-shuma-uṣur?

In 1936, when the Assyriologist Wolfram von Soden was first studying the Kummaya tablet and its scribe who succeeded his father, his brilliant teacher Benno Landsberger reminded him of the Wise Ahiqar and his son Nadin, a popular story in the Aramaic language set in the Assyrian court at the time of King Esarhaddon (681–669 bc). They also toyed with the idea that scribe and father in the Kummaya story might rather be identified with the famous Assyrian individuals Urad-Gula and his father Adad-shuma-uṣur, and it is this idea that I here follow up afresh, with certain new angles.

Urad-Gula's father was the very distinguished savant Adad-shuma-uṣur, Chief Exorcist in the Assyrian court at Nineveh. He himself had been Deputy Chief Physician to King Sennacherib (705–681 bc), and Court Exorcist under his successor King Esarhaddon (681–669), but thereafter things went bad. His downfall came rather promptly when Ashurbanipal came to the throne in 668, and from 30 October 667 to at least April 666 he was unemployed. Urad-Gula's professional biography is unfolded for us in a sophisticated literary letter-petition he addressed to King Ashurbanipal to plead for his reinstatement. The petition is an eloquently and allusively crafted document betraying a sharp and manipulative intelligence on the part of its author, as expounded by Simo Parpola in his Assyriological *tour de force* on the subject (Parpola 1987). We can follow from this self-promoting letter how things had deteriorated for Urad-Gula over a period of years; again, italics highlight points particularly pertinent for our investigation:

Esarhaddon on the throne
Initially, in the mind of the king's father, I was a poor man, son of a poor man, a dead dog, a vile and stupid person. He lifted me from the dung heap; I got to receive gifts from him, and my name was mentioned among fortunate men. I used to enjoy generous 'leftovers'; intermittently he used to give me a mule, or an ox, and yearly I earned one or two minas of silver.

Ashurbanipal Crown Prince
In the days of my lord's Crown-Prince-hood I received 'leftovers' with your exorcists; I stood at the window openings, keeping watch. All the days that I spent in his service, I guarded his privileges, I did not enter the house of a eunuch or a courtier without his permission, *I was looked upon as one who eats 'lion's morsels'. I appeased your god.*

Ashurbanipal on the throne
Now, following his father, the king my lord has added to the good name he has established, but I have not been treated in accordance with my deeds, I have suffered like never before and given up the ghost. Improper conduct, whispering about and revealing a secret are detestable things. I guarded the privileges of the king, *my lord, but I did not find benefactors, I endured [. . .] words, I made my office my night's resting place. I taught the servants, the non-eunuchs and eunuchs alike, submission, toil and fear of the palace, and what did I get for it?*

Professor Parpola's overview of the relationship between Ashurbanipal and Urad-Gula is indispensable to our enquiry. The following five points are central:

1. The shelving of Urad-Gula was deliberate. The king just did not want to see Urad-Gula in his palace. This attitude is hardly explicable without assuming a personal grudge between the two men, and reviewing

the evidence, which includes other cuneiform letters, that is very plausible.

2. Urad-Gula frequently came into contact with Ashurbanipal while the latter was Crown Prince, and the present letter confirms that the king had known the writer 'since the time he was a child'. Under such circumstances it is not at all unlikely that the future king would have grown to dislike certain personal characteristics in an exorcist continuously 'snooping around'.

3. Another passage in the present letter suggests that Urad-Gula not only displayed the most servile conduct while on duty at court, but may also have *known certain things* about the king that the latter would not have liked to become publicly known.

4. Other letters give the impression that Urad-Gula was a negative-minded, habitual complainer.

5. A more tangible cause for a personal grudge could be furnished by a letter that might refer to a miscarriage, possibly by the wife of the Crown Prince, for which Urad-Gula appears to have been held at least partly responsible.

Urad-Gula the high-born, excessively educated and once most elevated, kicked out of the court in 669 bc, and now disgraced, broke and desperate. We might imagine him also to be rather dangerous. We know of earlier moves that he made to reingratiate himself prior to this crafty document: two surviving letters were written on his behalf to Ashurbanipal by his father Adad-shuma-uṣur; a further letter, not found, was written by Urad-Gula him-self to be handed in at the right moment by the eunuch Sharru-nuri. To this campaign, we suggest, must now be added *The Underworld Vision of an Assyrian Prince*.

The core dream narrative, in Kummaya's own words, is sand-wiched between what we have called the Prologue and Epilogues.

What has not been considered by earlier writers is that this scribe does not just step on stage right at the end of the composition with a flourish, but is pinned down incriminatingly, right in the middle of Kummaya's lamentable decline:

> He [Kummaya] even went and opened . . . for the Scribe's son

I submit that this is Urad-Gula, son of Adad-shuma-uṣur. I suggest, therefore, that the *entire work* is, effectively, the work of Urad-Gula, who conceived of the whole as a vehicle to bring about his own exculpation and reinstitution, profiting in the process from the character, weakness and unfortunate decline of Kummaya, with whom he had been intimately connected since childhood. We will build the case against him shortly.

Who was the Prince?

Kummaya, spelled out syllabically in the cuneiform as *ku-um-ma-a-a*, is not a proper personal name. The Akkadian suffix *-a-a* can indicate a gentilic, like **Babilāya**, 'a Babylonian'; an abbreviation, like Betty for Elizabeth, or possibly even an affectionate diminutive. However it be construed, though, *Kummaya* is no royal Assyrian name. As a son of the king of Assyria, as we are told, the name given to the young prince at birth would unquestionably have been meaningfully constructed, like that of Ashurbanipal, 'Assur-has-given-an-heir'. This means that Kummaya is either a *nickname* or a *cover name*. Everybody knew full well the identity of the prince in this moral and biographical tale, but there was no need to name him.

Kummaya's father, as we have seen, was almost certainly mentioned by name in the early narrative, but the tablet is broken at the worst possible point: 'Kummaya, son of . . .' The king on the throne in Nineveh when this story takes place is not named in the surviving portions of the text. As noted, that king is referred to as the 'Shepherd', and the matching epithet 'Proud Shepherd' is used of the dead king lying in state in the Netherworld. It is this dead king who is identified to Kummaya as 'your father' by the god Nergal himself. We thus have two royal shepherds in succession, father and son.

The building of the Akītu-house attributed to the dead Assyrian king by Nergal has brought up the idea that the body is that of King Sennacherib (705–681 bc), who recorded this specific architectural achievement in his state cuneiform records. This would mean that Esarhaddon was the living king. On its own this does not seem to me to be quite compelling. More suggestive is Nergal's actual wording, for he uses not the common Akkadian noun for father, *abu,* but *zā'iru,* lit. 'begetter', which we have accordingly translated here as 'progenitor', which could therefore be understood as either Kummaya's father *or* grandfather. Either way, the pedigree embodied in Nergal's declaration establishes Kummaya beyond a shadow of doubt as the son of a king of Assyria. The evidence concerning the identity and behaviour of the scribe fits perfectly with the assumption that Esarhaddon is the dead king, and Ashurbanipal on the throne. Most previous writers have reckoned the dead king to be Esarhaddon, while identifying Kummaya as Ashurbanipal himself. This proposal is clearly impossible. The only logical conclusion from all this is that *Kummaya must be another of Esarhaddon's sons.*

Investigating Esarhaddon's Progeny

When Esarhaddon died in 669 bc he left behind at least *eighteen* children. Ashurbanipal, to be Assyria's greatest ruler, came to the throne in 668 bc. We only know one of Esarhaddon's queens for certain, Esharra-hammat, but there were surely others; we do not even know which of his children shared the same mother. One characterful and intelligent daughter, Sheru'a-eṭerat, stands out in particular. Disregarding those too young, it is within Ashurbanipal's six grown-up brothers that we must look for

Kummaya. The following list, brief though their biographies are, points the way unambiguously:

1. Sin-nadin-apli: In 677 Esarhaddon's oldest son; appointed Crown Prince; *probably deceased by 672 bc*
2. Shamash-shum-ukin: By 672 Esarhaddon's oldest son; from 668 bc ruler of Babylon
3. Shamash-metu-uballiṭ: Fate unknown
4. Assur-taqisha-libluṭ: *Probably deceased by 672 bc*
5. Assur-mukin-paleya: Appointed *sheshgallu* priest of the god Assur by Ashurbanipal by 668 bc
6. Assur-etel-shamê-erṣeti-muballissu: Appointed *sheshgallu* priest of the god Sin at the city of Harran by Ashurbanipal by 668 bc

Of these six brothers the only plausible candidate for our purposes is Prince Shamash-metu-uballiṭ, son of Esarhaddon. We know little about him. In an account document covering a ceremonial banquet at Nineveh he is the last identifiable offspring of Esarhaddon – listed after Crown Prince Ashurbanipal, sister Sheru'a-eṭerat and sons five and six – before the tablet breaks off. He also appears as one of two royal brother oath-takers in the important political Zakutu Treaty designed to ensure Ashurbanipal's safe accession to the throne; the other is Shamash-shum-ukin. Elnathan Weissert has pointed out that Shamash-shum-ukin and Shamash-metu-uballiṭ are referred to in this treaty as the 'older brothers', suggesting that the latter is Esarhaddon's third eldest son and, therefore, meriting my italics, *older than Ashurbanipal*.

Perhaps at some point, therefore, the boy had been heir-designate, while Shamash-metu-uballiṭ's own name, 'Shamash has revived the dying', could certainly reflect that he was or had been of such poor health that he was early passed over as Crown Prince by Esarhaddon in favour of the younger Ashurbanipal. This would give us an acknowledged son of the king, highly placed in the kingdom, discomfited at losing his chance at or right to the throne and troubled in his psyche, with a bitter tablet indeed that could hardly be swallowed. Were we writing a thriller, this psychological profile would fit Prince Kummaya rather closely. In the light of this, accordingly, I propose that Kummaya is the nickname for Prince Shamash-metu-uballiṭ, and the understanding 'Instead-of-sort-of-Chap', implied by the by-name Kummaya, might incorporate this very point. If our historical reconstruction is correct, the composition betrays who will have written it and how it suits the purpose for which it was designed.

Kummaya's Behaviour

It is possible that Prince Shamash-metu-uballiṭ, alias Kummaya, was only a half-brother of Ashurbanipal, but in any case, the boy would have grown to manhood in a complex court environment where favour and disfavour might fluctuate considerably with circumstance, and mortal danger loom inescapably when it came to succession. When we meet the prince he is enjoying a high administrative state position, from which we might conclude that he was considered worthy and capable with a role to play, given that he would no longer stand in direct line to the throne unless something very unexpected happened. Possibly Ashurbanipal made an earlier decision to provide him with something useful and safe to do. Kummaya's personality, however, turned out to have a deep flaw. Perhaps he was inwardly tormented by jealousy and resentment with so much once almost within reach that would always be denied him. Perhaps he was bullied and mistreated by his brothers, or humiliated by his father. On the other hand, maybe he exemplified this Holmesian dictum:

> There are some trees, Watson, which grow to a certain height, and then suddenly develop some unsightly eccentricity. You will see it often in humans. I have a theory that the individual represents in his development the whole procession of his

*ancestors, and that such a sudden turn to good or evil stands
for some strong influence which came into the line of his pedigree. The person becomes, as it were, the epitome of the history
of his own family.*

Either way, Kummaya was corrupted by the opportunities open
to him.

The Netherworld Description

We can take it, I think, that Prince Kummaya was properly literate
in cuneiform, having been, like his siblings, taught to read and
write within the palace as part of his princely upbringing. In
order for us to evaluate this unique Netherworld-account, two
points seem to me important: what experience is encapsulated
in this composition, and to whom do we owe its authorship?

Most of Kummaya's named gods are well known to us from
assorted Mesopotamian writings, but the striking 'rogues' gallery'
approach adopted – name and brief description – draws on an
existing composition. This is the esoteric religious work of the
first millennium known as the 'God-Type text'. It describes the
physical appearance and attributes of a sequence of gods and
demons and is a learned, priestly matter; familiarity with it
automatically bespeaks advanced acquaintance with cuneiform
theology and speculation. Here is a specimen god-type text entry:

*The turban of the head (is that) of . . . He has the horns of a
bovine. The hair is falling from [his] h[orns] down onto his
back. The face is human. The cheek is adorned. He has wings.
His front pair of feet are that of a bovine. His body is (that
of) a lion. He is walking on four (pairs of) feet. His name is
Shērum.*

Thanks to the insightful study published by Frans Wiggermann,
this recherché composition can be seen to shed direct light on

the prince's *Underworld Vision*. He showed that the layout of twenty-five named and described gods and demons reflects an intelligible, significance-loaded schemat, and was able to reconstruct a 'guidebook' diagram of a long rectangular space in which the figures are ranged around the walls with a predictable cumulative effect on the visitor:

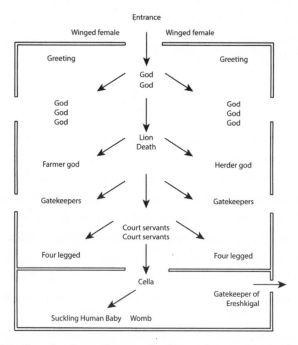

This diagram shows the temple plan with its statuary after the reconstruction in Wiggermann 2018: 356 Figure 2. Passage between the matching figures of gods right and left and other sinister entities led the visitor through and beyond into the crucial cellar, where his choice of path was between Life, symbolised by Womb and Suckling Human Baby, and the Netherworld, guarded by Ereshkigal's Gatekeeper. Redrawn by James Fraser.

With this example before us it is easy to see, unfolding in the account of Kummaya's experience, a complex Netherworld Visit ritual within the Nergal temple readily accessible to the Assyrian court. The overnight visit would involve, first, prayer and the procuring of an admission 'passport' from Queen Allatu or

Queen Ereshkigal, presumably conducted in an antechamber. Passing into the long principal chamber, the visitor is confronted by the avenue of Netherworld forces, carved as we might assume in the round at impressive scale, mounted on pediments, perhaps eerily lit from below, with carefully chosen incense, if not music, clouding the senses. Perhaps the ritual called for each statue to be named and rendered honour by the trembling visitor. After this protracted and traumatic exposure, the client reaches the narrow-doored cella at the end. Here he comes face to face with the throne and personage of Nergal, the Netherworld king, with his attendants, who will impose the judgemental address sought by the visitor, and his conclusion. It is here that the Wiggermann model and diagram fits particularly closely with Kummaya's experience, for the options available to the visitor at that final point, according to the God-Type text, are Life or Death; a passage to the right leads off directly to the first crucial gate, manned in the diagram by Ereshkigal's Gatekeeper, Ammakur, for those who must pass below. Reading between the awful lines of Nergal's address, it appears that he pardons Kummaya, saves him from perdition, and sends him out through the gate of Life back to the human world.

That we have no independent record of, or reference to, such a purgative Assyrian spiritual ritual in other tablets does not make this suggestion less likely. For one thing, it would be neither widely available nor an everyday affair. If we are on the right lines, the procedure was set up in such a way that whoever underwent it was totally convinced that they had been in the Netherworld and encountered its populace as a temporary ghost, to escape in retrieved human form. That is certainly what happened to Prince Kummaya.

A Parallel from Greece?

In this regard, attention must be drawn to the astonishing Oracle of the Dead, a vast subterranean replica of the Greek Underworld, that was discovered at Baia in southern Italy by Robert Paget in 1962, and recently investigated by Robert Temple. Here, long and descending passages with niches for lamps and a customised niche for Cerberus led down to the subterranean Styx River, where clients would be rowed across by a man dressed as Charon to disembark at the other side in the Netherworld.

There they would ascend to the séance to speak to the spirits of the dead and to Sibyl herself. This was clearly a highly sophisticated and no doubt profitable operation; in a disapproving later age it was all filled in and covered over to be utterly blotted out. It seems far from improbable that certain well-staffed Netherworld temples in ancient Mesopotamia might have offered similar facilities.

If my reconstruction is valid and correct, the living Kummaya's ritual reflects a process of judgement in the Netherworld administered to relieve misery. It is important to stress again that there is here no anticipation of the post-mortem choice between Heaven and Hell (on the basis of behaviour and sin) that subsequently worked its way into the world; the decision concerns, on the contrary, whether the penitent individual should be pardoned and continue *to live* – even if under strict supervision – or die and pass into the Netherworld proper.

The Nergal Temple, Tarbiṣu and the Netherworld Gate

We turn aside for one moment for one other bit of unusual cuneiform, a conventional-looking but wildly unconventional sale contract from Nineveh. It concerns a portion of land owned by one Likpuru, son of Lipugu. Likpuru, however, is no human being but a full-sized, human-headed, winged-bull *šēdu* of the temple-guardian type, standing at Kar-Nergal, 'Quay of Nergal'! The territorial location involved is set out with conventional precision, the adjoining fields and their owners listed, although the text is damaged, but the words 'graveyards' and 'adjoining the grave of . . .' can just be deciphered. On top of that, it is 'adjoining the Ulaya River of the Gate of the Netherworld (*Arallû*)', summed up as 'an area of gleaned field in the city of Zakūte of the Gate of the Netherworld'. The purchaser of the land is Ḫarḫanda, another winged-bull *šēdu*, who stands in the gatehouse of the temple, who has already paid over in full what is owed with the help of Arnaši-[. . .], the mother of the *šēdus* (and therefore Lipugu's) wife.

What this means in simple terms, I think, is that there was a temple of Nergal at Kar-Nergal that housed a well-known install-ation called the *Gate of the Netherworld*. This must be inside the main body of the temple, but there is also an outer Gatehouse. Lipugu is on protective duty at the Netherworld Gate itself, and Ḫarḫanda, his brother, at the outer Gatehouse to the Nergal temple complex. Land, for unknown reasons, is passing one from the other. The witnesses to this affair, however, named on the tablet's reverse, are *birds*, with *bird names* such *Ua-ua*, an owl from some other city, and *Qua-qua*, a crow between the walls; claw scratches take the place of witness seal impressions and bird-seed is the going currency. Opinions have varied rather strongly about this document, but I agree with Simo Parpola that these birds are likely to be Nergal cult personnel dressed in bird costumes re-enacting a Netherworld ritual in one of Nergal's temples at the Gate to the Netherworld.

But where is all this taking place? Since iconic Assyrian *šēdu*-figures are never found in Babylonia, the setting cannot be the Nergal temple in the south at Kutha. There is a city and province under Assyrian control called Kar-Nergal, which is located in the Western Zagros region; and the Ulaya River in cuneiform texts, also associated with the Netherworld, is often identified with the Ulai River of the Book of Daniel and the Eulaiois River of Greek sources, located in Susiana in Iran, but both can be ruled out as a location for the main Assyrian entrance to the Netherworld. The setting for such a complex symbolic ritual, carefully written up for the Nineveh library collections, cannot be located in a province so far east of the

Assyrian homeland. The *Gate to the Netherworld*, with burials clustered all around in the vicinity, implies a cultic installation within a major Nergal temple that would allow access to priests, worshippers or others, under certain circumstances, to the Netherworld itself. I suggest identifying the place Kar-Nergal as the temple complex at Tarbiṣu, a small city within the larger one, and the proposed site of Kummaya's remarkable experience.

The Gods of Egypt

What, meanwhile, is represented by the memorable Egyptian component among the Mesopotamian Netherworld gods waiting to meet the prince? There was Egyptian presence and influence at Nineveh, of course, but exposure to Egyptian visitors, conversations, descriptions or even acquaintance with Egyptian objects seems unlikely to account for the extent to which those specific alien features should come to be embedded in Kummaya's close description, produced under terms of maximum stress and horror. More probably, Egyptian gods were already deep in Kummaya's own mind, as if rooted through childhood tales, to emerge now out of his subconscious mind within his traumatic vision. Equally intriguing is the frontal prominence given to the great gods of Elam in Nergal's explicit statement. We have no way of knowing what this substitution for the chief Assyrian gods implies, politically or theologically, but for sure there is something specific and out of the mundane behind the inclusion of this passage. Here again, one senses input from a sophisticated and well-informed brain.

The Case against Urad-Gula: Summing Up

We have seen that Urad-Gula was a desperate man and that Kummaya's public and noisy character, with the court embarrassment he would have caused, lent itself to his inventive and crafty mind. Knowing Ashurbanipal since childhood, he would have been an equal *intimé* of Shamash-metu-uballiṭ/Kummaya, and sharply aware of the strengths and weaknesses of his character. More than that, his own hands were unclean. He was there with Kummaya on many occasions – that is how he was able to watch and document everything that happened so fully – while the abuse by him mentioned in the account overlaps suggestively with protestations made in his letter to Ashurbanipal, involving going where he had no business to be, and betraying secrets. It is conclusive in our judgement when one or two paired statements are matched:

> *Kummaya's story: [. . .] went and opened the [. . .] for the Scribe's son*

with

> *Urad-Gula's letter: I guarded his privileges, I did not enter the house of a eunuch or a courtier without his permission*

'Son of a scribe' in Akkadian can mean a member of the scribal profession, but this was not any old scribe. I have taken it to refer literally to Urad-Gula's father Adad-shuma-uṣur, given the fact that he, Urad-Gula, had previously accepted bribes and occupied the post of his father. Court eunuchs were undoubtedly privy to all manner of secrets.

> *Kummaya's story: He controlled the clever book-keepers, and especially the 'one who protects their lord's secrets'*

and

> *addressing Ereshkigal: 'Reveal for me the face of the secret, determine the . . .'*

with

Urad-Gula's letter: Improper conduct, whispering about and revealing a secret are detestable things.

Urad-Gula, close to the royal family of Assyria, had been bred from infancy in the role of advising, counselling, steering and manipulating at a high level. As a one-time top-flight exorcist, he would have been steeped in every aspect of esoteric learning, master of all that mortals could know of the Netherworld and its inhabitants. He would be versed in incubation temple rituals, when those in need of a message would sleep in a temple overnight with the most effective prayers and procedures. Urad-Gula would also be in a position to concoct a customised ritual of Netherworld type, with a malleable stooge under his control – part of a deep plan with a specific motive. Perhaps a special arrangement was contrived in the temple, designed to be lethally effective on Kummaya's frail psyche, with, perhaps, a twist of *anamiru*, the hallucinatory necromantic drug that allowed mortals to see what they would normally never see at all in this world. Slipped in Kummaya's drink or burnt over coals, *anamiru* might lend great effectiveness to the slightest whispered suggestion about the strange foreign gods that would be present, watching him.

That the Scribe referred to his own engineered expiation in his *Epilogue* as a *namburbû*, the procedure for undoing portended evil, shows that he conceived of the plan and put it into operation in terms of a professional undertaking, for *namburbûs* were at the heart of the exorcist's business, and often required highly specialised rituals to achieve their client's release. By his own admission, too, Urad-Gula enjoyed a special relationship with Nergal, king of Below. Somehow it must have been arranged that he would be waiting at the Netherworld Exit, able to claim credit and absolution for himself when Kummaya stumbled out into the sunshine. His reinstatement in the palace, if all went to plan, should follow thereafter.

The reader of this text can hardly doubt from the narrative that the Assyrian prince literally endured the personal career disaster that is described so powerfully and incriminatingly, only to be subjected to some orchestrated and traumatic ghostly ritual in the Nergal temple. That someone other than the prince composed the Akkadian account of the Kummaya story is clear from the imprecision with which the pronouns 'he' and 'I' switch throughout the narrative. If Kummaya's literary encounters in the Netherworld preserve any element of true experience, we can be sure that it was stage-managed, scripted and produced by Urad-Gula, an early precursor of Iago.

11

The Delicate Art of Necromancy

I can call spirits from the vastly deep.
Why, so can I, or so can any man;
But will they come when you do call for them?
                    Henry IV, Part 1, Act 3, Scene 1

Once in a while, despite the Mesopotamian preoccupation with getting rid of their ghosts altogether, some deeply compelling circumstance or question meant that a ghost had to be brought up from below to provide answers to pressing questions. Deliberately inviting a ghost up was, of course, playing with fire and a Pandoran undertaking in every way: no one could be sure who or what would arrive or just how easy it might be to send them back again. Necromancy – the art of summoning up the dead to learn what the future will bring – was one of many fortune-telling techniques in ancient Mesopotamia. The paucity of known examples might suggest that it was probably only under very unusual circumstances that anyone resorted to it, although that may not be true, for we know of several specialist types of necromancer.

'One who by charms can converfe with the ghofts of the dead; a conjurer; an inchanter,' wrote Samuel Johnson blithely of the word *necromancer* in his 1775 *Dictionary*, and it is thanks to the labours of his unsung predecessors, our cuneiform lexicographers working in clay, millennia before, that we command today the oldest possible vocabulary for necromancer. Ancient scholars collected words over many generations for virtually everything in Sumerian and Akkadian, listing them in orderly fashion for easy retrieval, and often explaining what they meant.

The result was shelves laden with priceless dictionary-tablets, the enduring backbone for cuneiform instruction in Mesopotamian schools, and equally indispensable to today's cuneiformists, four millennia later. One extensive work known informally as the 'professions' list is a hodgepodge of words for all the activities carried out in the world by men and, occasionally, women. This list includes professional necromantic terminology, both in Sumerian and Akkadian, from the beginning of the second millennium bc, and we are fortunate indeed to inherit such rarefied information. Note that there were two types of female specialists: perhaps a female practitioner would be preferred for bringing up a female ghost.

Guide to Sumerian and Akkadian Necromantic Terminology

THE PRACTICE
The verb 'to bring up', said of a ghost, is buru in Sumerian, explained as *šūlû ša eṭemmi* in Akkadian, 'to bring up a ghost'.

THE PRACTITIONERS
The generalist
Both Sumerian lú-gedim-ma and Akkadian *ša eṭemmi* mean 'ghost person', or, so to speak, 'ghost wallah'. Magical activity at large, as we have seen, was in the hands of *āšipu*-exorcists, and the *ša eṭemmi* was the ghost specialist within that broad field; it was *ša eṭemmis* who formalised the ritual and healing ghost compositions that we have benefited from in this book.

The specialist necromancer (male)
Sumerian has two words for necromancer: lú-balag-gá, 'one with balag drum', and lú-sag-bulug-ga, obscure to us, although the word sag certainly means 'head', and bulug might just be a variant form of balag, drum. Both are explained by Akkadian *mušēlû eṭemmi*, literally, 'one who brings up a ghost'. The throb of the

222

balag drum could be useful in a necromantic ritual, where a remote or uninterested ghost might need to be woken up from its daydreaming and attracted by some deep-register insistence.

The specialist necromancer (female)

The complex Sumerian term means literally, 'a woman who brings up an IGI.ŠID', an unknown term that obviously has to mean ghost. Her Akkadian equivalent, *mušēlītum*, is literally, 'woman who brings up (a ghost)', matching the male term, with the word ghost understood.

Black magician and necromancer (male and female)

The Sumerian translates as 'one who brings up a ghost', and the Akkadian equivalent is the *naršindu*. These *naršindus* are involved in dark magical activity, sorcery and witchcraft, but the cuneiform dictionaries tell us that both the *ša eṭemmi*, 'ghost person', and *mušēlû eṭemmi*, 'ghost-raiser', can sometimes be described as a *naršindu*, showing that necromancy could be a *naršindu* specialism. There might be a sinister implication to their ghost-intercourse. A wicked expert, of course, could cause true havoc in charge of a platoon of malevolent spectres who would do his bidding.

Black magician and necromancer (female)

This is the feminine Akkadian form *naršindatu*, *naršinnatu*, and there are plenty of cases of the *naršindatu* getting up to black magic practices.

Necromancer

Both the Sumerian and its Akkadian equivalent, *mušēlû ṣilli*, mean 'one who brings up a shade'. The Akkadian *ṣillu*, shadow, shade and likeness, just as in English, can mean ghost.

Two points come out of this quartet of necromancers. While this evidence from the ancient cuneiform dictionary dates to the Old

Babylonian period, about 1750 bc, it does not imply that this was the time when necromantic activity first appeared. The very fact that there are terms in the older Sumerian language, in one case two terms, hints at necromantic activity reaching back into the third millennium bc, remarkable in that we have so little information for fortune-telling or prediction of any kind in Sumerian sources. This means that the second-millennium Sumerian ghosts in Chapter 3, whose untroubled sojourn in the Netherworld was what everyone was hoping for, could equally well have been dragged up for intimate conversation by those who knew how, if need be. The very variety of distinct necromantic terms is suggestive of much activity, but none of these specialists is mentioned in our few necromantic documents. These consist of two private letters that refer to willing communication with ghosts, and three instruction-manual tablets that explain how communication with ghosts could be safely accomplished. Of these manuals, one is from Assyria in the north and two from Babylonia in the south.

LETTER 1: PRIVATE NECROMANCY — OLD ASSYRIAN PERIOD, 1950–1850 BC

Our first glimpse of the practice of necromancy anywhere in the world occurs in a private cuneiform letter in Akkadian excavated at the site of Kanesh (modern Kültepe) in Anatolian Turkey. The letter dates to between 1950 and 1850 bc and thus stems from the same broad period as the necromancer terminology collected above. The document belongs within archives of fascinating, one-sided and often 'modern-sounding' business correspondence. The writers are expat Assyrians from Mesopotamia proper out of the city of Assur, and permanently based at that time at a colony in Anatolia to develop fruitful, long-term trading; their letters cover every aspect of their financial transactions and undertakings. The one *necromantic* example translates as follows:

To Imdi-ilum speak,
Thus say Taram-Kubi and Shimat-Ashur:
'Here we are asking šā'iltu *female diviners,*
bā'irtu *female diviners*
and ghosts (spelled e-ṭe₄-me):
The god Assur has been keeping an eye on you:
You are too fond of silver,
Confound it! <. . .> your life!
You cannot even enjoy yourself in Assur city!
Please, when you hear (this) letter,
Come, look Assur in the eye,
Save your life.
Why don't you quote me the price of the textiles?'

The point here is enshrouded in the final, rather blunt line. The letter is an attempt to wrap up a laggard business deal with Imdi-ilum who, presumably, neither answers letters nor settles his debts. They write to the miser exaggeratingly, sarcastically even (*'we've tried this and this and this for a prediction'*), in an attempt to provoke a reaction and a response. The female *šā'iltu*, 'asker' diviners, probably specialised in dreams and are distinct from necromancers, as are the female *bā'irtu* diviners, who worked with liver omens. For the historian of necromancy, however, the mere mention of 'asking ghosts', using the flagship term *eṭemmu*, is crucial evidence. Even if this is just a literary figure of speech, the letter reflects familiarity with three contemporary branches of fortune-telling; other correspondence within the archive refers more than once to shaming the 'ghost in our father's house', when putting pressure on unscrupulous or lackadaisical partners. Old Assyrian family ghosts were present, accessible and touchy, not without influence, and they could also be communicated with.

LETTER 2: ROYAL NECROMANCY — LATE ASSYRIAN PERIOD,
SEVENTH CENTURY BC

The second necromantic case comes from a very different world, that of the Assyrian royal court and power centre at Nineveh in the seventh century bc. In fact, the letter was almost certainly written in 669 bc, right at the end of, or directly following after, the reign of King Esarhaddon (681–669 bc) whose burial (Chapter 3) and silent corpse (Chapter 10) we have already looked in on. It concerns the same weighty matter that was at play behind the experiences of Prince Kummaya: who was to succeed Esarhaddon as king of Assyria and king of the world?

This letter, much of which is poorly preserved, contains a report by an unknown writer to an unknown recipient within court circles. It is probable that Crown Prince Ashurbanipal himself is now speaking, and he is quoting the opinion of a ghost that can only be a dead queen:

> ... *reported as follows:*
>   *'She told me truthfully that*
>   *the gods Assur and Shamash*
>   *ordained me to be Crown Prince*
>   *of Assyria.'*
> *Her ghost blesses him in the same*
> *fashion with which he has revered*
> *the ghost:*
>   *'May his descendants rule over Assyria.'*

Esarhaddon died in November 669 bc, en route for Egypt. Prior to his demise, as we have seen, there had been complex and prolonged manoeuvring for the position of Crown Prince. Technically, Ashurbanipal's older brother Shamash-shum-ukin should have succeeded his father – if not Shamash-metu-uballiṭ/ Kummaya – but it was Ashurbanipal who was the preferred candidate, both of Esarhaddon, and of Naqi'a, the powerful Queen Mother. To that end, as already mentioned, treaties were drawn up to compel both Shamash-shum-ukin and other rulers under the aegis of the Assyrian Empire to acknowledge Ashurbanipal as king of Assyria when the time came. This letter dates therefore to the narrow interval of time between the death of Naqi'a and Ashurbanipal's formal installation on the throne, neither of which dates is known, and is an attempt by Ashurbanipal to force matters by means of his grandmother's vote. Perhaps there had been a plan for her to leave some written document of her own; at any rate, catching her in this way after she had died to secure her testimony suggests that the issue of succession at that point was still uncertain in Ashurbanipal's mind, to the point that any support was welcome.

The Crown Prince must have recruited the most loyal and discreet of individuals to carry out so subtle an enquiry, for the enormity of summoning the dead queen could only be undertaken in total secrecy, away from the all too watchful eyes of palace factions, individuals loyal to Shamash-shum-ukin and opportunist spies. The necromantic procedure could only have taken place in the building that housed the queen's tomb, most probably within the tomb chamber itself. This we must visualise as a corbelled subterranean vault with steps, with a stone sarcophagus to house the body, as in the case of the queenly burials from earlier reigns discovered at Nimrud discussed in Chapter 3. Access to the queen's grave chamber was probably from the harem section of the palace and few would have the right to enter; but no one would have halted Prince Ashurbanipal, who must have spent much of his early childhood playing there with his grandmother; he was her favourite. The ritual to call her up, then, must have been a dead-of-night and cloak-of-black affair.

The two letters, Old Assyrian and Late Assyrian, are separated by more than a millennium of time. We have no evidence for necromantic activity for the interval in between. This also means we have no grasp of how seldom or otherwise such activity occurred, for what written evidence survives and reaches the excavator and tablet reader is always fortuitous. All we can establish beyond dispute is that highly specialist necromantic practitioners, and thus their clients, were on stage and active before the commencement of the second millennium bc. It is only from the first millennium bc that we have any insight into necromantic procedure, and it is to the manuals and their magic words that we now turn.

NECROMANCY MANUAL *1* – LATE ASSYRIAN PERIOD, SEVENTH CENTURY BC

The first procedure tablet was also once in the Royal Library at Nineveh. It is the only item of necromantic activity among about 25,000 tablets and fragments, also indicating that such material was far from commonplace. The tablet is numbered K 2779 and consists of several ruled-off sections.

Summoning your ghost

We start off with the top Mesopotamian ghost-summoning spell, in which our familiar gedim-ghost appears three times. Try sounding these magic words out loud:

> *ni-ir-ḫa-ab ni-ir-ḫa-ab gedim ni-ir-ḫa-ab*
> *gedim igi-bar ni-ir-ḫa-ab*
> *gi-ir-gi ia-am-ma-ke₄*
> *igi-an igi-bar gedim am-ma-ke₄*

We are told the purpose for which this spell is needed:

> *An incantation to enable a person to see a ghost*

A very rough translation – for it is in strange Sumerian – reads:

> *(With) saḫab-oil, saḫab-oil, Oh ghost, saḫab-oil*
> *Oh ghost, be you visible (with) saḫab-oil!*

(Thereafter) hotfoot it back with the Netherworld oil!
Be you truly visible, Oh ghost from the Netherworld!

Specially mixed oil, sometimes called *nirḥab*, sometimes *saḥab*, is central in these manuals, and can be applied either to the necromancer's face, or to a figurine. This ritual goes with the spell:

You crush mouldy wood and fresh leaves of Euphrates poplar
in water, oil, beer and wine. You dry, crush and sieve snake-
tallow, white honey, a frog that lives among the pebbles, hair
of a dog, hair of a cat, hair of a fox, bristle of a chameleon,
bristle of a lizard, fingertip of a frog, gut-tip of a frog, the left
wing of a grasshopper, and marrow from a goose long-bone.
  You mix all this in wine, water and milk together with amñara-
plant.
  You recite the incantation three times and anoint your face
with the mixture.
  You will see the ghost and he will speak with you.

This mixture of ingredients is distinct both from common ritual material and from the normal healing pharmacopeia. The slippery concoction, infused with potent words, is applied to the officiant's face, and,

You will see the ghost and he will speak with you

This result is more than is implied by the caption to the spell, where just seeing the ghost is all that is promised.

Seeing and speaking
As we see from the second section, there is no need here to start by 'bringing up' this ghost. It might be one of those deceased family members, buried on the premises, who has already been seen by the client, half-glimpsed out of the corner of an eye. If so, the aim would be to *see it properly and speak to it properly,*

to discover what is troubling it, a striking and creative alternative to the customary aggressive-style expulsion of the anti-ghost rituals. Perhaps, on the other hand, the ghost is reckoned to be bearing a message or thought to be able to answer a question, and needs to be coerced into speaking up. We cannot, in other words, choose between, *What is the matter with you?* and, *Where are the gold bars buried?* At any rate the matter is not lightly undertaken. We know convincingly from the *If a City* omens translated in Chapter 5 just how dangerous seeing and hearing ghosts could be. We know also that such threatened danger could be averted with a *namburbû* ('its release') ritual, and the second ritual, with its spell, confronts this danger head-on:

> *In order to avert the evil in a ghost's cry you crush a potsherd from an abandoned tell-mound in water. He should sprinkle the house. Over three days he should make offerings to the family ghosts.*
>
> *He should libate roast barley beer. He should scatter juniper over a censer before Shamash, libate prime quality beer, offer a present to Shamash and recite as follows:*

> *O Shamash, Judge of Heaven and Netherworld, foremost among the Anunnaki! Judge of all the lands, Shamash, foremost and resplendent one! You keep them in check, O Shamash, the Judge. You carry those from Above down to Below, those from Below up to Above. The ghost who has cried out, whether of father or mother, whether brother or sister, whether a forgotten son of someone, whether a vagrant ghost who has no one to care for it, an offering has been made for him! Water has been poured out for him! May the evil in his cry go away behind him! May the evil in his cry not come near me!*
>
> *He should do this repeatedly over three days . . . broken*
>
> *He should wash his hands, purify himself and anoint himself with oil.*

IT IS FINISHED

This vital counter-measure to 'avert the evil in a ghost's cry' raises an important question: is this just conventional magical material for when someone hears a ghost, which is included here in view of what is going on; or does it mean that, even when intercourse with a ghost is deliberately engineered as in the opening ritual, steps will still have to be taken to disperse the intrinsic danger that follows automatically?

Conventional dues are first paid to the family ghosts and spirit master Shamash. Behind the water-sprinkling to clear the house is the point that vagrant ghosts frequented ruined cities, and crushed potsherds from such places, which were always lying about (and still do), are not infrequently prescribed for ghost-banishing purposes. The spell is to establish whether the speaking ghost is a family ghost or that of a stranger, and it is needful to declare that food and drink offerings have been properly carried to preclude delay in the ghost's return.

Next quoted is the most relevant and direct *If a City* ghost omen (although it is not actually attested in our incomplete tablets for Tablet XIX), and the heading that shows this is a *namburbû*:

Omen: *If an eṭemmu-ghost cries out in a person's house: death in the person's house*

Heading: *If an evil apparition (lit. something that 'comes up') appears in a person's house, in order that this evil should not approach the person and the house:*

One similar tradition is known from a Tablet XIX omen (already quoted in Chapter 5):

If a ghost in a man's house cries out and one who can hear, hears it: overthrow of the house: the man will die and mourning (follow).

The necromancy manual next gives the right evil-averting *namburbû* procedure:

> *In the late afternoon he makes a ceremonial-offering to Shamash.*
> *In the morning, in the steppe, in a secluded place, you sweep*
> *the ground. You sprinkle pure water. You set up a reed altar*
> *and you put three portions of two (var. seven) each (cakes)*
> *made from flour. You scatter dates and fine flour. You add*
> *sweetmeat-cake with honey and ghee. You set up a libation*
> *vessel. You plant an arrow in the ground. You set up a censer*
> *with juniper. You libate beer. To the right of the offerings, in*
> *the shade of the west part of the house, you scatter . . . and*
> *cress. You libate roasted grain beer.*
>
> *You make him recite as follows,*
>
>> May the ghost that cried out in my house for evil purposes
>> not approach me!
>>
>> *To the left of the offerings, in the shade of the east part*
>> *of the house, you scatter . . . You libate . . . in the later*
>> *afternoon. You make him recite as follows, '. . .'*

The entire procedure is carried out adjacent to the client's house, underlining the point that the ghost for interlocution will be a family member, identifiable and on the premises, the whole operation conducted on home territory.

Do observe the arrow in the ground. Obviously, it must have been driven in point-down, constituting a slightly comic **THIS WAY** notice-type hint.

History Behind Necromancy Manual 1

K 2779, *Manual 1*, is in Babylonian-style cuneiform, one of many similar-looking magical tablets commandeered from the Babylonian south for Ashurbanipal's library collections, long after his accession (and his own necromantic experience). Perhaps the king had sought it out. It arrived at Nineveh as part of an ordered series, for library tablets that belonged together were given running numbers in a surprisingly modern way for logical storage and easy retrieval. The first line of K 2779, the old spell *nirḫab nirḫab*, occurs as the catch-line, indicating that it came next in the tablet Sm. 810, also from Nineveh. The two tablets, therefore, run in library sequence, with K 2779 following Sm. 810, which is also a *namburbû* for use with dangerous omens. It is quite possible both were written by the same scribe.

The Namburbû Tablet SM. 810

A man is sufficiently startled and alarmed by a bird flying into his house to consult a specialist exorcist, to clarify what the event might portend and, more importantly, deal with it. Sm. 810 contains the

> namburbû *for the evil of a dove or strange bird which has entered a man's house, or has hovered over the man, that the evil may not affect the man*

A ritual and recitation are given. At the end of it all, the anxious individual has only to recite the spell *I am pure, I am clean*, and go straight home, and the evil of those birds will not approach him.

K 2779 is, unusually, only inscribed on the obverse. The scribe noted *It is finished* after the second incantation and ritual, showing they form a unit separate from what followed. It has thus been assembled from three, originally independent sources:

1.   The necromantic spell and ritual. This is a *proactive* procedure and at odds with the characteristic *reactive* nature of the *namburbû* system.
2.   The general ghost-cry *namburbû*.
3.   The specific domestic ghost-cry-predicting-a-death *namburbû*.

Whoever compiled this tablet ringed the necromancy ritual and spell around with necessary safeguards and inserted it within the greater, multi-tablet *namburbû*-work. If we peer at the tablet itself, we see that:

- The scribe states that the tablet he was copying was *broken* at the end of the penultimate line of the second incantation.
- He missed out a sign or two himself – unless they, too, were broken without indication – in the last line.
- Half of one line to the lower left seems to have been partially erased.
- A further two lines of text from the third ritual which he overlooked were written in afterwards on the left edge.

These not-quite-finished points would be frowned on at the capital library and not pass muster with the exacting standards of the librarian-king, but they tally with the strangely uninscribed space on the reverse in showing that necromantic manuals were in flux, and good magical sources in short supply. Since K 2779 was excerpted from a longer native Babylonian compilation, it is fortunate that part of that interesting work is known from *Necromancy Manual 2.*

Necromancy Manual 2 – Babylon, Sixth Century BC

Perhaps seventy-five years after Ashurbanipal's death a very able scholar-scribe at Babylon copied out – in his best handwriting and on excellent clay – our *Manual 2*. Originally it had two full columns of writing each side, but only part of each on the obverse survives today and almost nothing of the reverse. It must have been an earlier copy of this same Babylonian necromantic *grimoire* from which the spell and ritual in K 2779, later taken to Nineveh, were excerpted. The number of this Babylon tablet is BM 36703.

Talking things over

In the first incomplete lines there is mention of a roaming ghost that is obviously the problem to be addressed. A flour offering put out under the stars included some particular dust. A juniper censer is set up, and two spells are referred to, but the words are lost. The second is recited seven times over an oily preparation that includes a certain crushed mineral and blood, and,

> *You anoint your face before Shamash, and when you call (to him) he will answer you*

The Akkadian verb here means 'to cry' and 'to call', and is often said of the ghosts themselves in the omens. Whether or not the ghost becomes visible is not stated, but that, of course, was not essential for conversation and would compound the danger. The ritual thus has the same basic purpose as the spells in the preceding manual; here, too, there is no question of bringing up a ghost; the 'roaming' ghost is a type we know, and already on the loose, and the necromancer is hoping to deal once and for all with an unhappy individual who has overstayed its welcome and resisted dismissal.

This incantation then follows:

> *Who are you? Who are you? (Sumerian)*
> *Who are you? Who are you? (Akkadian)*
> *You who constantly seek out sweet life,*
> *Whether you are an evil spirit, an evil šēdu-demon,*
> *An evil ghost, an evil gallû-demon . . .*

. . . oh evil ghost . . .
Oh evil ghost!

This short spell asks outright, *Who are you?*, twice, both in Sumerian and in Akkadian. This is a quite different approach from the standard 'saturation bombing' method of, *Whether you are a . . .*, summarised in the next lines, but exemplified in the elaborate ghost lists of Chapter 5. It is quite remarkable that the opening to the 'conversation' is given in Sumerian as well as Babylonian. No one in ancient Iraq at this period, the sixth century bc, had spoken Sumerian for *a good thousand years*, so this implies that an unknown ghost might prove to be some very-long-dead individual out of the very dustiest of depths, reminding us of the ghostly Sumerians in the Netherworld described by Enkidu.

This passage, and the beginning of *Manual 1*, indicate a shift in thinking about how best to handle ghosts. If precautions are taken, the idea is to identify the ghost properly with the aim of talking to it and, surely, sorting things out. The ritual that follows is obviously the next step to make progress if it doesn't work.

If . . . do/does not answer you,
You . . . will not answer you . . .
You recite the incantation Great . . .

The ritual is also, sadly, fragmentary, but mentions excrement of a wild ox, and a part of a bear, used in some installation.

Bringing up a ghost
In *Manual 2* column ii, in contrast, we are presented with some-thing very choice and important. Here we receive clear instructions for bringing a ghost up from the depths with the unambiguous aim of *asking it questions*. This is more than just having a helpful chat; it is necromancy in the classic meaning of the word.

Here is what survives of this useful spell:

May he bring up a ghost from the darkness for me!
May he revivify the dead man's muscles!
I call upon you, skull of all skulls,
May he who is within the skull answer me!
O Shamash, who can open the darkness!

Although the first crucial lines are missing, what survives opens a window on a very dramatic and startling procedure. Appeal is made to Shamash, our familiar sun god and ghost-master, to animate a ghost so that it can make its way up from the darkness below to enter into an oiled and waiting human skull, the mouthpiece that will enable him to deliver answers. This is no ploy to pin down straightforward conversation with a resident ghost on the rampage, but a fully deliberate method of bringing up a ghost who would otherwise have stayed where it was, for one's own purposes.

This is the necessary ritual:

Its ritual: *You crush a male and female partridge, dust from a crossroads, dust from a jumping steppe-cricket and an upturned potsherd from a crossroads in anointing oil.*
  You mix it all together and leave it to stand overnight.
  In the morning you anoint either the ghost (figure) or the namtaru *(figure) or the skull, and you call upon him and he will answer you.*

Again, the anointing oil mixed with certain ingredients is to stand overnight under the stars. When the skull in question is anointed *the following morning*, you call to him and he will answer. The oil is not applied to the living operator, as before, but to the bony medium of communication. It is not clear whether the arriving ghost would be seen.

One can only imagine that the skull used for this ritual needed to be that of the deceased individual with whom contact was desired. Any client who underwent this operation at the hands of a necromancer would be in pursuit of a specific individual, almost certainly a family member, and in many cases – given underfloor burials – it might have been quite possible to retrieve that person's skull for the purpose. It feels doubtful, one might think, that a ghost jerked from its remote resting place would be content to fold itself into someone else's skull, even temporarily. The words of the incantation are addressed to the ghost within the skull from which the voice would emanate, with or without the hollow click of teeth.

Facing and interrogating the talking skull of someone once known personally and now dead was probably not undertaken lightly even by a necromancer, let alone a Babylonian house-holder. Perhaps it is for that reason that the ritual is to be enacted in the bright light of morning. This is not without its implications, for even if the atmosphere swirled with heavy smoke and incense, the client would see everything that was going on. If the skull was not, in fact, accessible, the magic oil with its irresistible pull could be applied to one of two substi-tutes, the individual's *eṭemmu*-ghost, or his *namtaru*, with the same result. Both must obviously be pre-prepared models or figurines. That a likeness of a person's ghost could be convinc-ingly modelled in clay we know already from the illustrated tablet in Chapter 7. The *namtaru* figurine also appears in *Necromancy Manual 3* below, as well as a modelled figure in an anti-witchcraft ritual where it is one cubit high, possibly a dwarf. The god Namtar we have met in the Netherworld, where he is vizier and messenger to Queen Ereshkigal; his Sumerian name means Fate-Decider. Here, however, we are dealing with the plain Akkadian noun *namtaru*, loaned from Sumerian, for which the Assyrian dictionary from Chicago (*CAD*, Vol. N, 247–9) offers, 1. death, fate; 2. (a demon, bringer of death). Such a *namtaru* is an evil force, listed in incantations among inimical demons and devils, but here the word can obviously have neither meaning. It is perhaps closer to 'messenger', implying that the deceased who has been summoned communicates by proxy. At any rate, a man's *namtaru* is distinct from his *eṭemmu*, even if, in this context, they can be functionally interchangeable.

Either type of figurine would need to be recognisable as the intended dead individual rather than merely generic. This would require its name either written in cuneiform on the body or, as in *Manual 3* below, simply named out loud. Since we assume that the incoming ghost could speak through either medium, the figurines presumably had mouths open.

The incantation that follows is the Babylon version of the chief ghost-intercourse incantation *nirḫab nirḫab*, with illuminating spelling variations, which is here also described as 'a spell to enable a person to see a ghost'. The same ritual as that in K 2779 Ritual 1, 'You crush mouldy wood . . .', is then given, but here it concludes,

You will see the ghost and he will speak with you;
you can look at the ghost and he will talk with you

But two broken lines remain,

'They panicked, they panicked. The ghost covered [. . .]'

Ghosts are known to tremble in fear at the sight of a forbidding staff in the *Epic of Gilgamesh*, as we have seen (Chapter 10), and I have a sneaking suspicion that this is a reference to that famous text.

The third set of necromantic instructions comes from the southern city of Uruk.

Necromancy Manual 3 – Uruk, Fourth Century BC

This tablet, W 22758/2 from Uruk of the fourth century bc, is the latest in date. Here also two short procedures originally on

two small tablets have been combined on a larger one. The first
is to make a man's *namtaru*, as mentioned above, speak; the
second contains the *Ritual for the Land-of-no-Return*.

Seven herbs are listed for the right oil to persuade a *namtaru*
to speak. At Uruk the *namtaru* is obviously the preferred necromantic medium, in contrast to the Babylonian skull or the
ghost-figure. The spell is in Sumerian. The operation is under
the supervision of his namesake, the great god Namtar, and Bilgi,
a by-name of Shamash. This supports the idea that the *namtaru*
acts as a messenger. The spell, described as 'incantation to make
a man's *namtaru* speak', then follows:

> *This* namtaru *speaks; this* namtaru *speaks;*
> *Joyfully this* namtaru *speaks to procure desirability;*
> > *it is for the gods to make fate sweet*
> > *You recite the incantation seven times over the oil; you anoint*
> *(the* namtaru*) and whatever you ask him he will tell you*

The word translated 'desirability' is the abstract nam-ḫi-li, which
usually refers specifically to sexual allure; it is not impossible
therefore that a message here is sought about the client's future
chances with a lover: *Will I succeed?* The *namtaru* intercedes,
therefore, on his owner's behalf, with the telling point: *Whatever
you ask him he will tell you.*

This ritual follows:

> *You go to the river bank and pinch off clay, saying,*
> > *'Namtar of So-and-so, son of So-and-so.'*
> > *You crush seeds of (three named) plants and mix them*
> *together in oil. You recite the incantation over it. You anoint*
> *your face several times.*
> > *You make enquiry of her and it will speak with you.*

The *namtaru*'s identity is established by formally pronouncing
its owner's name and that of his father aloud over it. The feminine

pronoun in the last line is clearly written and unlikely to be a mistake. Perhaps the speaker is addressing his dead wife, and the *namtaru* replies on her behalf.

A double ruling separates what follows from this material, indicating that it is drawn from the second source. It has a formal introduction, 'When you perform the Ritual of the Land-of-no-Return', and this is the procedure:

> *You set up two portable altars before Shamash and Pabilsag and fix on twelve food portions each. You pile up dates, flour, figs, grapes, honey and butter and pressed oil. You fill four libation vessels with equal quantities, two with wine, one with milk and one with beer and set them up before the offering installation. You place a water basin in position. You pour out mixed together sieved barley and clay. You set down . . . repeatedly. You libate beer. You recite the incantation. You libate milk and wine. This is the procedure for . . .*

This operation takes place outside the client's house, and is reminiscent of the well-controlled necromantic procedure with helpful arrow at Nineveh. There is no question of anybody's going *down* to the Netherworld; something is to come *up*. Altars are set in place for Shamash and Pabilsag, the old Sumerian god of the venerable city of Larak. The lost end of the ritual cannot be restored with certainty, but what is brought up by the ritual is the ghost with the answer, as becomes clear shortly. Apparently six hundred food offerings have to be set up in front of the house for the Anunnaki gods of the Netherworld, who are known in the later first millennium bc to number that many. Then,

> *You crush* anamiru *plant in oil and anoint your face. You recite the incantation three times over it and the ghost will make your prediction* (purussû).
>
> *If he remains silent it is unreliable; you must perform a* namburbû.

The incantation explains about how this essential *anamiru* plant came into the world:

> *Enmesharra, Ninmesharra, father and mother of all the gods,*
>   *Endashurimma, Nindashurimma, father and mother of all*
> *the gods,*
>   *Enkum, Ninkum, father and mother of all the gods,*
>   *Lord of all lands, fierce king, king of justice,*
>   *'What wrong have I done him, that you made (me) as clay?*
>   *My arms are exhausted, prince of Ekishnugal,*
>   *I, O great gods, did do this!*
>   *Do you look! Bring tranquillity to my heart!'*
>   *He goes up the mountain, he goes down the mountain,*
>   *They tore out the* anamiru *plant by its roots.*
>   *He saw the gods, his brothers.*
>   *He prostrated himself, speaking a word to him:*
>   *'With you his assembly pronounced justice!'*
>   *He threw it down, and anointed his face.*
>   *He anointed his eyes.*
>   *'Bring me your decision!'*

> *Incantation in order to see a ghost and to get a prediction*

The *anamiru* plant is crushed in oil and the incantation recited three times. Anointing the face will make the Anunnaki speak and give you a decision.

> *If it is silent it is unreliable. You must perform a* namburbû.

The Akkadian term for the outcome means, variously, decision, verdict and prediction, and in the present context most likely refers to asking the ghost's advice about some proposed plan. In the first ritual the ghost provides the answer, but the operation can also be addressed to the assembled Netherworld judges, the Anunnaki, who will also bring a decision. Perhaps the idea is that the Anunnaki debate the issue below and it is the ghost who brings up their conclusion. If so, the question or questions must have been submitted or communicated before the ritual. Also interesting is the repeated stipulation that silence in the ghost or the Anunnaki is 'unreliable'; perhaps a more sympathetic translation would be 'doubtful'. Probably it means that without parley they cannot be sure of who the ghost was. In any case, things cannot be left to drift, and a *namburbû* is essential in both cases.

The Plant Anamiru and its Origin

The incantation, in Akkadian, embodies an old myth about the *anamiru* plant, how it came to the attention of gods and men, and how it can compel an answer for those who control it and ask. The original mountaineering expedition procured the plant and the heroic god who went for it, his face anointed with *anamiru* in oil, gained a verdict from the divine assembly. It is this answer-inducing power that is recruited in the present instance. The incantation is explicitly in order to see a ghost and get a decision. A layer of meaning is wrapped up in the plant's very name, *anamiru*, for any schoolboy would naturally construe it in Akkadian as *ana āmiru*, 'for the see-er', which is exactly what *āmiru* is, the English seer. Botanically the plant is unidentified, although it does occur in the cuneiform list of plants and is used among medical herbs. Application of this substance renders the ghost, brought up from below, *visible*. The same old incantation occurs in four other first-millennium Babylonian tablets, and the wording circulated in a very unstable form, often corrupted or misunderstood; the translation offered here is the best compromise to get sense out of it.

Necromancy in Use

We are fortunate that these few first-millennium necromantic passages survive in cuneiform. Their function and the level of gravity behind them are not necessarily identical in all cases. The milieu varies between matters of state and the private lives of private individuals. Ritual passages allow the sufferer to confront a ghost face to face for conversation or pluck one from below to interrogate it. These activities contrast with the less formal use of an oiled *namtaru* messenger at Uruk to get an angle on courtship or contact a lost beloved (if that is indeed the case), a very different proposition from wrenching a ghost out of retirement to engage in conversation through its own, stiffened jaw.

Of the procedures that we meet here, the Babylonian ghost talking out of a skull has wider implications for the ghost historian, as we shall see in Chapter 12. The professionals were not over-confident of their powers or the success of their operations: the admission is, that even with best *anamiru* oil at Uruk, no one could be sure that any answer would come. This blend of expertise and humanity is another indication that ghosts were believed in completely.

What we cannot assess on available evidence is how rare or commonplace the mechanism of talking to the dead or interrogating them for information might have been during the centuries of our anti-ghost literature. The profusion of Old Babylonian specialist necromancers in the early second millennium suggests that, as already remarked, such activities were not uncommon among the ancient Mesopotamians, or inaccessible to private persons. The startling abundance of evidence for necromancy in the Greek and Roman literature and society that comes afterwards stands in direct contrast, for a modern account of it fills an entire volume, and classical necromantic activities are so far embedded in society that rumours, accusations and slanders about them are a major social theme of their own. It is perfectly conceivable that a more brisk and lively cuneiform trade in parleying with the dead – despite the great drive just to send them away – has simply largely remained under the cuneiform radar. At least in Mesopotamian circles, we can trace no sense of attached stigma or wrongdoing.

Finally, there is the matter as to how, or why, the Mesopotamian dead should be thought by their descendants to know about what was going to happen. It is unlikely that, even if the great gods in Heaven were fully up to speed on the minutiae of the Great World Plan, the individual dead (such as someone's great uncle) could be privy to the future in general: it was hardly their concern. The god in charge of dropping hints and clues to human diviners was Shamash, as we have often seen in this book, who inscribed daily coded messages into the surface of sheep livers that would yield meaning to experts charged with interpreting such things. It is Shamash who is always in the ghostly background and who here brings up the required skull-ghost himself, and one can only imagine that it is in the course of such upward journeying that they talked things over. There is also the question of whether a given ghost, family member or not, would necessarily tell the truth if they did know it. People often don't, after all.

12

The Biblical World

*'tis mad idolatry to make the service greater than the
  god*
                    Troilus and Cressida, Act 2, Scene 2

We have drawn from the Mesopotamian landscape and its writings the model for our classic picture of man's relations with ghosts. The dead are buried, sometimes below floors, sometimes in cemeteries. The individual's *eṭemmu* – ghost or spirit – goes *below*, to a Netherworld whose location and visualisation varies, the destination where the peaceful dead maintain their existence and wait for the great recycling process to touch them. They can expect in the meanwhile to receive offerings and be remembered. This model comes with the following points:

1. Certain ghosts cannot settle. They have a grievance: *primary* is unsettled business carried over from life or involved with their death or burial; *secondary* is neglect of or breakdown in offerings and prayers.
2. Visits from ghosts are not always disastrous, but the professional has a whole repertoire of procedures to send them back, drive them out, or bodily remove them from a seriously affected victim.
3. Ghosts can be brought back at the hands of a qualified necromancer with access to the necessary procedures, to answer questions before being sent back again.

There is no question but that the Mesopotamian resources that illuminate this subject are vastly more extensive, focused and numerous than those of any of the contemporary cultures of the ancient Middle East, including Egypt. Across the board, archaeological evidence for burial practice is, of course, often plentiful, in some cases perhaps, even over-plentiful, but it is in the field of written documents from the surrounding cultures that there is a disastrous shortfall. We can judiciously, nevertheless, visualise a common background system of ideas and activities concerning death, burial and the world to come that was broadly shared by the cultures of the ancient Middle East, and reflected in archaeology. Domestic folk belief, with its healers and practitioners, will always have involved gods and goddesses, demons and ghosts, spells and magic words, amulets, figurines, rituals, superstitions, and all the other timeless human paraphernalia that are so explicitly visible in ancient Mesopotamia, and with which ghosts are inevitably bound up. Cultural differences obtained, of course, and sometimes these are plainly in view. But we will probably not go far wrong if we hold this broadly sketched ghost-Netherworld system as the common backdrop to the lives, events and history of the Middle Eastern cultures of the second and first millennia bc.

Old Testament Ideas

When it comes to ghosts in particular, the Hebrew Bible is a most complicated source. When the Hebrews arrived in the land of Canaan, they encountered a quite *deplorable* number of flourishing *abominations* in widespread use that the Deuteronomist was quick to itemise:

> *When you come into the land that the* Lord *your God is giving you, you must not learn to imitate the abhorrent practices of those nations. No one shall be found among you who makes a son or daughter pass through fire, or who practises divination, or is a soothsayer, or an augur, or a sorcerer, or one who casts spells, or who consults ghosts or spirits, or who seeks oracles*

from the dead . . . Although these nations that you are about
to dispossess do give heed to soothsayers and diviners, as for
you, the Lord *your God does not permit you to do so.*

Deuteronomy 18:9–14

With the exception of passing children through fire, which never
took root in Babylonia, all these dreadful practices had long been
ineradicably entrenched in Mesopotamian society, as we have
seen, and this prescriptive statement establishes very helpfully
that a matching reliance on fortune-telling and intercourse with
ghosts and spirits prevailed before their arrival in Canaan too.
There was, accordingly, a clash.

People who read their Bible usually depend on one familiar
translation and seldom consider other versions or interpretations.
But the translations of the *RV (Revised Version)* and the *New
Revised Standard Version (NSRV)* are often surprisingly divergent,
and when it comes to biblical ghosts, awareness of this fluctuation
becomes important. In the background are much earlier translations, into Greek (the Septuagint) or Aramaic (the Targums), for
example, and on top of that the inherited opinions of ancient
commentators, scholars and theologians, not to mention their
later counterparts.

The Hebrew Netherworld and its Ghosts

The prophet Isaiah, cutting the wicked Babylonian
Nebuchadnezzar down to size, outlines what will happen at the
latter's demise:

> Sheol *beneath is stirred up*
> *to meet you when you come;*
> *it rouses the* shades *to greet you,*
> *all who were leaders of the earth;*
> *it raises from their thrones*
> *all who were kings of the nations.*

> All of them will speak
> and say to you:
> 'You too have become as weak as we!
> You have become like us!'

Isaiah 14:9–10

Sheol (Hebrew *šeʾôl*) is the Old Testament term for Netherworld, easily defined from the scattered references as the place of darkness where the spirits of the dead go. The origin and meaning of the word are uncertain, and so the proper noun Sheol is used in English. In this prophetic passage we see that the ghosts of the world's former leaders and kings are assembled side by side with the general dead, their former status enduring and acknowledged, ready to welcome a newly dead tyrant. A dead king clearly expected to be greeted by his peers on arrival. There is a direct echo here of the dead kings of Mesopotamia encountered clustered together by Enkidu in the Netherworld in Chapter 8, matched by King Esarhaddon's funerary text in Chapter 3, where offerings are made to the *malkī*, dead kings, whom he would shortly be meeting, including his own dynastic ancestors Sargon and Sennacherib.

Telling phrases in the Old Testament filter through to give us some physical idea of Sheol. The dead went *down* to get there, it is fitted with gates and bars at which they have to wait to enter and to keep them in, it has depth and those who go down to Sheol do not come up. The lyricist has other names for the Netherworld: Pit, Abaddon ('Doom'), Darkness and Land of Forgetfulness.

Hebrew Ghost Words: Rephaim

The first biblical word for ghost is Rephaim (Hebrew *rēp̄āʾîm*), a plural noun translated 'shades' in the *NRSV*, recalling the same image for a ghost sometimes used in Babylonian, *ṣillu*. Job talks about the shades trembling below; Isaiah states that the dead do not live and the shades not rise; the Psalmist asks: 'Do you work wonders for the dead, do the shades rise up for you?'; while Proverbs does not hesitate to remind us that the way of the loose woman leads down to death, her paths to the shades. These passages embody the understanding that the Hebrew dead went down to their Netherworld, Sheol, and while there, in the *assembly* of the dead (Proverbs), were conceived of and referred to as Rephaim, 'shades'.

Rephaim at Ugarit

This Hebrew term Rephaim recurs also in texts from the surrounding world. Excavations in the 1920s at the north-Syrian Bronze Age port site of Ras Shamra, ancient Ugarit, uncovered clay tablets, including literary and religious texts, of the thirteenth to twelfth centuries bc. The script was cuneiform, but cuneiform simplified into a set of signs far away from the Mesopotamian system; the language proved to be an unknown Semitic tongue and decipherers were soon at work. A whole new ancient literature was uncovered, in a language closely related to Hebrew, with subject matter that often overlapped excitingly with the Old Testament. Included are texts that refer to the *rpum*, clearly related to the Hebrew *rĕpā'îm*, perhaps originally sounding like *rapi'um*. It has long been assumed that this Ugaritic word *rpum*, especially when found in conjunction with *ars*, earth, referred to the spirits of the dead in the local idea of the Netherworld, although the range of textual contexts for *rpum* has subsequently made this specific interpretation less certain.

Rephaim at Tyre

Six hundred or so years later, however, in about 490 bc, the same word Rephaim resurfaces among the Phoenicians, where the shades of the dead are certainly meant. Here, in Lebanese Tyre, King Tabnit very roundly curses anyone thinking of defiling his tomb:

> *May you have no living seed under the sun and may there be*
> *no resting place for you with the Rephaim!*

While that of his son Eshmunazar II threatens the despoilers even
more explicitly:

> *May they not have any funeral couch with the Rephaim, may*
> *they not be buried in a grave, and may there be no son or*
> *offspring to succeed them!*

Rephaim is also used as a gentilic or 'race' term in the Hebrew
Bible for the aboriginal giants who were thought to have inhabited Canaan long before the Hebrews got there. Why the same
word – one form from a shared linguistic root – should have two
such distinct meanings is unclear. It has been suggested that
Rephaim originally just referred to these primeval populations
with their own royal heroes, later becoming democratised to refer
to the dead in general. That may be, but it cannot be concluded,
as some have proposed, that the shades in Sheol are just those
of dead kings.

An architectural terraced structure at the Northern Mesopotamian Hurrian city of Urkeš (Tell Mozan), which predates
the third-millennium temple and functions down into the second
millennium, revealed deep funeral offering pits that were thought
by the excavators to reflect the summoning of Netherworld deities
in the milieu of the Hurrian underworld god Kumarbi. In Hurrian
texts, the term *āb* or *pi*, which seems to apply to this feature,
has been connected with another Hebrew word, *'ôb*, to which
we now turn.

Hebrew *'ôb*

Hebrew has this second word for ghost, *'ôb*, the etymology of
which is also unknown, and about which there has also been an
utter flurry of inconclusive discussion. The difficulty is conveyed

by consulting the trusty *Hebrew and English Lexicon of the Old Testament* of Messrs Brown, Driver and Briggs, published in Oxford in 1953, where *four* meanings are attributed to one and the same word:

1. Skin-bottle
2. Necromancer
3. Ghost
4. Necromancy

Ignoring the bottle, it seems improbable to me that one extraordinarily loose noun in any language could mean ghost, ghost-raiser, and the art of ghost-raising all at once. That the Hebrew *'ôb* means 'ghost', parallel to Babylonian *eṭemmu*, is incontrovertible in, for example, Isaiah 29:4, and that is all we need here:

> *And being below you will speak from the Netherworld,*
> *and from the dust your speech will be low;*
> *and your voice will be as a ghost ('ôb) from the Netherworld,*
> *and from the dust your speech shall twitter.*

The substance of this Hebrew passage would, of course, be completely lucid to any passing Babylonian, with the dead squeaking and gibbering, bird-like in the dust, the eternal *eṭemmu*.

Hebrew yiddĕʿonî

In many biblical passages the Hebrew *'ôb* is paired with the word *yiddĕʿonî*. The trouble here is that no one is at all sure what this word means either. It is sometimes translated 'familiar spirit', supposedly deriving from the common verb to know, although this etymology is very doubtful. Other common Bible translations of *'ôb* and *yiddĕʿonî* are:

- familiar spirit and wizard (*RV*), i.e. one ethereal; one human
- medium and wizard (*NSRV*), i.e. both human
- divining spirit and enchanter (Greek Septuagint), i.e. one ethereal; one human

Familiar spirit is an absurd translation, dragging in the old European witches' animal familiar at the bidding of any self-respecting, dark-arts practitioner. Nor can we for a moment argue, *à la* Babylon, that a 'familiar spirit' is the ghost of an extended-family member as opposed to some unknown ghost. *Wizard*, with all its later accretions and associations for us, can equally be neither defended nor sustained for a moment. The important point here is that neither term refers to a human practitioner; they refer rather to the *forces* with which they deal.

It seems to me obvious that '*ôb* refers to a ghost of human origin and *yiddĕ'onî* to a spirit of non-human origin, or, to put it more plainly,

'ôb *means* ghost *and* yiddĕ'onî *means demons.*

Any practitioner who operated in such spheres would be dealing with evil spirits or demons just as much as ghosts. What else were there, after all?

Old Testament Ghosts and Demons

While the Old Testament is obviously immersed in, and speaks for, its contemporary world, it is at the same time effectively detached from it. Minimum 'column space' is afforded by the compilers to the distasteful features that they condemned, and anything to do with ghosts, spirits and demons falls headlong into this category. The received account is not that of the ethnographer but is hyper-critical and agenda-selective, and it fatally diminishes and distorts the picture of real life among the wider population of Israel and Judah. Underpinning the whole is the deep-seated culture of the Canaanites who preceded them. Behind the biblical narrative, the same system of ideas and activities had long flourished, suppressed from view by the censorious reformer. Household gods and goddesses in their own place were not *idols*, but legitimate and trusted helpmeets. Only sometimes can we glimpse all this, but the 'other-world' tapestry can be taken for granted, running under the received narrative. When we are fortunate, archaeology can re-animate the squashed-down reality.

As a direct result, the Old Testament is conspicuously reticent about demons and evil spirits. Later Hebrew magical texts, we may point out, refer unceasingly to demons, *šēd*, pl. *šēdîm* (loaned from Babylonian *šēdu*), who are all over the place and everyone is worried about them, but it is singular that there is no corresponding word in biblical Hebrew for demon. Given this, I suggest that *yiddě'onî* is a *cover name for evil spirit or demon*, assuming reluctance to mention them within the Hebrew text and thereby afford status to the evil or forbidden. There are other examples of this device, whereby mention of the offensive can be avoided, such as *Ish-bosheth*, Man of Shame, being substituted for the name *Esh-Baal*, which incorporated the hated alien god Baal. Perhaps *yiddě'onî* should be understood along the lines of our *What's-his-name*, or *Whatchamacallit*. That the actual meaning of this cover name is lost goes a long way to explain the extraordinary confusion about the varying translations of these words in the Old Testament. Thus, respectfully, I would translate Leviticus 20:6 as,

> *The soul who turns to ghosts and demons to go whoring after them, I will set my face against that soul and cut him off from among his people.*

This 'whoring' after evil forces parallels whoring after foreign gods. It is the *forces*, again, not the agents, that is meant.

Necromancy for the King

With '*ôb* = ghost firmly in mind, let us pursue ghosts further, with King Saul and the *so-called* 'Witch' of Endor in 1 Samuel 28:3–16. On the death of Samuel, extreme and dramatic danger from Philistine aggression led the king to take the most extraordinary steps.

> 3 *Now Samuel had died, and all Israel had mourned for him and buried him in Ramah, his own city. Saul had expelled* ghost and spirit *from the land.*

I take it that Saul, head of state and the highest authority, outlawed ghosts and spirits, as opposed to the individuals who had truck with such activity. Was Saul's action a reaction to the death of Samuel, his court prophet, or had the strictures already been long imposed? The verb can be simple perfect, *Saul turned away*, or pluperfect, *Saul had turned away*. Either the writer sets the scene for what follows or Saul had not wanted to be bothered by fraudulent message-bearing seers after Samuel had gone. The Philistines, meanwhile, were massing their forces:

> 5 *When Saul saw the army of the Philistines, he was afraid, and his heart trembled greatly.*

> 6 *When Saul inquired of the* Lord, *the* Lord *did not answer him, not by dreams, or by Urim, or by prophets.*

No help was forthcoming from the king's three-arm intelligence service: dream interpreters, visionary prophets and fortune-tellers (who apparently only used the *Urim* component of the two-part, lot-throwing *Urim* and *Thummim*). Revealingly, none of these miscellaneous offices could function without divine support, showing that in and of themselves – in biblical terms – they were sterile.

> [7] *Then Saul said to his servants, 'Seek out for me a woman Ghost-Mistress, so that I may go to her and inquire of her.' His servants said to him, 'There is a woman Ghost-Mistress at Endor.'*

Note, crucially, that the original Hebrew is *ba'alat 'ôb*, literally 'Ghost-Mistress', while the conversation also implies that there was more than one Ghost-Mistress in the country. Saul thus reveals himself to be a dyed-in-the-wool subscriber to necromantic consultation, convinced of its validity and taking it entirely for granted. He also knew that whatever the official position, ghost and spirit operators were still in business, and his own servants knew immediately whom to see and where to go.

> [8] *So Saul disguised himself and put on other clothes and went there, he and two men with him. They came to the woman by night. And he said, 'Divine for me by means of a ghost ('ôb),' and bring up for me the one whom I name to you.'*

The two men accompanying the unhappy king are the ancestors of Rosencrantz and Guildenstern. The request, in context, is entirely normal-sounding; Saul knew not only that it would work in principle, but also that the Ghost-Mistress could summon whomever he named.

> [9] *The woman said to him, 'Surely you know what Saul has done, how he has* cut off the ghosts and the spirits *from the land. Why then are you laying a snare for my life to bring about my death?'*

The Ghost-Mistress declares herself fearful for her life, which may or may not imply that Saul's public dictum carried the threat of the death sentence. It is the obfuscation of meaning as transmitted by the various translators that has made our Lady of

Endor into a *witch*. The sobriquet is ill-founded and she will probably be typecast forever among the top-ten witches of history. *Get me a Ghost-Mistress!* the king had said . . .

> [10] *But Saul swore to her by the* Lord, *'As the* Lord *lives, no punishment shall come upon you for this thing.'*

> [11] *Then the woman said, 'Whom shall I bring up for you?' He answered, 'Bring up Samuel for me.'*

There is a feel here of a secretary at the keyboard looking up in enquiry, waiting for details to type in under *Search*. Neither party sees anything out of the ordinary in all this.

> [12] *When the woman saw Samuel, she cried out with a loud voice; and the woman said to Saul, 'Why have you deceived me? You are Saul!'*

The Ghost-Mistress did not recognise the disguised Saul when he confided to her whom he was seeking, as might be expected, but only when Samuel appeared. That is indeed strange. Also, the Ghost-Mistress herself was shocked when the ghost became visible, although judging by the following line she did not at that moment know it was Samuel.

> [13] *The king said to her, 'Have no fear; what do you see?' The woman said to Saul, 'I see a divine being coming up out of the ground.'*

Her term 'divine being' is the word for god, as used in the plural form in the Old Testament to mean the god of the Israelites and refer to those of other nations. Many have discussed this line.

> [14] *He said to her, 'What is his appearance?' She said, 'An old man is coming up; he is wrapped in a robe.' So Saul knew that*

it was Samuel, and he bowed with his face to the ground, and did obeisance.

This does not mean that Saul recognised Samuel by virtue of his being a cloak-wearer, but that must have been the moment when he first glimpsed the prophet for himself.

¹⁵ *Then Samuel said to Saul, 'Why have you disturbed me by bringing me up?'*

This, if I may say so, is my favourite line in the whole Hebrew Bible. It is so utterly *credible*. Samuel, venerable and a little uncertain on his feet, recently deceased, his life's work done, is settling in down below, meeting dead old friends, securing his billet, lying back and daydreaming gratefully, and . . . *the door-bell rings*.

Saul answered, 'I am in great distress, for the Philistines are warring against me, and God has turned away from me and answers me no more, either by prophets or by dreams; so I have summoned you to tell me what I should do . . .'

Nothing to be done. The Ghost-Mistress insists on feeding the king and his bodyguards before they leave – also an oddly disturbing vignette – but Saul is finished.

The Place Endor

Endor (Hebrew *Ey'n Dor*) is a real place, in Manasseh, conventionally located between the Hill of Moreh and Mount Tabor, as shown on the adjacent map, although the location is disputed today, with several candidates proposed. The Israelites under Gideon had trouble in defeating the Midianites and were ultimately successful at Endor (Judges 7:1; Psalm 83:11). The site must have been significant and its name obviously in use long before the arrival of the Hebrews. But what about the name?

The plain meaning of the two Hebrew words that make up

En-dor is *Well of Generation*. We learn that it was under the charge of the Ghost-Mistress; it provided direct access, as everybody knew, to the Netherworld and was obviously the long-established, central port of call in the land for those needing such services. This picture allies itself closely with the Babylonian Netherworld access point at Kutha, as discussed in Chapter 9, and the Assyrian Netherworld Gate perhaps located at Tarbiṣu, and the neighbouring ancient history of female Mesopotamian necromancers. At the same time, its very name, *Well of Generation*, implies that the deep Babylonian belief (for which see *Afterword*) that the spirits of the dead remained in the Netherworld until, one at a time, they were required to give life to a new baby child, was shared also by the pre-Hebrew Canaanites.

The Narrative

We are fortunate that this episode clearly survived within the Hebrew Bible without apparent interference or editing, and it astonishes me that Shakespeare never turned his attention to so dramatic and timeless a scene.

The luckless Saul, of course, perished the next day in conflict with the Philistine enemy. This point bears on how the narrative came into being. The supreme literary quality of the Endor episode is, to me, its realistic nature, at once gripping and somehow convincing. To my mind the passage can be neither backdated 'creative writing' nor a made-up, 'historical' episode, as it is often characterised. The only possible author of the record as we read it in its own terms is one of Saul's two companions. They witnessed an historical event like no other, and the published account is exactly that of the silent observer. No one else but the Ghost-Mistress knew what had happened. Guildenstern, then, or Rosencrantz, confiding to some chronicler engaged on recording dynastic history, spilled the beans. In our hunt for the ghost world of the ancient Middle East, the affair at Endor is of unparalleled importance. Its description, in conjunction with the written Babylonian accounts of necromancy, acquires the status of prime testimony.

The Response

Many later writers, Jewish and Christian alike, wrestling with ghosts and underworlds, have found royal necromancy at Endor quite indigestible. According to the summary of Saul's career in the biblical 1 Chronicles 10:13, he died for being unfaithful to the Lord and, moreover, *enquiring of a ghost*. But in the later Deutero-canonical book of Sirach, the whole episode is thoroughly bowdlerised:

> *Even after he [Samuel] had fallen asleep, he prophesied and made known to the king his death, and lifted up his voice from the ground in prophecy, to blot out the wickedness of the people.*
> Sirach 46:20 (*NSRV* version)

In 1979 Klaas Smelik published a very illuminating article summarising the deft ways in which theologians of both persuasions wriggled so desperately out of accepting the narrative as presented. None of these authorities seems to have considered reading the account as a literary record and taking it at 'face value' – as I have done experimentally in this book – and they have explanations for every bit of the dismantled story. The point here is that the Saul at Endor episode and its later treatment encapsulates the very transition from the stage when ghosts were believed in perfectly to when naive ghost belief is no longer deemed acceptable. Later theological interpretation does all it can to disguise what the text plainly tells us, that a famous Old Testament king went to call up a famous dead Old Testament prophet with the help of the local professional necromancer. And up he came. In that world, around the turn of the first millennium bc, that is what people did.

Necromancy Beyond, and Skulls

Later there is also discussion of necromancy between certain
Talmudic rabbis. In the oral traditions of the *Mishnah*, compiled
from the beginning of the third century ad, the chapter 'Sanhedrin'
looks at the death penalty by stoning for necromancers caught
in the act, with their own special interpretation of the *yiddĕʿonî*:

> A baʿal ʾôb *[ʾGhost-master'] is the* pithom *[from Pythia, the
> Greek oracle at Delphi] who speaks from his armpit. The* yiddĕʿonî
> *is one who speaks from his mouth. These two are stoned; while
> he who enquires of them transgresses a formal prohibition.*

In Greek, *baʿal ʾôb* at Endor is sometimes translated engastrim-
uthos, ventriloquist, referring to the practitioner's technique, and
this is the idea behind the rabbinic dismissal of both necromancers as frauds. The corresponding Talmudic *Gemara* discussion
distinguishes between two necromantic techniques in the hands
of what they now call a *baʿal ʾôb*, the Ghost-Master. Here we
meet the male title equivalent to that of *Our Lady of Endor*, the
Ghost-Mistress. This incidental reference gives us a brilliant
glimpse of the persistence of the activity and the survival of
master-specialists, whose heritage reaches back uninterruptedly
into biblical times and forward into the Middle Ages:

> *Our Rabbi taught:* baʿal ʾôb *denotes both him who conjures up
> the dead by means of soothsaying, and one who consults a skull.*

In the mid-fifteenth century ad, the scholar-rabbi Bar-Tenura is
still somehow able to give more details about this skull technique,
giving us, in effect, a précis of the procedure in the Babylonian
Necromancy Manual:

> *He takes a skull of a dead person after the flesh has decomposed,
> and he offers incense to it, and asks of it the future, and it answers.*

This testimony demonstrates how ancient ghost ideas and materials quietly and determinedly survived to underpin the complex sea of traditions that make up later Jewish magic. Since necromancy by skull is not a widespread or commonplace activity in magic it is reasonable to suppose that Jewish acquaintance with the art goes back to the sixth century bc and the period of the Babylonian Exile, when many ideas and procedures were adopted through the influence of the Babylonian cuneiform academies in the fields of magic and medicine, and textual interpretation. The results of this evolving tradition, in which astrology and angelology come to play their part, are epitomised in this Jewish invocation from the Middle Ages:

> *Stand before the grave and recite the names of the angels of the fifth camp of the first firmament, and hold in your hand a mixture of oil and honey in a new glass bowl, and say,*
>
> *'I conjure you, spirit of the grave, Nehinah, who rests in the grave on the bones of the dead, that you accept this offering from my hand and do my bidding; bring me N son of N who is dead, and make him stand erect and speak at me without fear, and have him tell me the truth without fear, and I shall not be afraid of him; let him answer the question which I shall put to him';*
>
> *and the deceased will immediately appear. But if he doesn't, repeat this invocation a second time, and if necessary, a third. When he appears, place the bowl before him, and converse with him. Hold a myrtle wand in your hand.*

In later Judaism, open discussion of the fate of the dead, or ghosts, or the world to come, was traditionally avoided, but magical writing, spells and amulets have continued uninterruptedly until modern times.

By the time the New Testament was being written in Greek, the parallel exclusion of ghosts from sacred narrative is almost complete. When Jesus walked on the water, however, we are presented with the clearest evidence (respectfully italicised below) that, nevertheless, everyday belief in ghosts was instinctive, uninhibited and uncontrollable:

> *Immediately he made his disciples get into the boat and go on ahead to the other side, to Bethsaida, while he dismissed the crowd. After saying farewell to them, he went up on the mountain to pray. When evening came, the boat was out on the sea, and he was alone on the land. When he saw that they were straining at the oars against an adverse wind, he came towards them early in the morning, walking on the sea. He intended to pass them by.* But when they saw him walking on the sea, they thought it was a ghost and cried out, for they all saw him and were terrified.
>
> Gospel of Mark 6:45–50

A similar description appears in the Gospel of Matthew. Here, too, there is a good deal of worry by scholars and theologians about what the text, and Greek *fantasma*, really mean here, but it seems to me that the disciples who were present on that occasion just thought they had seen a ghost.

13

A Brief Enquiry as to What the Inhabitants of Mesopotamia Believed About Their Netherworld and the Ultimate Fate of Those Who Languished in Same

Now pile your dust upon the quick and dead
Till of this flat a mountain you have made
                                        Hamlet, Act 5, Scene 1

The Cosmos, Heaven and Below

It behoves us to offer the reader a summary look at the central beliefs of the ancient Mesopotamians about the world in which they lived, what was above them when they were alive, and what awaited them when they were dead.

Starting at the beginning, Heaven is above, Earth is in the middle and the Netherworld beneath. With regard to death, burial and ghosts (and all that *they* could lead to), here we are mostly concerned with the Netherworld. The general word for sky, heavens and Heaven in Sumerian is an, like the name of An, the ancient head of the pantheon, in Akkadian *šamû*. Actually, cosmologically speaking, there were three Heavens: Upper, Middle and Lower. The gods inhabited the upper levels, a form of heaven that could, rather satisfyingly, be reached by a stairway echoing that of the great temple towers called ziggurats, the high architectural feature of the main Mesopotamian cities, supposed to reach as near to Heaven as possible (later renowned as the Tower of Babel in the Book of Genesis):

Namtar came up the long stairway (simmiltu) of Heaven
When he arrived at the Gate of Anu, Enlil and Ea.
Anu, Enlil and Ea saw him:
   'What have you come for, Namtar?'

Lower Heaven is the sky, where the astral bodies visible to man, the sun, moon and stars, followed their much-observed circuits. The constellations, much studied by the watchers of Babylon, were considered to be 'drawn' on the face of Lower Heaven. The intervening heavenly floors as well as the stars themselves were fashioned of exquisitely coloured or translucent stones, reddish *luludānītu*, bluish *saggilmut* and greenish jasper, from top down.

Their, and our, earth was called ki in Sumerian, *erṣetu* in Akkadian. The terrestrial disc of the Mesopotamian world was sometimes thought to be supported on pillars resting on the Netherworld. The heart of the terrain to be explored side by side with ancient Mesopotamian guides stretched from the west to the mountains in the east, north beyond our Armenia, south beyond the Gulf. It is represented graphically in the famous Map of the World, which depicts the terrain as round, which is surely how they conceived it, ringed by a cosmic river, with Babylon in the middle of everything and mountainous regions arrayed remotely beyond the rim in eight directions.

The Netherworld, too, had its Upper, Middle and Lower levels. The Upper sometimes housed the Igigi gods; the Middle was the Apsÿ, the sweet water resources under the Earth and the abode of Ea, god of wisdom. At the Lower level were to be found the six hundred Anunnaki judgement gods. At other times the Igigi could be in Heaven, too.

The Netherworld as a whole is often described as a great city, called urugal or erigal in Sumerian, walled around with gates. Within it there are palaces, a temple and other structures, but not for the huddled masses, of course. It was dark inside, as indicated by its name kukku = *kukkû*, 'darkness'. On the other hand, having emerged through the Eastern Gate at dawn to cross the sky, the sun god Shamash would exit at nightfall through the Western Gate, passing through the Netherworld by night to judge the dead below, presumably leaving a trail of brilliance.

To reach the Netherworld the path of no return brought the traveller to a river. It seems to have no name in Sumerian, but the Akkadian is clear in this philosophically resigned-sounding remark:

> Our fathers gave in, travelled the road of Death
> They crossed the River Ḫubur, *as the old saying goes*

The dead had to be ferried across the Ḫubur to reach their destination by Humuṭ-tabal, acknowledged as *Netherworld Boatman* by Prince Kummaya in Chapter 10. The parallel with Charon, who ferries the Greek dead across the Styx to Hades, obviously suggests itself, but the importance of the Mesopotamian figure, the river and the journey is hardly comparable in importance judging by the paucity of allusions in cuneiform texts. Some arrive at the chillingly named Gate of Captives. One spell that details how an exorcised demon should be committed to the Netherworld shows us in reverse gate-order what met all new immigrants and stresses the finality of crossing the waters:

> The gate of the Land-of-no-Return,
> > The seven Gatekeepers of Ereshkigal,
> > > Namtar, vizier of the vast Netherworld, at the Gate of
> > > the Bound,
> > > The gate of the vast Netherworld,
> > > > The great devils,
> > > > > Nedu, Chief Gatekeeper of the Netherworld
> > > > > Ningishzida, chamberlain of the Netherworld,
> > > > The Anunnaki, the great gods,
> > > > > The great chamberlain of Allatu,
> > > > > > The stream of the great Netherworld

Once crossed over, in other words, never to return! *Supposedly* . . .

There are many cuneiform names for the Netherworld, some of which are esoteric and seldom encountered; these five are regularly used:

1.   Sumerian kur, the oldest term, always written with an early pictographic sign from the end of the fourth millennium bc, which is usually taken to represent mountain or mountains. The word kur is also applied to any 'foreign country', in contrast to kalam, '*the* land', meaning Sumer. On top of that, kur, more or less as a proper name, refers in Sumerian literature to the Netherworld where the dead go. Some scholars have suggested that, at an early date, the Netherworld was linked to 'mountains in the east', located behind the real Zagros mountains on the eastern frontier. Today, this interpretation has been largely rejected, and most scholars believe that Sumerian kur lay downwards, below the Earth, in keeping with the unambiguous tradition in later literary passages such as the *Descent of Ishtar*.

2.   Sumerian ki is literally 'place'. It can refer both to the Earth on which they walked as well as to the Netherworld *under* the earth, ki with 'capital letters', so to speak. Despite this apparent looseness, it is usually clear enough which meaning is intended. The Akkadian equivalent, erṣetu, earth, shares the two meanings.

3.   Sumerian kur-nu-gi$_4$-a, Akkadian erṣet la târi: Land-of-No-Return. The 'no-return' point applies to human beings; gods could come and go into the Netherworld, but they did not do so lightly, and when they did there was usually a story attached. It is these stories that give us our best view of the *Great Below*. Demons likewise

could come and go freely, in and out of the Netherworld, and did so. Ghosts, once resident, were not supposed to at all, but some did nevertheless.

4. The Sumerian name Irkalla is a Netherworld name also used for Queen Ereshkigal herself, and Ganzir, Queen Ereshkigal's Netherworld Palace, is also used to stand for the Gate of the Netherworld and even the Netherworld itself.

A variety of Netherworld personnel have flitted in and out of this book. The principal actors are Queen Ereshkigal and King Nergal, her husband, with the following staff at their disposal: Ningishzida, Chair-Bearer, Namtar, Chief Help and Messenger, Nedu (or Neti or Biti), Chief Doorkeeper, Hushbisha, Steward, Sharsharbid, Butcher, Etana, Vizier and, of course, Gilgamesh, Judge

There were plentiful, unpleasant, non-human, *utukku*-type demons also in the Netherworld. Some present a clear identity, such as the Baby-Snatcher (*Lamashtu*), the Grabber (*Aḫḫāzu*), the Lurker-in-the-Toilet (*Shulak*) or the Croucher (*Rābiṣu*), while others are less distinct. It is unlikely that these undesirables mingled freely among the assembled ghosts below like so many pickpockets, and in any case most placid ghosts would probably be frightened of them and see them for the gangsters they were. Probably the demons had their own subterranean quarters whence they could certainly come and go as they pleased. Dreams also inhabited the same cavernous Netherworld, because they too had to be 'brought up' when a message was solicited in a dream ritual, either lifted by one of the Four Winds, or ascending by means of a special Ladder.

The formal and official route through the gates by which the dead were to be admitted was not, however, the only way in or out. Shamash the sun god, especially familiar with the ways under the world, knew of a handy *chink* in the Underworld (see Chapter 9) that would allow Gilgamesh's friend Enkidu to be wafted back up to the world. Ghosts, too, make use of the *crevices*. Both words confirm that the dead were not supposed to escape, and it is only with close knowledge of the terrain and certain 'back-door' options that most of the ghosts who returned probably made their way back.

Being Below

In Chapter 8 it has been stressed that there is a perfectly intelligible chasm between the image of the Netherworld presented by literature and that implied by burial customs and grave goods. The strong literary tradition of the Netherworld Descents and sort of scene that greeted the new arrival cannot, however, be brushed under the carpet as unrealistic or non-authoritative in its context. The accumulative impression one gets of the Mesopotamian Netherworld is that it was a bit of a railway terminus; everyone is waiting around interminably, in a particularly intense kind of despair, for it is never articulated *what they are waiting for*.

We have emphasised that there was no post-mortem judgement of morals to be endured by a human spirit on arrival, let alone backward-looking punishment; the shadowy entrepôt was thus no waiting-room where the dead hung about waiting for good news (upwards) or bad (further downwards). They were already 'down'. The importance and impact of this, even if it is a purely literary tradition, cannot be exaggerated. Mesopotamia contains nothing that corresponds to the contemporary and profusely documented Egyptian ideas about the fate of the dead in the Underworld; neither is it in any way antecedent to the later post-Judaeo Christian system of judgement and punishment, often visualised as lasting eternally. There is no hint of moral assessment or moral judgement in anything that concerns death or the Netherworld in ancient Mesopotamia, a society altogether liberated in comparison with the victims of punitive destiny that was to prevail in later times, imposing all its remorseless, uncharitable and entirely pointless misery.

If there is no courtroom drama waiting in the end, how are we to understand it all? It would be strange if the Netherworld construction simply existed as described, meaning an unending shadowy but goal-less sojourn in the company of an ever-swelling multitude of drifting spectres. The purpose of it all, by and large, is not considered by writers on the Mesopotamian scene either, but once posed it compels an answer.

Access to the Netherworld for the goddess in the *Descent of Ishtar* is regulated by the formidable sequence of Seven Gates. Ishtar, unless admitted, will knock down the door herself, with dire consequences:

> I *will raise up the dead to devour the living,*
> *The dead shall outnumber the living!*

The threat is very meaningful. It is not simply that releasing the floodgates will see the world overwhelmed by liberated zombies, streaming remorselessly up the escalators to take over. What would happen is that the delicate balance between Life and Death that prevails under normal conditions would be overthrown with irreversible consequences for the world. Underpinning this passage is, I believe, the conception in Babylonia that the life force itself was *finite*, with the corollary that the birth of a new baby was always predicated on the death of an adult person. The system was thus a never-ending cycle that involved the recycling of the *eṭemmu* essence, round and round, in a timeless and divinely regulated process.

The clearest evidence is provided by a learned work of scholarship that originated in academy classrooms at Babylon. Here advanced students in cuneiform lore destined for a position in which master-level literacy was essential would study classical literature in Sumerian and Babylonian with their scholar-teacher. Much attention was lavished on the meanings of words and the individual cuneiform signs used to spell them, and classroom exposition in or around the sixth century bc attained a very high level of textual exegesis; a skilful scholar with traditional texts at his fingertips could prove black to be white to everyone's satisfaction through the ingenious manipulation of signs and their usages. One of these passages concerns the ominous implications that follow when a Babylonian doctor, hurrying through the street to visit a sick patient, sees a bit of baked brick on the way:

> *If an exorcist spots a kiln-fired brick on the way to a sick person's house, that sick person will die*

This chance sighting of an insignificant item of rubble might hardly seem replete with danger to us, but a Babylonian specialist trained in interpretation would draw several deep messages from it. The technique involved taking the four cuneiform signs used to write the word 'baked brick' and reinterpreting them using several philological tricks to produce two quite new interpretations beyond the literal meaning:

Interpretation 1: A person who had successfully returned from a river ordeal

Interpretation 2: A pregnant woman.

Individuals 1 and 2 both hover on the cusp between life and death. The ordeal survivor cheats death and the pregnant woman is busily creating a new life. What unites these two passers-by in the street is the underlying conception of the cycle of life, with the specific point that a new life is dependent on a new death. For last-minute rescue or new birth to go forward, the patient awaiting the doctor's arrival has to die.

The underlying system is not reincarnation but rather what we might call recycling. The bodiless, personality-and-intelligence-bearing, one-third matter that remains after death – equal in some way to female divinity – sustains the *eṭemmu* human spirit in a recyclable state until needed for a new birth. The conception is of a finite number of human spirits in circulation, reflecting the idea that the material of life, like any other natural resource – especially water – is not boundless. It does seem hard to divorce the *eṭemmu*-ghost of ancient Mesopotamia from what is usually referred to, in common understanding, as a soul.

The Netherworld gates in the formal literature lock into this idea, for they function not only to keep the unwanted from coming in, but also to let out the wanted, on demand and under control, to animate new babies. From this point of view, a ghost's stay in that Netherworld was not a sentence to unending and unendurable Limbo, but an interval in the great cycle, waiting to be called, to start it all over again. It is this that gives the force to Ishtar's famous threat to break down the Netherworld gates so that the dead would overwhelm the world and outnumber the living. The system required delicate calibration, under divine control, to ensure the survival of human life on the planet. The effects of unleashing that tidal wave of undirected and frustrated motley on the world would be disastrous and was never to be thought of.

14

Afterword

That affable familiar ghost
Which nightly gulls him with intelligence
                    Shakespeare, Sonnet 86

As we have seen, ghosts – the spirits of the dead – have walked by our side since the beginning of our time. They are there in our first ancient writings, and can be suspected, or glimpsed, far earlier than that; while the human ideas, brought out of the ground dressed in cuneiform to have life breathed into them, reflect a belief system that will be intelligible, accessible and even familiar to any modern reader who has interest in the subject.

Our story has brought us from the shady beginnings to the edge of the classical world, the terrain of the three great mono-theistic religions, and the beginning of successive new ages of ideas, theories and philosophies. Ghosts beyond Mesopotamia known to the Egyptians, the Greeks and the Romans can claim their counterparts ever after right across the span of the world; it is a simple matter to demonstrate the universal presence of ghosts in people's minds and lives, dreams and writings.

Should we believe the media, ghostly incarnations of the dead apparently roam with undiminished energy today, too, slipping and sliding about the world to startle, warn or torment, and behaving, as one might say, in time-honoured fashion. Modern ghost experiences – true or imagined, promoted or derided – represent the contemporary expression of an age-old belief system.

Human beings, after all, continue as a single species, with what they share in common, hopefully, still outweighing their differences. Shared humanity cannot be disguised by the cosmetic and superficial – dress, language or religion; it concerns ancient and inherited attributes that persist beneath, inside the complex human animal. Belief in ghosts is as old as time and hovers around a core part of human make-up; it continues unabashedly today, suppressed or submerged though it may be, as strong as ever.

This, the first ghost system that we can document in history, sets the stage in many ways for what came later. Central is the conception that ghosts tend to be restless due to unhappiness, returning to a scene of their former life and seeking closure for injustice, cruelty or violence. Coupled with this is the conviction that they can be dispelled by those who know how.

One crucial change that we can perceive over four thousand years of accumulated tradition is the loss of what I see as ghostly innocence. In ancient Mesopotamia, belief in their well-established and well-documented system was simple and un-questioning: ghosts were taken for granted as a fact of normal life and nobody, as far as we can judge, scoffed at another for 'believing' in them. This point must be accorded considerable respect.

This 'phase' had actually prevailed, in my opinion, for hundreds of thousands of years, and represents a deep-seated and ineradicable inheritance for, and influence on, human beings today. With the arrival of the second phase the innocent ascrip-tion to the original belief system grew unstable, its innate simplicity was abandoned, and the matter became subject to theological dispute, psychological evaluation and ultimately scientific scepticism.

Since the nineteenth century endless attention has been paid to the whole business of ghosts by writers, investigators, scient-ists, mountebanks, fakers and filmmakers. One feature that often surfaces today is the truly ancient idea that ghosts return to the spot where once they lived, or where they had come to a prema-ture end. They still are, it seems, unhappy or unable to rest, tied somehow to the 'scene of the crime' in an effort to assuage malaise or seek closure on injustice. This broad 'explanation' recurs so regularly in such widely differing contexts that it could be seen as a central component of the whole modern ghost tradition. What fascinates me is the overlap with the ancient Babylonian view at the beginning of it all.

The topic of ghosts in our world divides individuals in the same way as does religion: there are believers, disbelievers and don't-knowers. Believers are bolstered by libraries of records from perfectly normal people who say they have seen a ghost and describe the circumstances to the best of their ability. Agnostics, who carefully refrain from dogmatism, calmly acknowledge that there *may* be such things as ghosts and that there *might* be some explanation beyond their understanding, and that *maybe* some whitecoat one day will even settle the question one way or another scientifically. Disbelievers wave away the subject peremptorily with, *I just don't believe a word of it and I never will and there is no point in talking to me about it.* For the Disbeliever, anyone who says they saw a ghost therefore must be,

Lying
Inventing
Mistaken
Delusional
Hysterical
Hallucinating
Drunk
Drugged
Delirious
Hypnotised
Influenced by external images
Repeating something heard
Regurgitating something read
Undergoing freak weather conditions

Experiencing a trick of the light
Experiencing a trick of the dark
Affected by stress
Undergoing financial worries
Undergoing marital problems
Overworking
or
Eating unwisely

Use of the *must have been* clause to dismiss something inexplicable is, needless to say, a sign of weakness. To abnegate bulk testimony, ancient or modern, written or spoken, about seeing a ghost requires sustaining four separate strands of disbelief at the same time:

1. I don't believe there was anything.
2. I don't believe in ghosts anyway.
3. I don't believe he saw anything.
4. I don't believe anything he says.

Two of these are simple disbelief, but two have to be levelled – quite unjustly – at the witness himself.

Descriptions by people throughout history and across the world of their seeing ghosts are, of course, essentially *anecdotal*. But one man's anecdote is another man's evidence. The point is, what should the historical investigator make of such disinterested anecdotal records of ghost experiences? Such accounts are not presented for scientific criticism or judicial appraisal: they operate on a different level. Records, of course, can be truthful or untruthful, accurate or inaccurate, complete, censored or distorted. But to dismiss *all* anecdotes of this kind outright as lying, invention, delusion and so forth – widely spread as they are over millennia and continents – requires one or other of the following two assumptions:

1. All human 'ghost-seeing' testimony everywhere is modelled on the same detailed but artificial construction about the dead. This blueprint has been everywhere impressed on people's minds for at least five millennia of time, so that *everyone who has ever thought that they have seen a ghost has been deluded in the same way.* Or:

2. There has been a conspiracy in every human population since the ancient Babylonians whereby *Group A all try to make Group B believe that ghosts exist* and they themselves have seen them, even though this is wholly untrue, motivated by some unimaginably persistent and inexplicable motive.

If neither 1 nor 2 rings true we are left with the conclusion that an atom, a fraction or even a respectable proportion of the inherited record by people from all over the world for centuries of time who say they have seen a ghost and tried to describe it to someone else should represent reality.

My personal conclusion, lounging against this colourful tapestry, is that most, possibly even all human beings everywhere *really, truly* (as they used to say in books) *believe in ghosts.* Visibly on top, wobbly inside or buried underneath. The conviction that some part of a human being triumphs over annihilation by death and the dissolution of the body is intrinsic to the species, hard-wired at the deepest level from the start, and inextricable. If some part exists and survives, why should it not, sometimes, be visible? The inevitable corollary of the survival of the spirit is the existence of the ghost. It is all one system.

To our untroubled and self-conscious Babylonian informants, the *eṭemmu* is both,

1. That animating element (which we call a spirit) which, combined with clay, i.e., flesh and blood, produces a human being. And:

2. That component of a dead person (which we call a ghost) which, post mortem, is supposed to live on quietly in the Netherworld, but which sometimes returns to the world and interacts with the living.

They were *one and the same thing*, in other words.

Against this venerable precedent it is hard to comprehend why the same elementary understanding does not prevail today. Given that *all the world's religious systems* maintain unabashedly and unapologetically that *the life force survives death* in human beings, their spokesmen cannot, to my mind, with any authority simultaneously deny the existence of ghosts as if they are something distinct. The 'spirit' and the 'ghost' are one. Perhaps the gentlest way to express this would be to suggest that a dead person's *spirit* is called a *ghost* simply and only when it happens to be *visible*.

Sometimes a Babylonian fortune-telling procedure had to be repeated three times to ensure an unambiguous answer. Ritual did not always succeed, as is clear from this Babylonian saying, which is occasionally added as an afterthought at the end of a set of cuneiform instructions:

He who can see will see
He who can hear will hear

The unflinching matter-of-fact attitude to *eṭemmus* reflected in cuneiform sources suggests overwhelmingly that the Mesopotamian belief in ghosts was literal. It would be a mistake to conclude that their thinking about ghosts or undertaking to deal with them was shrouded in any process akin to symbolism or equivalent to mysticism; ghosts were just one of those things.

One final point must be reiterated about the enduring nature of the Babylonian *eṭemmu*. As indicated in Chapter 13, deep-thinking cuneiform theologians versed in the ancient cuneiform classics reckoned that the life resource was finite and that it circled eternally. For one individual to be born, another had to die. It is an idea of great power and effect for us today, and a source of unexpected comfort.

> *In this way do we conclude our*
> *study of the first ghosts,*
> *and how they arrived.*

> *They have been here ever*
> *since.*

15

User's Guide: Telling Your Ghost from Your Demon

Will Fortune never come with both hands full,
But write her fair words still in foulest terms?
                    Henry IV, Part 2, Act 4, Scene 3

Finally, safely corralled together here out of harm's way, we allow living space to examine the very cuneiform signs used to write the Mesopotamian words for *ghost* and *demon*, for, as referred to in Chapter 1 and depended on in Chapter 9 with regard Gilgamesh and Enkidu, much can be unwrapped from within them. As we have seen, the Sumerian and Babylonian languages, although completely unrelated one to the other, were written with the same cuneiform script and were closely interwoven in literature, learning and lexicography. One aspect of this inter-locking relationship was that words were not infrequently loaned from Sumerian into Akkadian, and sometimes vice versa. This applies transparently to the terms for ghost and demon, which existed first in Sumerian and then in Akkadian; that they are borrowed is easy to see by comparing the words. Nouns in Akkadian end in *-u*; final Sumerian consonants, here -m and -g, are doubled and sometimes softened in Akkadian derivatives:

	Sumerian	Akkadian
Ghost	gedim	*eṭemmu*
Demon	udug	*utukku*

The oldest forms of the sign for ghost occur from about 2500 bc, roughly speaking the period of the Royal Graves of Ur. Scribes include it in lexical lists and, of course, incantations; at that early stage it is not sure in several cases whether the sign represents ghost, GEDIM or demon, UDUG. In the third millennium bc one sign was probably sometimes used for both. The later emergence of two distinct forms results from the need to avoid ambiguity in magical texts: nobody wanted to confuse ghosts and demons for a minute. It is only from the Old Babylonian period, about 1750 bc, that the two signs are clearly differentiated.

The Classic Sign Forms of the Mature Script

In the mature period, and certainly throughout the first millennium bc, two closely related, large Sumerian signs were used to write the words gedim = *eṭemmu* and udug = *utukku*. Their structure is created by large wedges acting as a frame to contain smaller wedges. At first sight these two cuneiform signs might seem not only daunting but also easily confusable with one another. On close inspection there is, indeed, only one slight difference between them. Nevertheless, the composition of the two signs is revealing and important for the ghost-hunter to disentangle. We are helped in this by a long-vanished Babylonian teacher-scholar of cuneiform writing, who compiled an important didactic sign list (called *Syllabary B*) in which one section investigates these very signs. Two component parts are separated out, and the names of each in Sumerian and Akkadian given. This can be laid out in typescript:

Sumerian name	Cuneiform sign	Akkadian Name	Translation
šu-uš-šá-na		šu-uš-šá-an	one third
gi-dím		e-ṭím-mu	ghost

Sumerian name	Cuneiform sign	Akkadian Name	Translation
šá-na-bi	𒑷	ši-i-ni-pu	two thirds
ú-tug	𒌓𒌇	ú-tuk-ku	demon

In each case the frame of the sign that creates the long structure is a numerical fraction, for GEDIM one-third (šuššana), for UDUG two-thirds (šanabi). First shown above are the fractions drawn in their normal proportions. The distinction between the one-third and two-thirds fractions is expressed by the number of vertical wedges standing upright on the horizontal base wedge; either two equal-sized, for one-third, or two equal-sized plus a third small one tucked in between, for two-thirds. In the signs for ghost and demon, they are written with the normally short lower horizontal wedge greatly extended to the right in each case.

The extra component inside each sign consists of the two simple signs IŠ and TAR. These are crucial, and the composition of GIDIM and UDUG makes remarkable use of them.

IŠ and TAR

IŠ consists of: two horizontal wedges,
one diagonal and two verticals.

TAR consists of: two horizontal wedges
and one diagonal.

Like all cuneiform signs, of course, both IŠ and TAR have more than one sound value and more than one meaning. When they are taken together as simple phonetic or sound signs, they often spell the word *iš-tar*. This usually refers to the famous goddess Ishtar, but it can also be understood as the Akkadian noun *ištaru*, goddess or female divinity.

In each sign, however, the TAR element is written in a very stylish way *inside* the 'split-opened' IŠ, between the two widened-out vertical wedges, sitting on top of the long lower wedge. Assyriologists convey such a writing of one sign inside another as if one is multiplied by the other, i.e. 'IŠ ø TAR.' The result can therefore be represented as:

$$\text{GEDIM} = \text{1/3 IŠ ø TAR}$$

$$\text{UDUG} = \text{2/3 IŠ ø TAR}$$

What Does This Tell Us?

The cuneiform sign used to write Sumerian GEDIM, ghost, or Akkadian *etemmu*, can therefore be analysed as the fraction ⅓ next to *female divinity*. This harmonises beautifully with the literary account of the Creation of Man that prefaces the Flood Story in Chapter 1, where the intelligence that unites with clay and blood to animate a human individual is considered both divine and feminine, and constitutes one-third of the complete being. When the individual dies, the two-third physical substance of the body returns to the earth and the surviving one-third, the *etemmu*, or *spirit* as we would refer to it today, slight, diaphanous and like the wind, goes below.

The counterpart sign for UDUG = *utukku*, normally a wholly malevolent, demonic entity, breaks down in contrast into the fraction ⅔ next to *female divinity*, equated with the gift of divine intelligence. This raises an interesting – but unanswerable – question. If alien demons possess a higher measure of divine intelligence than human beings, what is their other third made of? Demons, unlike men, are immortal, as is evident from the fact that all exorcists could ever do was drive them temporarily away whenever they appeared but never kill them, as mentioned in Chapter 9. This unkillable quality must therefore be due to the unidentified, 33.33 per cent, high-octane component of their make-up, forever denied to human beings.

Urban Misery

We can here spare a thought for the pitiful type of wandering ghost who has no provider of funerary offerings, who eats pot scrapings and crusts of bread thrown away in the street. The fear of the fate that awaited those abandoned by their descendants to root haplessly in the highways and byways for sustenance is also encapsulated within the cuneiform sign GEDIM itself. The interior signs IŠ and TAR that write the noun for goddess *iš-tar* can also be interpreted with a second layer of meaning. When IŠ is pronounced saḫar, Sumerian for 'dust', and TAR pronounced sila, Sumerian 'street', we encounter a neglected ghost fatally condemned to what he can find for himself in the *dust* of the *thoroughfare*.

Entrance by Ear

We have seen that ghosts bent on medical malice entered the human body above all via the ear. A learned tradition discussed among Babylonian scholars clarified the point. This is not surprising, for physical access must be by one or other orifice, and human beings usually sleep with at least one ear unguarded. The speculative among Babylonian scholars found confirmation for this idea from a particular, shorthand way of writing the crucial ghost word gedim = *eṭemmu* in cuneiform. The complex sign gedim that we have just dissected is the most common spelling:

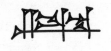

gedim = *eṭemmu*

A simpler alternative, given the flexibility of the cuneiform script and the rule that there was usually more than one way to write the same sound, was to use a much rarer but much less complex Sumerian sign, which could also be pronounced as 'gedim'. The tidy-minded Assyriologist differentiates this as **gedim₂**:

gedim₂

Here again we take recourse to dismemberment. It is easy to see that this cuneiform sign consists of two components:

BAR

and

U

By the peculiar facility of exegesis that was natural to all well-educated Mesopotamian scribes, the sign gedim₂ (written U+BAR) can be understood to mean 'ear-opener'. The first Sumerian sign BAR corresponds to the Akkadian verb *petû*, 'to open', while Sumerian U corresponds to the Akkadian noun *uznu*, 'ear'. In this way the nasty tendency in evil-minded ghosts to penetrate their victims' ears is thus intrinsic to one aspect of their complex cuneiform identity.

Endnotes

In nature's infinite book of secrecy
A little can I read
    Antony and Cleopatra, Act 1, Scene 2

Author's Note

P. xi *Peter Blakebrough saw one . . .* And what follows is the record
he made for me for this book, which tallies exactly with the
original account that so struck me before:

> I shared a bedroom with my brother. The landing light, a
> shaded bulb of low wattage, would have been on, the
> bedroom door substantially ajar. It was not unusual for
> friends of my parents visiting for the evening to come to
> look in on us in bed and, should we be awake, to exchange
> a few drowsy words with us.
>
> One night, my brother asleep, I became aware of an
> elderly lady, dressed in black, seated on the upright chair
> between mine and my brother's bed. I was not unduly
> surprised, for the reason stated above, but her iteration of
> the phrase 'go away', while not especially threatening or
> even insistent, was sufficiently out of the ordinary for me
> to recall it in the morning and for me to ask my mother
> who the lady, for lady she was, had been. I may have been
> sleepy, had awakened, but I was sure I had not confused
> dream with waking. My mother told me no one but the
> family had been in the house. She asked me to describe her:
> long black dress, tall, thin, softly spoken, stern. My mother,
> not a gullible woman or prone to dramatic interpretation,
> must have mentioned this to our neighbour, who said my
> description would fit that of the solicitor's wife who had

lived in the house up until about ten years before we lived there. The neighbour would not have been as sceptical as my mother. My mother told me what the neighbour had said and the matter was left there. This was when I was a child and I recount it here some sixty years later. The most obvious explanation is that this was a dream. I would accept that but my memory was and is that it was not something I dreamt. Thus it becomes a ghost story, though I am by no means convinced of the existence of ghosts.

Peter J. Blakebrough *scripsit*
Tuesday 14 August 2018 at 17.52

Importantly, neither Peter nor his mother knew anything about the earlier inhabitant of the house or her physical appearance. That she told him to 'go away' is remarkable in that ghosts are only seldom recorded as speaking, and his bedroom had previously been hers, after all.

P. XI   *shadier vaults of the British Museum* . . . See Angell and Gooding 2018 for certain ghosts that have been on offer in that august institution. Many years ago a séance was conducted on a December afternoon to establish who it was who had been haunting the ill-lit Mesopotamian Brick Store in my own department's basement. According to the then Keeper – I, sadly, was not invited – it was a long-dead staff member still unable to rest because of the backlog in object registration.

P. XII   *evidence in Greek and Latin* . . . Dip, for example, into Ogden 2001 or 2002, or Johnston 2013, or the works behind them.

Chapter 1: Ghosts at the Beginning

P. 1   *the very word for ghost* . . . Full details of the cuneiform sign and its suggestive features are safely located in the *User's Manual*, right at the end of the book!

P. 2   *the development of abstract thought* . . . On which see, for example, Clottes 2016.

Elephants, the most celebrated of mourners . . . See Bradshaw

2009: 10–13. In addition to chimpanzees, they are in company in this respect with wolves, otters, dolphins, sea lions, geese and even magpies, according to King 2013.

P. 3   *knuckle-trailers* . . . Neanderthals have much better press these days, and are championed not only in an appreciative selection of T-shirts, but in presentations of remarkable new and accessible data on the internet.

P. 4   *dug down into a lower layer* . . . Pomeroy et al. 2019: 11–26. The news made the *Guardian*: *Scientists discover Neanderthal skeleton that hints at flower burial* (February 18 2020); see also Marshall 2020.

DNA findings show that there was interbreeding . . . Interesting here is the so-called Lagar Velho Portuguese boy, buried about 24,500 BP with pierced shell and red ochre, whose skeleton has been considered to be a hybrid of early modern human and Neanderthal features. If the disappearance of the immensely long-running and adaptable Neanderthals, usually placed between 400,000 and 40,000 BP, coincided, very broadly speaking, with the arrival of incoming *Homo sapiens*, as people say it does, one cannot help but wonder whether the newcomers did not just kill off all the Neanderthal men and carry off all the Neanderthal women, thus contributing permanently to our gene pool, and establishing the pattern of characteristic human behaviour for invading populations with regard to those who were there first that has prevailed ever since. The find in Israel near Nesher Ramla of a cranium and jawbone from an individual who lived between 140,000 and 120,000 years ago is now announced as a previously unknown type of hominid ancestral to the Neanderthals.

P. 5   *of an afterlife* . . . Grave goods are sometimes interpreted as no more than food and drink for the 'journey', but journeys always proceed from one point to another, and the conclusion is the same: something was going somewhere. Archaeologists, followed by *Wikipedia* on Grave goods, are much given to discussing objects in graves as indicators of class or status, tributes to an individual, offerings for ancestors or simply things that individuals valued during their lives. Undoubtedly all such interpretations can be valid and crucial; what is argued here is that they all grew out of and beyond the indispensable starting point, the human acknowledgment of existence in the great beyond, and it is that Great Beyond that is important. See also Chapter 4 below.

P. 8   Prism A *Inscription* . . . Lines vi 70–6; the full and dramatic account is translated in Novotny and Jeffers 2018: 250.

P. 9   *Assyrian specialist Barbara Porter* . . . There are good discussions of this matter in Porter 2009: 220, and now Simpson 2020: 152, 154.

Chapter 2: Ancient Mesopotamia: Home to the First Ghosts

P. 13   *Mesopotamian cuneiform* . . . Syllabic signs, such as *bu* or *az*, recorded words syllable by syllable, which were then joined up together in reading, as if we were to write *ca-ra-va-an* to spell 'caravan'. Ideas signs indicate materials, such as stone, or whole words in one sign, such as king. For a relaxing induction to the wonder of cuneiform writing and the beauty of tablets of clay let me recommend Finkel and Taylor 2015, available now also in French and Chinese translations.

P. 14   *two versions of this Akkadian cuneiform story* . . . Translations of both passages may be found in Lambert and Millard 1969: 58–9; George and Al-Rawi 1996: 170–1.

Assyriologically speaking, the brilliant idea that *uppu*, drum, means *heartbeat* in this creation context was announced in Kilmer 1972: 162–3. The Akkadian *uppu* was obviously borrowed from the older Sumerian onomatopoeic thud word ub, *drum*. In the later version of the creation passage, *uppu* is troublesomely replaced by the inappropriate verbs *li-pa-a* and *i-pa-a* (verbal root *apû* A, 'to become visible'), which have no conceivable meaning in this context. To explain the verbs *li-pa-a* and *i-pa-a* I deduce a new Akkadian verbal root **apû* B, 'to throb, thrum, beat', also derived from the old sound word ub, to mean 'to make an ub-sound'. This allows us to harmonise the two versions, which need to express one and the same message at so significant a point in human genesis.

P. 16   *the bane of mankind* . . . For the Sumerian account of *The Death of Gilgamesh* consult Cavigneaux and Al-Rawi 2000: 17;

George 1999, Vol. 2: 203. On the Mesopotamian word for death in all possible contexts see Sibbing-Plantholt 2021.

Tablet of Destinies . . . This most interesting and fateful document of reckoning is often referred to and was no doubt often at the back of everybody's mind; it was described by King Sennacherib himself, Ashurbanipal's grandfather, as follows:

> *The bond of supreme power, dominion over the gods of Heaven and Netherworld and kingship over the Igigi and the Anunnaki (Netherworld gods), the secret of the Heavens and the Netherworld, the link of the Canopy of Anu and Ganzir (Netherworld names), the leash of the multitudes . . .'* (George 1986: 134, 138–9).

There was also, more worryingly, an incriminating *Tablet of Sins*; this is hardly ever mentioned, but reference could be made to it by supervisory gods when necessary; see Finkel 1983.

the allotted span was not an absolute fixture . . . This idea is worth considering. When pressed about prediction, the deep ten-year-old meditator Teddy in J.D. Salinger's remarkable short story of that name captures something of living in a partly but not rigidly pre-ordained existence:

> *I told them places, and* times, *when they should very, very careful. And I told them certain things it might be a good idea for them to do . . . I didn't say anything was inevitable*

as well as the estimate of his own date of death:

> *It will either happen today or February 14th, 1958, when I am sixteen. It is ridiculous to mention even.*

Ages of Man . . . The site of Sultantepe where this remarkable tablet was found is about 15 km south of Urfa in southern Turkey; the cuneiform text was published in Gurney and Hulin 1964, no. 400.

P. 18   *plentiful in the cuneiform world* . . . Good Assyriological
reading material here includes Bottéro 1980; Castellino 1955;
Charpin 2012; Cooper 1992, 2009; and Lambert 1980.

Chapter 3: The Death and Burial of Kings

P. 22   *the gold did not quite measure up* . . . Years ago, in a different
world, there was just such a skeleton-and-gold vitrine in the
vestibule of the Aleppo Museum in Syria, where arriving visitors
of all ages were spellbound at once and the *whole point of
archaeology* was at once self-explanatory. Probably no other
exhibit in the gallery ever had the same impact.

P. 25   *undergone heat treatment* . . . See the report by Baadsgaard,
Monge, Cox and Zettler 2011: 'It is possible Ur specimens were
heated (or smoked) to reduce putrefaction and enhance preser-
vation' (p. 11). Corpse heating for this purpose is reported
elsewhere: Late Bronze Age Qatna, near Homs in Syria (see
Chapter 13), and with one of the queens at Nimrud; see below,
this chapter. In this we have to follow the scientists.

  glorious museum exhibits and party wear . . . Some years ago
now the Metropolitan Museum shop in New York took to selling
costly replicas of these golden Ur headdresses, and a fellow curator
told me of a smart fundraising reception in which two ladies
unknown to one another turned up bedecked with the same
Sumerian finery, each much discomfited for the rest of the evening.

P. 26   *would become explicable* . . . I still favour this idea, first maintained in Finkel 2014: 81–3.

P. 27   *The Sumerian composition Urnamma A* . . . This is a fine and
highly suggestive piece of literature that deserves a more inviting
nickname; see the edition and translation in Flückiger-Hawker
1999 and 'Revisiting the Dead Ur-Namma' in Chapter 8.

P. 29   In the tablet just the key Sumerian words are translated into
Akkadian, written in helpful small signs underneath:

  im-bi ba-bar
  ša-ar-šu i-di-ip
  His wind has blown away

  And the crib . . .

im = *šāru*, 'wind'; bi = *šu*, 'his'; bar = *edēpu*, 'to blow (away)';
ba-, *i-* = verbal bits.

P. 30   *and the Maiden* . . . This text is discussed in Cohen 2005:
69–70.

P. 31   *The wind ~ spirit (im ~ gedim) interplay* . . . This idea, and
its reflex in administrative documents, has been developed by
Dinah Katz, who has written copiously about Sumerian death
and underworld matters; see especially Katz 2005; 2007 and 2014.

P. 32   *fear of vivisepulture* . . . For events of just this kind remembered among the Iraqi Mandaeans see Drower 1937: 363–5. A
most interesting general survey of this matter and the ingenious
devices it has stimulated in recent times is Vollum and Perry 1905.

      Incantation to Utu . . . The incantation is of 266 lines. The
excerpts translated here mostly follow those in the excellent
primary study published in 1991 by Bendt Alster. Further pieces
are given in Geller 1995. In some lines I have avoided the question
marks needed in a technical study of a Sumerian composition in
order to put across the essential message of the quoted text.

P. 33   *he cannot defend himself* . . . The man in his tomb cannot
pray. This sober verdict occurs in a learned scholar's commentary
touching on ghost spells; see Geller 2016: 394.

P. 37   *past deeds and misdeeds* . . . It has, in other words, nothing
to do with the all too familiar trope of eternal punishment after
death for all the added-up misdemeanours during life inflicted on
the long-suffering human race by later religious systems.

      Amy Gansell . . . Passages quoted after Gansell 2018: 78–9.

P. 38   *spirit* (ziqīqu) . . . On this word, distinct from *eṭemmu*, ghost,
see the notes to Chapter 15 below.

P. 39   *post-mortem heating* . . . Reportedly Queen Atalia's body had
been subjected to a temperature of 150–250 °C for many hours;
Baadsgaard, Monge, Cox and Zettler 2011: 11.

P. 40   *in royal oil. I sealed the opening* . . . Passages in cuneiform
refer both to oil and salt for preserving a dead body; Alexander
the Great, on the other hand, was committed to honey.

Chapter 4: Everyday Houses, Burials and Ghosts

P. 43   *sixth-century*-bc *house plan* . . . For a good overview see Baker 1995, 2014; Novák 2000.

P. 44   *basic types* . . . This information derives from the useful overview in Potts 1997: 230–1. The Akkadian word for tomb or grave is *kimaḫḫu*, loaned from older Sumerian 'exalted (*maḫ*) place (ki)'. This Sumerian word ki also stands for the earth under one's feet as well as the Netherworld, as discussed later. Another Akkadian term for grave is *qubūru*, from the verb *qebēru*, 'to bury'.

P. 45   *tactful gifts* . . . The handful of silver offered to Shamash in Chapter 5, which occurs in other similar texts, does have a rather bribe-like feel.

P. 46   *archaeology suggests* . . . This is certainly true of the royal Assyrian burials in the previous chapter.
Caitlín Barrett . . . Author of the most lucid and beneficial published discussion of this grave matter; on funerary goods see Barrett 2007: 10–19.
for adult burials . . . Children, of course, will normally have less.

P. 49   *is called* 'If a City . . .' The Akkadian name for this multi-tablet collection of omen data is *Shumma Alu*, which means literally 'If a city'. I have made appreciative use of the reconstructions published by Sally Freeman (Freeman 1998, the first of three volumes) of the *Shumma Alu* omens quoted here and in Chapter 5. Three dots are substituted for editorial brackets and minor restorations are not indicated in order to present as readable a translation as possible.
If a City *Tablet XVI* . . . The first line of this tablet warns, quite justifiably in view of the omens that follow, *If a man worries every day about building a tomb, that man will be constantly disturbed.*
given month of the year out of thirteen . . . As with all calendrical matters, Mesopotamian divination experts took account of 'Second Addaru' (i.e. XII/2), which had to be intercalated after the final month Addaru (XII) once every nineteen years to keep the lunar calendar of the Babylonians in sync.

P. 51   *really quite off-putting* . . . There are other incomplete omens within Tablet XVI that cover a projected tomb in the garden, an unfinished tomb, breaking into a tomb, using fire to enter a tomb, showing one's tomb to a prominent person; then several about a tomb doorway, seeing something or not seeing it, and then hearing rumbling. Then follow three tantalising part-omens: a *rotating corpse*, a *changing corpse* and a *missing corpse*, irresistible thriller material requiring lurid covers.

P. 52   *private cuneiform tomb inscription* . . . This still-eloquent tomb inscription is kept today in the Vorderasiatisches Museum in Berlin, and numbered VA 3111. It is written on a 'truncated cone' of clay about 11.5 cm in height. The second, broken example is VA 3114. Drawings of both are given in Messerschmidt and Ungnad 1907: 1, 54. For the conundrum of the interesting funerary texts from Susa in Elamite Iran, which are written in Akkadian cuneiform, see Wasserman 2019, and, generally, Bottéro 1982; Jonker 1995.

Chapter 5: Living with Ghosts

P. 57   *ghost-trouble procedure* . . . LKA no. 84; Scurlock 2006: no. 217.

P. 60   *a gallû* . . . The *gallû* is sometimes translated as 'sheriff-demon'. One exorcising spell describes him as a 'goring ox, a *big ghost* (*eṭemmu rabû*), a ghost who always climbs over all the houses' (Geller 2016: 202). I cannot locate another 'big ghost' anywhere; but *gallûs* and *eṭemmus* should be incompatible given their internal make-up, as demonstrated in Chapter 15. Not infrequently, the two are mentioned as here in the same breath as *rābiṣus*, 'croucher-demons'. In the Sumerian *Inanna's Descent* (Chapter 8), the *gal₅-lá*, demon-cum-official types, manhandle the goddess going in and out of the Netherworld; these are the ancestors of later *gallûs* and *rābiṣus* and all constabulary individuals. Possibly, in the exorcist's mind, they are thought likely to be hanging about with errant ghosts, and hardly safe company in themselves.

P. 61   *entitled* Evil Demons . . . The exorcist's essential tool, published in Geller 2016. These lines occur in Tablet IV 84–91 and 130–53.

P. 62   *out-laws* . . . This innovative neologism, to accommodate the full range of unclassifiable connections that come with serial marriage, was coined by the Danish Sumerologist Thorkild Jacobsen, and it is worth promoting.

tribal allegiance . . . The seventh-century-bc Assyrian document that refers to killing a murderer on top of his victim's grave in lieu of compensation for the bloodshed comes right out of that tribal world (*CAD* Q 293).

ghosts 'roving', and 'roaming' . . . The distinguishing ghostly terms in Akkadian are *murtappidu* and *muttaggišu* respectively.

P.63 *a timeless theme* . . . See, for example, Campbell Thompson 1908: 18–23, or the *churel*, 'the peculiarly malignant ghost of a woman who has died in childbirth', in Chapter 8 of Kipling's *Kim*.

P. 64 *Night after night* . . . Text after Farber 2014: 155, translation mine. Lamashtu was the most articulated and identifiable of the forces of evil between the rivers. Note, incidentally, that the only Hollywood film in which ancient Mesopotamian evil is taken to be alive and kicking, the monstrous production of 1973 entitled *The Exorcist*, attributed the spectacularly disfiguring possession of a young but increasingly green girl by a 'demon', who appeared right at the outset of the film, when most people were probably still parking or leaving their coats. This so-styled 'demon' in fact was our good Pazuzu, a hero to human beings and definitely on our side, for the very sight of Pazuzu was anathema to Lamashtu, and he could always be relied on to see off the savage, baby-consuming demoness Lamashtu. That poor Pazuzu was blamed for what happened in that film is nothing short of solicitor-activating slander.

astronomical report . . . Conveniently *CAD* M/1 120.

No Man's Land . . . See Finkel and Rey 2018.

has been suggested . . . See Westenholz 1970: 30; an interesting overview and discussion of the treatment of war dead is Richardson 2007.

P. 66 *'I raised my head'* . . . Text quoted after George 1999: 151.

There were prisons . . . For a good survey of the Mesopotamian penal institutions see Reid 2016. The prison that features so prominently in the Old Babylonian Sumerian literary composition

Nungal in the Ekur has sometimes been considered to lie in the Netherworld, partly because the goddess who ran it, Nungal, who was in charge of punishment and prisons, was herself a Netherworld goddess. She was daughter of Queen Ereshkigal and married to the god Birdu. Nungal controlled the Tablet of Life and carried supervised judgement on the wicked, but the hymn is actually concerned with the Water Ordeal that was ordained by the courts to establish guilt or otherwise. This was not, therefore, an afterlife court trying an individual's earthly behaviour.

P. 67   *Study of fever . . .* The work of Marten Stol (2007).

P. 68   *those responsible could list all the reasons . . .* That the reasoned and reasonable understanding of the history and behaviour of ghosts presented in these cuneiform sources represents human thinking on a wide and enduring scale is easy to demonstrate. The breakdown of the section 'Part II. Restless Dead' (Johnston 2013) into '4. The Unavenged: Dealing with Those Who Die Violently', and '5. Childless Mothers and Blighted Virgins: Female Ghosts and Their Victims', speaks for itself. One sample passage, quoted from a world away in space and time, Tibet of the early twentieth century ad, makes the point succinctly:

> *In certain circumstances the spirit of a dead man* (namshe) *does not go to the King of Hell but remains behind, haunting the place where the man died. This angry ghost is then known as a* Dre. *It may be said that there are four sets of circumstances which produce* Dre. *First is the case of men who have been killed by the sword or other weapon. Second is that of the rich man of material mind who is indifferent to the promptings of his soul and who, even on his death bed, does not think of where his soul may be going, but only of all the possessions he is leaving behind. Third may be classed those who die suddenly of a seizure; these are believed to have been killed by a spirit. And fourth come those who have died a violent death by accident or suicide. The* Dre *of the fourth class are known as Rock Spirits, Water Spirits, Fire Spirits and Wood Spirits. The ghost of a man killed by falling from a rock lives in the*

rock and tries to kill other men in the same way. The ghost of a man who is drowned lives in the water and tries to drag in anyone walking nearby. The ghost of a man who has been burnt to death haunts the place and causes fires. And the ghost of a man who has hanged himself on a tree lives in the tree and tries to induce others to follow his example . . .

> (Source: G.A. Combe, *A Tibetan on Tibet: Being the Travels and Observations of Mr Paul Sherap (Dorje Zödba) of Tachienlu; with an Introductory Chapter on Buddhism and a Concluding Chapter on the Devil Dance.* London, 1926: 78.)

P. 69   *already in the house* . . . These and similar lines have usually been translated, 'If a ghost does such-and such in a man's house' (thus Freeman 1998), rather than, as the Akkadian reads and is understood here, 'If a ghost in a man's house does such-and such.' The more direct translation communicates the vital point that the ghost is already in the house and thus a family ghost.

P. 73   I follow Sally Freeman here in restoring 'will die' and 'will be lost' at the end of some lines in this section.

     the fear of premature burial . . . This omen and its implications are already discussed in Chapter 3.

P. 81   *Funerary offerings* . . . The Akkadian terms for the three crucial funerary responsibilities are *kispu*, offerings, *naq mê*, water-pouring and *šuma zakāru*, pronouncing the name. For the history of the institution, which can be traced throughout the second and first millennia bc, see the full account in Tsukimoto 1985.

Chapter 6: Ghost Magic 1: Words and Deeds

P. 86   *the world of modern times* . . . An old volume about Middle Eastern and other amulets that grew out of long experience of being a British Museum curator is that of Budge 1930, which can still be read with interest.

     If a person . . . Translated after the Nineveh tablet shown in Fig. 7; textual quotations that follow are from this same tablet unless otherwise noted.

P. 87　*There are no others known* . . . These two modest and, perhaps to some, unimpressive-looking objects remained unstudied in the British Museum, after Theophilus Pinches recorded their arrival and sketched them, for nearly a hundred and fifty years until Christopher Walker, long my esteemed cuneiform colleague, came upon them one day and mentioned them to me. They are, for the ghost-hunter, *jewels beyond price.*

P. 89　*Magical Sevens* . . . The number seven evinces the peculiar and consistent valency in Mesopotamian magic that it possesses in many later cultures. For cuneiform examples see Horowitz 1998: Chapter 9.

　　　　For the tablet CBS 8235, and the related spells from other tablets studied in greater detail, see Cavigneaux and Ar-Rawi 1994: 73–82. It is interesting to compare the repeated Sumerian sign for ghost, gedim, in the second line of this early tablet with the later forms of the similar signs gedim for ghost and udug for demon discussed in Chapter 14. In the amulet it certainly means ghost and not demon, as is made clear from amulets with the same, or closely similar inscription.

　　　　Certain sophisticated amulets . . . Two of these are quoted in Horowitz 1998: Appendix B, but there are many other examples.

P. 91　*The Zimzilaḫ tablet* . . . This inscription is published in Lewis and Jewell 1982: 66 no. 12. Thanks go to Chris Dissinger for the new photograph published here. Some discussion of this matter was already given in Finkel 2014: 62–3.

P. 94　*Akkadian hymn to Gula* . . . See Lambert 1967; a new study of this text filling in many of the gaps will come from Enrique Jiménez.

P. 95　*British Museum tablet K 2175+* . . . Scurlock 2006: no. 232.

　　　　If the sufferer often sees dead persons . . . These words are not actually written out here, but conveyed by the shorthand *ditto*. Cuneiform number 2, two vertical wedges, was used for ditto, like our paired inverted commas. Since the document sequenced closely similar entries it was pointless to write out identical words each time. This is a common device with serious scribes, and breeds a feeling of kinship across the millennia in a modern reader.

P. 99   *In the absence* . . . Quoted from Geller 2016: Udug-Ḫul Tablet IV: 40–2.

P. 100   *Assyrian seventh-century letter* . . . Scurlock 2006: no. 230.

P. 102   *seats are provided* . . . Something about the seating difficulties here reminds one of family weddings when all the participants are simple flesh and blood.

P. 103   *This is the diagnosis* . . . Quoted after Köcher 1964: nos 228, 229 and Köcher 1971: no. 323.

P. 105   *as a 'Hand'* . . . Some occurred already in the *If a City* omens in Chapter 5. For a full discussion of the various *Hands* that occur in the healing texts see Heessel 2007.

P. 107   *short bead incantations* . . . Available in Farber 2014: 155; 103; 188: lines 57–62.

Chapter 7: Ghost Magic 2: Pictures and Conversations

P. 110   *Many workers* . . . Including Robert Biggs, Hans Güterbock, Walter Farber and, especially, Daniel Schwemer; it was Scurlock 2006: no. 20.

Evil-Panic ghost . . . In Akkadian *hajjattu*. The *mukil-rēš-lemuttti*-demon, who, literally, 'raises an evil head', is also mentioned in the ritual. There was fortunately a *benevolent* version, too, called the *mukil-rēš-damiqti*, but interestingly, we do not hear so often about that.

P. 113   *four cuneiform tablets* . . . That from Assur is Köcher 1964: no. 202; that from Sultantepe, Gurney and Hulin 1964: Vol. 2 no. 286, and that from Uruk, von Weiher 1976: no. 83. The Babylon tablet is published here for the first time.

P. 115   *infuriatingly broken and unreadable* . . . As far as I can see the traces just cannot be the remains of the signs *a-ba-ak-na-na*, which is what is clearly written in the following Babylon version and what we might expect.

P. 118   *the throne feet* . . . The correct placing on the tablet of this crucial drawing fragment, then unnumbered, was discovered forty years ago by my old friend Martha Roth.

P. 119   *So-and-so* . . . The Sumerian word for So-and-so, French *untel*, is spelled *nenni*, *nennu* and *nenna*; the Akkadian equivalent is *annanna*, with the feminine form *annannītu*. It sounds as if the words must be connected, even if the Akkadian looks like *this-this.*

state image . . . Excavations conducted in area WC at Nippur in the early 1980s produced a terracotta mould, for which the excavator's description (kindly drawn to my attention by Michael Roaf) can here be quoted (Gibson 1981–82: 45–6):

> . . . *a baked clay mold for the making of bronze (?) plaques. The mold shows a man wearing a conical helmet and holding a staff. The staff is decorated with six balls and a long tassel. The details and style of the figure seem closest associated with Babylonian kings such as Merodach Baladan, who ruled in the eighth century. The mold may be a relic from this or an earlier Babylonian king, but it might also be a depiction of Shamash-shum-ukin in Babylonian style.*

An image produced from this Nippur mould would be flat backed and not stand up. Several uses for such an image can be envisaged, ranging from political propaganda to tourist trinkets: the need for reproducible icons of Babylonian kingship in troubled Nippur may be far removed from the world of magic and healing, but it is certainly instructive to compare the range of attributes with those shown in the Abaknana drawing.

P. 122 *ever-so-slightly insane* . . . For the madness of Nabonidus see Beaulieu 2007. Word even reached a scroll-writer at Qumran on the Dead Sea in the first century bc.

P. 123 *Lucian, the second century satirist* . . . The translation of the Greek quoted here is that of Fowler 1905.

    Menippus reflected a Babylonian name . . . See Geller 1997: 58–60.

P. 124 *well-preserved example* . . . Köcher *BAM* 3 no. 323; Scurlock 2006: no. 226 and 218.

P. 127 *Overlap in wording* . . . Such overlap between say an *eṭemmu*-ghost and *mimma lemnu* in banishing texts is not uncommon, and in fact it is difficult to know the extent to which a given passage can always be meaningfully analysed from this standpoint.

Many texts of this broad genre have been put together and worked into compilations and so may sometimes embody a certain 'cut-and-paste' quality, but a structured and quite elaborate ritual such as this can be taken at face value and its internal integrity trusted. For the *mimma lemnu* or *Any Evil* entity see Schwemer 2010.

K 6073+ . . . This is the tablet K 6073 + Bu. 91-5-9, 132. The second fragment was published in the nineteenth century in Gray, 1874: pl. 12. K 6073 was joined thereto many years ago by R. Borger.

The scribe records . . . It reads GABA.RI KUR *aš-šur* KI *ana* DÙ ŠIR *za-mar* SAR. The sign ŠIR is clear and presumably a disguised writing for ŠÌR = *riksu*.

Chapter 8: The Descents of Inanna and Ishtar and Other Netherworld Stories

Plate 7 (inset) *endless argy-bargy . . .* The best reading on this whole issue, together with an assessment of Inanna/Ishtar's presence in the realia of funerary archaeology, is Barrett 2007. For the known modern history of the relief see Collon 2005.

P. 135 *He should have old . . .* This is Shakespeare's wording; it stands for what we would call, 'a fine old time'.

P. 138 *exercise material, in mastering literary Sumerian . . .* I cannot help but feel that the image of the goddess Ishtar, undoubtedly a peach in every way, being forced to remove her clothing, garment by garment, until she was entirely naked, is one of the elements of the Descent cycle that guaranteed its interest during Sumerian text-reading classes. There is something disturbing, on top of that, about the terracotta *Queen of the Night*, probably depicting Ishtar once arrived in the Netherworld, that heads this chapter; it is, in comparison with modelled clay work in general, decidedly erotic.

Reflect, too, on the line, *qâtka šūṣamma luput ḫurdatni*, 'put out your hand and touch our vulva!', which is what the same Ishtar said explicitly to Gardener Ishullānu in Gilgamesh Tablet VI: 623, 69. It is interesting that this line is one of only two quotations from the *Epic* that found its way into a late learned commentary text in the Babylon Academy. The ancient cuneiform scholar explains the medical expression 'her vulva is loosened' by quoting this very Gilgamesh line from Tablet VI, with its rare word *ḫurdatu*. While fully admiring the scholarship displayed in Frahm 2011, where this matter is discussed (p. 104), I do not deduce with him, from the very fact of the quotation, that 'the commentator had a solid knowledge of the literary texts handed down in Mesopotamia's "stream of tradition".' It seems more probable to me that the Goddess of Love saying 'feel my cunt' would stick in the minds of every single cuneiform schoolboy over every other line of the whole of Gilgamesh and any text they ever read afterwards, never quite going away, but for altogether different reasons.

P. 139 *the classical composition* . . . Quite unintelligibly, this major work of Sumerian literature has been the subject of no comprehensive modern treatment. Like all workers in the field of Assyriology, I have used, most gratefully, the edition by W.R. Sladek that formed his 1974 Johns Hopkins University PhD thesis entitled 'Inanna's Descent to the Netherworld'.

P. 140 *astral identity: she is Venus* . . . For the Venus aspect of the goddess Inanna and how it is reflected in her stories, see Cooley 2008.

the gate to the Netherworld . . . On the gates of mythology see Ragavan 2013.

when the frisky gardener Shukaletuda . . . Edited and translated in Volk 1995; Cooley 2008: 167.

P. 141 *narrator, with voices, moving figures and music* . . . An astonishing and riveting performance of the *Descent* was staged in London on 14 February 2017 by a visiting Noh theatre company, with words part Sumerian part Japanese. The cast was as follows:

Inanna: Nadiah Sorait; Voice of Ninshubur, Narrator and Shamisen: Nanafuku Tamagawa; Galaturra: Kenichiro Okutsu; Kurgarra: Haruki Sasame; Chorus and Percussion: Yoshio Oshima and Kaoru Izumi; Ereshkigal: Haruko Sugisawa; Voice of Ereshkigal, Narrator: Kousuke Tsuji; Neti: Kentaro Okutsu; Nokhan flute: Satoshi Tsukitaku; Percussion: Mariko Kitagawa; Keyboard, Computer: Satoru Wono.

P. 142   *a sculpture* . . . For this interesting idea about the Inanna cult in action see the discussion in Buccellati 1982.

P. 144   *the sacred customs* . . . The 'customs' quoted at Ishtar by the doorkeeper do not imply that the Mesopotamian dead were buried naked. This is a different matter altogether.

P. 145   *dirt from under his fingernail* . . . See Kwasman 2017–18: 209, fn. 18.

P. 146   *convoy of demons* . . . These are the gal$_5$-lá demons, who reappear later as *gallûs* in Akkadian; notes on Chapter 5 above.

P. 149   a *zikru* . . . The Akkadian word used, not accidentally, means both 'male' and 'name'.

Aṣušu-namir – *an* assinnu . . . The *assinnu* (apparently an effeminate male figure) is paired with the *kulu'û* as members of Ishtar's cultic personnel in the context of this story, and they correspond in some measure to the kurgarra (*kurgarrû*) and galaturra (junior *kalû*) figures who occur significantly in *Inanna's Descent*. All this has been looked into in refreshing and close detail in Peled 2014.

P. 150   *seventh-century-bc Assyria* . . . Translations of the whole story are Dalley 1989: 154–62; Foster 2005: 403–413

The site of Kutha . . . For an account of nineteenth-century excavations at Kutha, Tell Ibrahim al-Khalil, see Reade 1986: 112–16.

P. 152   *excavated at Amarna* . . . The find proved to be historical treasure in the form of diplomatic correspondence between the Egyptian court of Pharaoh Amenophis III (about 1386–1349 bc), and the Middle Eastern states that then formed part of his extensive empire. Their importance led Sir Flinders Petrie to excavate seriously at the site, where he found supplementary cuneiform materials in the court's *House of Records*, where back correspondence of sensitive content was filed for later retrieval. *Adapa and the South Wind* is also translated in Dalley 1989: 182–8.

P. 155   *In 1990 Wilfred Lambert* . . . Under the title *A New Babylonian Descent to the Netherworld*, where 'new' as so often in Assyriology means 'hitherto ignored'.

Chapter 9: Gilgamesh, Enkidu and the Netherworld

P. 159   *Gilgamesh, Enkidu and the Netherworld* . . . Essential reading
here is Gadotti 2014, the most enlightened study by far published
on this ancient composition with the Sumerian text made truly
accessible to the translator. It is she who has established beyond
doubt that *Gilgamesh, Enkidu and the Netherworld* stands at the
beginning of the Sumerian Gilgamesh cycle, and who shares my
own conviction that Enkidu was, crucially, alive during his
Netherworld trip, although she did not consider the implications
taken further here or my own view of the text's real meaning. I
entirely repudiate the Sumerological approach of, say, Thorkild
Jacobsen, who dismisses the narrative as a hodgepodge of separate
mythological strands poorly thrown together, denying the text
any integrity. To my mind *Gilgamesh, Enkidu and the Netherworld*
comes down to us intelligible and meaningful as a whole, and,
granted the hallmark repetition of passages within a work of
cuneiform literature that was once purely oral, is succinct and
pared down. The text was a staple of early second-millennium
cuneiform classrooms. As we will see, certain passages within its
narrative exhibit revealing variations in wording depending on
the site at which the tablet manuscripts originated. The variant
readings in the Sumerian manuscripts of this composition, especially regarding the different categories of ghosts, are very
interesting for the would-be translator.

P. 162   *Two-thirds of Gilgamesh was divine* . . . See Finkel 2014: 343–4.

P. 164   *in Sri Lanka* . . . See, for example, the nineteenth-century
description in Parker 1909: 629–30 (Kalli Keliya).

P. 170   *beam* . . . there is a pun here between Sumerian ùr, the word
for roof-beam, and Akkadian *ūru*, 'vulva'.

P. 172   *A man who does not value his god* . . . For this proverb, known
to Sumerologists as *UET* VI/2 no. 299; see Alster 1997: 316.

P. 174   *my small stillborn* . . . Bendt Alster, under the heading 'The
Benefit of an Early Death', has seen reflected in this the progres-
sion from stillborn children, who never came to consciousness,
to the man who lived but died early, an anticipation of the Greek
notion that it is better not to be born, and if you do, to die young;
see Alster 2005: 339–41.

P. 179 *special royal enclosure* . . . The same idea surfaces later in the description of the royal Assyrian funeral in Chapter 4 and the statement of Isaiah in Chapter 12.

Cuneiform King Lists . . . For all the rulers of ancient Mesopotamia we know, recovered by *decades* of Assyriological labour and neatly ranged in order, see conveniently the chapter by J.A. Brinkman in Oppenheim 1977: 335–48.

P. 182 *just to make sure we notice* . . . *Pace* George 2003, Vol. 2: 902.

P. 183 *'Enki-creator'*. . . Nineteenth-century translators of the *Gilgamesh* narrative such as George Smith put the Sumerian name into Akkadian as Ea-bani, with the same meaning. This reading has long been rejected, but more recently Jean Bottéro and Simo Parpola have independently argued that the spelling with -dù, 'to create', was deliberate and meaningful, and taken Enki as the father, and since I came on the idea independently in writing this book, I entirely agree with them. For all details as to the spelling and meaning of the name Enkidu, see George 2003, Vol. 1: 138–44.

Chapter 10: Part 1: An Assyrian Prince in the Netherworld

P. 185 *The Underworld Vision* . . . This composition was first published, translated and discussed by Wolfram von Soden as long ago as 1936, with an English translation soon after in Heidel 1946: 132–6; more recent editions with translations are Livingstone 1989 and Fadhil 2012, with a very useful new hand-copy of the inscription; translation also in Foster 2005. The translation given here has, of course, profited from work by all these scholars but, like my new interpretation of the document for this book, also profits from improved readings. Contrasting discussions are Ataç 2004; Sanders 2009, Loktionov 2017, while it is Bach 2018 who goes on to consider the science fiction question.

Full of breaks and holes . . . There is more than one large and inconvenient hole in the obverse of this tablet – which is also distorted in itself – with the consequence that matching the beginnings, middles and ends of lines 16–25 is not straightforward. Despite the transliteration and selfless copy of Anmar Fadhil, where the alignments differ, I still follow the von Soden and Livingstone reconstruction of this section, which produces better sense of what remains and is quite important for the argument here. The width of this tablet, of landscape rather than portrait orientation, means that the lines when complete were probably too long to read comfortably without a fingertip, an unusual feature in a cuneiform tablet. Also noteworthy is the lack of any 'library' information at all, such as the title or number of lines, the name of the scribe and that of his father or the place and date of writing as is conventional in literary Assyrian tablets.

P. 188 *dead pig carried hung from a pole* . . . In fact, contemporary cuneiform omens make it clear that encountering a pig in the street could be bad news.

P. 189 *(modern Sherif Khan)* . . . See Curtis and Grayson 1982 for the Nergal temple there.

P. 190 *hallowed form of divination* . . . This was probably apparatus for reading oil on water; see Lambert 1967.

P. 191 *a full-blown 'night vision'* . . . It is not certain whether the expression *tabrīt mūši* implies that Kummaya was actually asleep or awake in a visionary state; see Oppenheim 1956: 201; 225–228 *House of* [*Death*] . . . The restoration follows line 33, where the two signs É IDIM = *bīt mūti* that make up this remarkable expression are fully preserved, remarkable in that such a telling phrase seems to occur nowhere else in cuneiform.

P. 192 *Death had the head* . . . This has given rise to a long discussion of the very nature of this composition in Bach 2018, with very different results from mine.

Death . . . Here again, Sibbing-Plantholt 2021.

P. 193 *The fateful Ferryman* . . . On this figure and his relationship with Ur-šanabi see George 2003, Vol. 2: 500–501; Horowitz 1998: 355–7. For his role with witches see Schwemer 2010.

P. 197 *Bibbu, Slaughterer of the Netherworld* . . . Gilgamesh, in Tablet VIII of the *Epic*, presented this intimidating figure with a two-edged weapon, a dagger fitted with lapis lazuli and possibly a sea-mineral, to facilitate his work; George, Vol. 2: 860–1 for more about him.

P. 200 *the Egyptian-type divinities we have already encountered* . . . Thinking also of the body of Osiris in the Netherworld, uniting each night with the sun (discussed in Loktionov 2017).

anti-sorcery spell . . . This occurs in Tablet II, lines 161–4 of the Akkadian magic compilation *Šurpu*, 'Burning', see Reiner 1958: 17; Loktionov 2017: 50–51. The clay tablet sources for this magical compendium are mostly contemporary with Kummaya's text and afford no indication of when and how these Elamite gods moved into such a powerful position. Yabru was acknowledged as the 'Anu of Elam', and Ḫumban sometimes equated with Enlil, so probably the three equated to the top Mesopotamian trio Anu, Enlil and Ea, but the first appearance of these names in magical texts, acknowledging and re-establishing their Elamite status and importance, can only have taken place at a point of international harmony and no doubt reflect a specific reason.

considered completely trustworthy . . . Foreign gods certainly did take up residence and become acculturalised in Mesopotamia; war booty could always include captured images from outside temples that might come to be the recipient of cult offerings and even find a place in the official theological lists into which the numerous gods of the home pantheon were organised. Diplomatically they were useful bargaining material too. Sennacherib's armies wreaked havoc in Elam, but we don't know whether his spoils included local gods; later, in about 657 bc, Ashurbanipal made a list of the Elamite gods captured when he conquered Susa.

P. 201 *let this be my expiation* . . . This revealing and crucial remark contains the same term *namburbû* that recurs in this book. It is a loan from Sumerian nam-búr-bi, meaning the release from predicted or anticipated evil consequences of an event or deed effected by exorcistic manipulations.

Chapter 10: Part 2: Who was the Prince?

P. 204 *Wise Ahiqar and his son Nadin* . . . For translations of the sources for this interesting narrative see Conybeare et al. 1913. The existence of this story shows that there was an Assyrian market for Aramaic translation out of cuneiform Akkadian of stories about the rich and famous in the capital, since the Aramaic language was increasingly widely spoken and doubtless many more people could read it than Assyrian cuneiform. The same applies to the long section in the Aramaic Demotic Papyrus Amherst 63 (conveniently Kottsieper 2009), which includes a story about the fatal build-up to the later war between Ashurbanipal and his rebellious brother Shamash-shum-ukin, in which their sister Sheru'a-eṭerat plays a diplomatic role. This royal-brothers story must have first existed in Akkadian, been translated into Aramaic and written out as Aramaic in demotic script for the Egyptian market. It was probably a bestseller at railway-bookstall status. One could imagine that the Kummaya story might have undergone similar treatment.

follow up afresh . . . These identifications were referred to by Foster as speculative, without further consideration (Foster 2005: 811).

P. 207 a *nickname* or a *cover name* . . . The Akkadian form *kūm* is adverb, conjunction and preposition, meaning 'instead', 'otherwise' and 'instead of'. I imagine this provides a clue to its meaning; see below.

P. 208 *identifying Kummaya as Ashurbanipal* . . . This was the view of von Soden (1936: 7–8), followed by Livingstone (1989: xxviii), possibly (Ataç 2004: 69) and Foster (2005: 833); see Loktionov 2017: 41, for earlier discussions of the royal father's identity.

P. 209 *Assur-etel-shamê-erṣeti-muballissu* . . . This name, meaning Assur-prince-of-Heaven-and-Earth-is-the-one-who-keeps-him-alive, is perhaps the longest Assyrian personal name known. One does wonder what his mum called him.

Elnathan Weissert . . . For this highly important point, and the whole matter of Esarhaddon's sons and their order and careers, see Weissert 1998; Novotny and Singletary 2009: 171 and references given there.

own name, 'Shamash has revived the dying . . .' That the prince was under the protection of Shamash could explain Ereshkigal's asking him why he had not applied to the latter for help with his problem (see line 36).

P. 210 *this Holmesian dictum* . . . Made to Dr Watson during the *Adventure of the Empty House*.

P. 211 *like his siblings* . . . For the cuneiform education of Esarhaddon's children see Livingstone 2007.

P. 211   *the* 'God-Type text' . . . Properly the *Göttertypentext*. The formal literary connection between Kummaya's descriptions and this learned treatise was pointed out in Bach 2018: 76–9, and the specimen text quoted here is after his p. 78.

    insightful study . . . The text itself was earlier treated in Wiggermann 1996, but his own innovative and lucid exposition in Wiggermann 2018 is nothing short of brilliant.

P. 213   *replica of the Greek Underworld* . . . see Paget 1967 and Temple 2002.

P. 214   *wildly unconventional cuneiform sale contract* . . . See the illuminating study of this inscrutable text in Kwasman 2017–18, where earlier efforts are appraised.

P. 215   *the mother of the šēdus* . . . Panayatov 2020: 147. What is interesting, *en passant*, is that the paired monumental and silent *šēdus* who once stood on guard in temple, palace and other gateways of Assyrian cities were evidently conceived not only to be alive, but to be one interconnected family! A later chronicler recorded a divine *kāribu* adorant-figure positioned at the right-hand side of a temple door, probably at Babylon, as having been seen to move (Grayson 1975: 138, 16).

    the Ulaya River . . . See on this Potts 1999 and Panayatov 2020: 147. It carried off Lamashtu!

P. 216   *Egyptian presence and influence at Nineveh* . . . See conveniently Loktionov 2017: 51–52 and references. None of these separate factors seems to explain the physicality and detail of the gods in the vision, or the temple.

    childhood tales . . . Assyrian kings, we know, availed themselves plentifully of royal concubines, who were resident in the *bēt isāte*, the women's apartments or harem (Parpola 2012). If, and only if, Kummaya's mother happened to be an Egyptian girl, and the baby had been allowed to live in her care, it would be the most natural thing in the world had she taught the child her own tongue and talked to him about Egypt's landscape, gods and pyramids.

    The modern personal name Kambish is sometimes attributed an 'ancient Egyptian etymology', supposedly meaning 'the Kambujien', or 'Crown Prince Kambuja'! Despite investigations, this is at present entirely unsubstantiated, but *si verum est* would fit perfectly as the origin of the nickname Kummaya from an Egyptian mother whose son was legitimately expected to be king himself one day!

P. 218 *His reinstatement* . . . As pointed out by Simo Parpola, we have no idea whether or not Urad-Gula's self-promotion letter campaign proved successful, and we lose sight of him almost entirely thereafter; one reference shows that he was probably dead by 649 bc.

P. 219 *scripted* . . . Attention has already been drawn to the absence of clues from the tablet itself. It is certainly not the author's first draft and so we can probably not extract insight from the hand-writing itself. It may also be significant that, while the document came to light at Assur, no copy of its inscription is known from the Nineveh libraries. This is unusual and meriting consideration. Perhaps Ashurbanipal was disgusted by it.

Chapter 11: The Delicate Art of Necromancy

P. 221 *a Pandoran undertaking* . . . On disturbing the Mesopotamian dead see Livingstone 1991.

P. 222 *brings up a ghost* . . . The word for ghost is an unread Sumerian sign, probably GU_4, meaning ox (in Kummaya's Netherworld the Chief Ghost is described as having an ox head), but also a well-known equivalent of *eṭemmu*, ghost; the tablet, found at Sultantepe, will need to be checked. The reading and interpretation of *naršindu* as necromancer as well as black magi-cian is new to this book. By the way, the sign ÍD- in *MSL*, Vol. 12: 226 is used to spell the sound 'nar-' in *naršindu* because Sumerian íd, river, is *nāru* in Akkadian; it is a *dreadful* sort of clever Dick pun.

P. 224 *translates as follows* . . . See Tropper 1989: 69–76 and Michel 2001: 470 for earlier translations. 'Confound it!' is a guess, given that the sign sequence written on the tablet, *za-zi-ir*, is inexpli-cable. I wonder, therefore, if it is not a swear-word somehow connected with the verb *nazāru*, 'to curse'. 'Your life', notwith-standing, is in the accusative case. It has been fun to discuss this letter afresh with my Old Assyrian colleague Mathilde Touillon-Ricci.

P. 227 *his grandmother's vote* . . . On Queen Naqi'a and her political effectiveness see Melville 1999.

P. 228 *ia-am-ma-ke₄*. . . This word probably contains the Netherworld name Ammatu, which probably underpins the Akkadian feminine noun *ammatu*, 'earth', the name of Queen Abatu in Chapter 5. See Horowitz 1998: 282.

> *to enable a person to see a ghost* . . . Sumerian gedim igi-bar-ra. The same Sumerian igi-bar, to see, occurs twice within the spell. Note the repetitive pattern of this old item of magic, *Word A, Word A, Word B, Word A*.

P. 230 *The second ritual* . . . See Tropper 1989: 91–2; Scurlock 2006: 178–9.

P. 231 *an evil apparition* . . . The noun is written as Sumerian zi-ga, Akkadian *tebû*, 'to rise up'; while the reading or form of the derivative word is unknown the meaning is clear.

P. 233 *Sm. 810* . . . See Caplice 1967: 34–8, and for *namburbû*-type tablets and literature in general, Maul 1994.

> *the evil of a dove or strange bird* . . . Stefan Maul has made the interesting suggestion that these oddly behaving birds might themselves be ghosts in a form that reflects the wingéd dead in the classic Netherworld visions; see Maul 1995: 220.

P. 238 *his Sumerian name means Fate-Decider* . . . The nam element for an abstract is the same as in nam-búr-bi = Akkadian *namburbû*. For the dwarf *namtaru*-figure in the witchcraft passage see Panayotov 2020: 147. Greek necromantic parallels use a doll (Ogden 2001: 214–15, where this very Babylonian *namtaru* passage finds mention).

P. 239 *illuminating spelling variations* . . . *i sa-ḫa-ab* for *ni-ir-ḫa-ab*, *gedim-e* for *gedim* and *igi-bar igi-bar-bar* for *igi-an igi-bar*, where igi-an is probably a mistake for igi-bar (confusion of AN /BAR). *Manual 1* tablet and catch-line read ni.IR.ḫa.ab, but in *Manual 2* ni.SA.ḫa.ab (confusion of IR/SA).

One other source for this spell is the contemporary *zabbu* tablet BM 76671 (Finkel 1983: 12–13); the *zabbu* – and his fellow ecstatic *maḫḫû* (both with female equivalents) – wandered about the place, going into trances and making pronouncements, as with certain Old Testament prophets. BM 76671 prescribes the same spell in order to procure a sleep message, with the explicit variant *i-giš* (signs ni.giš) instead of plain *i* (ni), helpfully showing that oil must be understood in all the versions. For the *zabbu* ritual, crushed human and canine bone, wolf dung and rancid fat are mixed with fish oil, naphtha, ghee and cedar resin, and the result: 'You anoint his face and he will fall into a sleep-trance.'

W 22758/2 from Uruk . . . The text is published in von Weiher 1982: 100–103, no. 20.

P. 241 *The Anunnaki* . . . See Chapter 13.

P. 243 *'for the see-er'* . . . The English word seer is, of course, a 'see-er'.
four other first-millennium-bc tablets . . . As with the first necromantic incantation, this old spell also surfaces in different but related contexts, of which the most revealing is to solicit a fortune-telling dream.

P. 244 *as we shall see in Chapter 12* . . . To complement *necromancy by skull* we must note here an Assyrian ghost-dispelling ritual where a skull is used, in contrast, to *get rid of* a family ghost. The haunted person is instructed to recite the incantation, 'You, ghost of someone . . .' right in front of a skull; for this, and other Mesopotamian ritual use of skulls including a cure for grinding your teeth in your sleep, see Finkel, 1983/1984: 13–14. A seventh-century-bc letter from the Assyrian court at Nineveh asks:

> . . . *shall we bring these skulls that are required for the ritual? We have wrapped them in* kusippu-*cloth and in [. . .] and have left them inside* . . .

although here we have no clue as to what this ritual was. See Parpola 1983: no. 178. Later Aramaic magic inscriptions to exorcise demons were sometimes written in ink on a human cranium; see Levene 2006 and earlier literature.

an entire volume . . . This is Ogden 2001, referred to above, and highly interesting it is too, especially Chapter 12, 'Reanimation and Talking Heads', with lovely necromantic skulls.

Chapter 12: The Biblical World

P. 248   *this broadly sketched ghost-Netherworld system* . . . See here, for example, Jacquet 2012 and the other contributions to that volume.
the Hebrew Bible is a most complicated source . . . Otero 2012 is fascinatingly involved.

P. 250   *Sheol (Hebrew* še 'ôl) . . . Later, in the Hellenistic period, Sheol takes on a different mantle; it becomes the destiny of the wicked, who go there to await the Final Judgement – the good meanwhile assembling in Paradise with the same idea in mind – and the name becomes identified with Greek Hades, or Hell.
idea of Sheol . . . Gates, Isaiah 38:10; waiting about, Job is excellent reading on the topic.

P. 251   *Rephaim, 'shades'* . . . From Job 26:5; Isaiah 26:14; Psalm 88:11; Proverbs 2:18, 9:18.
texts that refer to the rpum . . . See Tropper 1989: 123–60; Levene 1984; del Olmo Lete 1999; Wan 2009: 49–55.
in conjunction with ars, earth . . . I agree with Theodore Lewis (1992: 104) that Hebrew *'ereṣ* here (cognate to Akkadian erṣetu, earth and Netherworld) is a synonym of Sheol, although there is a mountain of printed discussion about this (as every word in the Hebrew Bible); Wan 2009 gives an overview with references.
King Tabnit . . . For this and the following inscription see Donner and Röllig 2002 (KAI 13 and 14).

P. 252   *two such distinct meanings* . . . See Lewis 1999: 228–9.
at Hurrian Urkesh in Syria. . . See on this, Kelly-Buccellati 2005: Collins 2004: 55.

P. 259   *the location is disputed* . . . The useful summary 'Endor' (village) on *Wikipedia* lists the following proposed sites: (a) Jezreel Valley south: Khirbet Jadurah, Tell Qedesh/Tell abu Qudeis (b) Jezreel Valley north: Tell el-Ajjul/el-Ajyul/Agol; Indur/Endur/En-dor; Khirbet Safsafeh/es-Safsafa.
Well of Generation . . . This translation of the name and the whole of this interpretation are, I believe, new to this book. It does mean that for those who are concerned to locate Endor on the ground once and for all there is no necessity to look for an ancient well or watercourse. The traditional Canaanite entry to

the Netherworld is likely to have been complex with, at the very least, a cave entrance and, obviously, deep tunnelling. I see, in finishing this chapter, that some *Wikipedia* writer identified the Hebrew as 'eye' rather than 'well', and 'generation' in the name Endor, but without drawing any conclusions therefrom.

P. 260 *backdated 'creative writing'* . . . It has been argued that the Endor story is a late composition, inserted . . . *non credo*!

P. 261 *Deutero-canonical book of Sirach* . . . This work was composed between roughly 220 bc and 100 ad but not accepted by all. See also Ecclesiasticus 46: 20 and Smelik 1979: 161.

wriggled so desperately . . . A big sticking point was reluctance to attribute the raising of Samuel to a necromancer rather than to comfortably divine intervention. The earlier rabbinic view was that necromancy worked but was wicked. Then, they say, the Ghost-Mistress recognised Samuel because he rose *face up*, as the dead do in front of a king. As for the means at her disposal, all they knew was that 'she did what she did, and she said what she said, and raised him'. Later interpretations are more detached, suggesting she supplied the words of Samuel herself in awareness of the effect her statements would have. Christian theological ideas about Saul at Endor also find the narrative indigestible during the first millennium ad, and settle on three possibilities: 1 Samuel was in fact brought up by the Ghost-Mistress; 2 Either Samuel, or a demon pretending to be him, was brought up by divine command; 3 A demon deceived Saul with a treacherous prophecy off its own bat. Later still Samuel Johnson, now less sympathetic on necromancy than in Chapter 12, quoted *Browns Vulgar Erroures, b.* I in 1755 with evident approval,

The refurrection of Samuel is nothing but delufion in the practice of necromancy and popular conception of ghosts

More information as to the persistence of this activity comes from Chapter 65 of Talmudic *Sanhedrin*:

The Sages taught: the category of a necromancer includes both one who raises the dead with his zekhur *(a tool? an incantation?), which is a form of sorcery, and one who*

inquires about the future from a skull. What is the difference between this type of necromancer and that type of necromancer? When one raises the dead with his zekhur, the dead does not rise in its usual manner, but appears upside-down, and it does not rise on the Sabbath. By contrast, when one enquires about the future from a skull the dead rises in its usual manner, and it rises even on the Sabbath.

Discussions consider whether the summoned voice is really heard at all or imaginary, and conclude that the necromancer sees the spirit but does not hear it, the person that evokes the spirit hears its voice but does not see it, and others present neither see nor hear it.

P. 263   *Jewish invocation from the Middle Ages* . . . See Trachtenberg. For later Jewish magic see Bohak 2008.
In later Judaism . . . *Encyclopedia Judaica*, Vol. 6: 739; Trachtenberg 1939: 223.

P. 264   *good deal of worry* . . . See, at length, Combs 2008. In John's account the idea that what they had seen was a ghost does not crop up.

Chapter 13: A Brief Enquiry as to What The Inhabitants of Mesopotamia Believed About Their Netherworld and the Ultimate Fate of Those Who Languished in Same

P. 266   *Namtar came up* . . . These lines are quoted from the myth *Nergal and Ereshkigal*, discussed in Chapter 8. For the stairway (*simmiltu*), see Horowitz 1998: 66.
Map of the World . . . See perhaps Horowitz 1998: Chapter 2, but then, swiftly, Finkel 2014: 261–76.

P. 267   *old saying goes* . . . Quoted after Lambert 1960: 70: 16–17.
One spell that details . . . Udug-Ḫul Tablet XI: 110–119 (Geller 2016: 389).

P. 268   *esoteric and seldom encountered* . . . For details of all the Netherworld names and their meanings see Horowitz 1998: Chapter 12.
has been largely rejected . . . See on this matter, with regard to earlier interpretations, Artemov 2012.

P. 269   *the Four Winds* . . . Dreams are to be added to the survey of conveyance by wind in Jiménez 2018.

P. 271   *life force itself was finite* . . . For the full and nimble philological acrobatics performed at the Babylonian Academy in the fifth century bc that led to this conclusion see Finkel 2014: Appendix I, 335–41, from which this discussion has been abbreviated. It is possible that one esoteric text from Assur (quoted in Horowitz 1998: 16–17) also refers to this idea, for it states that the upper surface of the earth is home to the *ziqīqū ša naphar nišī*, 'the spirits of all mankind'. The term *ziqīqu* means phantom, or evanescence, and *not* the ghost of a dead person; a lucid description in one spell, talking of phantoms, says 'they are neither male nor female but drifting *ziqīqū*'. I think that the surface of the earth being full of all the *ziqīqū* refers to endless new lives generated out of recycled *eṭemmus* in accordance with the great scheme. See also on *ziqīqu* Chapter 9, with regard to Enkidu's strange experience.

P. 272   *a river ordeal* . . . This ancient system (which was to have a long history, if not imitators) was practised in ancient Mesopotamia from at least the second millennium onwards. It sought to establish guilt or innocence by throwing the suspect into some turbulent stretch of river to see whether the River God would establish his innocence by saving him. In this case the person had been vindicated, and the man is on his way home, holding on to his life portion.

    not reincarnation . . . This, as I see it, involves only, *à la* Boyle, the source material. There is no known cuneiform evidence that could be taken to reflect awareness of past lives or experience. Consideration of this idea would not be completely unexpected in a philosophical Babylonian, however, for the structure of cuneiform omens is predicated on how *events* repeat themselves tirelessly throughout history, and could therefore stimulate or support such a proposition.

Chapter 14: Afterword

P. 280   *The 'spirit' and the 'ghost' are one* . . . In this regard, it would appeal to the Martian encyclopaedist mentioned at the outset of this book; that which always used to be referred to in Christian doctrine – at least when I was a boy – as the *Holy Ghost* now often becomes the *Holy Spirit*.

Chapter 15: User's Guide: Telling your Ghost from your Demon

P. 283   *the very cuneiform signs* . . . For details about these signs see Steinert 2012: Chapter 11; Schwemer 2020: 154–5.

P. 288   *the peculiar facility of exegesis* . . . Details about this matter already found their way into Finkel 2014: 337–9, but it is even more essential for the present enquiry.

Bibliography

They are the books, the arts, the academes,
That show, contain and nourish all the world
                    Love's Labour's Lost, Act 4, Scene 3

Alster, B. *Proverbs of Ancient Sumer*, Vol. 2. Maryland, 1997.

Alster, B. 'Incantation to Utu', *Acta Sumerologica Japonica* 13 (1991): 27–96.

Alster, B., *Wisdom of Ancient Sumer.* Maryland, 2005.

Angell, N. and Gooding, F., *Ghost Stories of the British Museum.* London, 2018.

Artemov, N., 'The Elusive Beyond: Some Notes on the Netherworld Geography in Sumerian Tradition', in C. Mittermayer and S. Ecklin, *Altorientalische Studien zu Ehren von Pascal Attinger.* mu-ni u$_4$ ul-li$_2$-a-aš ğa$_2$-ğa$_2$-de$_3$. Orbis Biblicus et Orientalis, Vol. 256. Göttingen, 2012.

Bach, J., 'A Transtextual View on the "Underworld Vision of an Assyrian Prince"', in S.V. Panayotov and L. Vacín (eds), *Mesopotamian Medicine and Magic: Studies in Honor of Markham J. Geller.* Leiden, 2018: 69–92.

Baker, H.D., 'Neo-Babylonian Burials Revisited', in S. Campbell and A. Green (eds), *The Archaeology of Death in the Ancient Near East.* Oxford, 1995: 209–21.

Baker, H.D., 'House Size and Household Structure: Quantitative Data in the Study of Babylonian Urban Living Conditions', in H.D. Baker and M. Jursa (eds), *Documentary Sources in Ancient Near Eastern and Greco-Roman Economic History. Methodology and Practice.* Oxford 2014: 2–23.

Barrett, C., 'Was Dust their Food and Clay their Bread? Grave Goods, the Mesopotamian Afterlife and the Liminal Role of Inana/Ishtar', in N. Laneri (ed.), *Performing Death. Social Analyses of Funerary Traditions in the Ancient Near East and Mediterranean.* Chicago 2007: 7–65.

Bayliss, M., 'The Cult of Dead Kin in Assyria and Babylonia', *Iraq* 35 (1973): 115–25.

Bohak, G., *Ancient Jewish Magic: A History.* Cambridge, 2008.

Bottéro, J., 'La mythologie de la mort en Mésopotamie ancienne', in B. Alster (ed.), *Death in Mesopotamia. XXVIe Rencontre Assyriologique internationale.* Mesopotamia Copenhagen Studies in Assyriology 8. Copenhagen, 1980: 25–52.

Bottéro, J., 'Les inscriptions cunéiformes funéraires', in G. Gnoli and J.-P. Vernant, *La Mort, les morts dans les societes anciennes.* Cambridge, 1982: 373–406.

Buccellati, G., 'The Descent of Inanna as a Ritual Journey to Kutha?' *Syro-Mesopotamian Studies* 4/3: 3–7.

Buccellati, G. and Kelly-Buccellati, M., 'Urkesh as a Hurrian Religious Centre', *Studi Miceni ed Egeo-Anatolici* 47 (2005): 27–59.

Budge, E.A.W., *Amulets and Superstitions*, Oxford and London, 1930.

Campbell Thompson, R., *Semitic Magic: Its Origins and Development.* London, 1908.

Castellino, G., 'Rituals and Prayers against "Appearing Ghosts"', *Orientalia NS* 24/3 (1955): 240–74.

Cavigneaux, A. and Al-Rawi, F.N.H., 'Charmes de Sippar et de Nippur', in H. Gasche (ed.), *Cinquante-deux Reflexions sur le Proche-Orient Ancien offertes en hommage à Léon De Meyer.* Mesopotamian History and Environment Occasional Publications II. Leuven, 1994: 73–89.

Cavigneaux, A. and Al-Rawi, F.N.H., *Gilgameš et la mort. Textes de Tell Haddad VI, avec une appendice sur les textes funéraires sumériens.* Cuneiform Monographs 19. Groningen, 2000.

Charpin, D., 'Les vivants et leurs morts dans la Mésopotamie paléo-babylonienne: L'apport des textes archives', in J.-M. Durand, T. Römer and J. Hutzli (eds), in *Les vivants et leurs morts.* Fribourg and Göttingen, 2012: 19–32.

Clottes, J., *What is Paleolithic Art? Cave Paintings and the Dawn of*

Human Creativity (translated by O.Y. Martin). Chicago and London, 2016.

Cohen, A.C., *Death, Rituals and the Development of Early Mesopotamian Kingship. Towards a New Understanding of Iraq's Royal Cemetery at Ur*. Ancient Magic and Divination 7. Leiden, 2005.

Collon, D., *The Queen of the Night*. British Museum Objects in Focus. London, 2005.

Combs, J.R., 'A Ghost on the Water? Understanding an Absurdity in Mark 6:49–50', *Journal of Biblical Literature* 127/2 (2008): 345–58.

Conybeare, F.C., Rendel Harris, J. and Lewis, A.S. (eds), *The Story of Ahikar from the Aramaic, Syriac, Arabic, Armenian, Ethiopic, Old Turkish, Greek and Slavonic Versions*. Cambridge, 1913.

Cooper, J.S., *The Lagash-Umma Border Conflict*. Sources from the Ancient Near East, Vol. 2.1. Undena, 1983.

Cooper, J.S., 'The Fate of Mankind: Death and Afterlife in Ancient Mesopotamia', in H. Obayashi (ed.), *Death and Afterlife: Perspectives of the World Religions*. New York, 1992: 19–33.

Cooper, J.S., 'Wind and Smoke: Giving Up the Ghost of Enkidu, Comprehending Enkidu's Ghosts', in M.-C. Poo (ed.), *Rethinking Ghosts in World Religions*. Leiden and Boston, 2009: 23–32.

Cooley, J.E., 'Inana and Šukaletuda: A Sumerian Astral Myth', *KASKAL* 5 (2008): 161–72.

Curtis, J.E. and A.K. Grayson, 'Some Inscribed Objects from Sherif Khan in the British Museum', *Iraq* 44/1: 87–94.

Dalley, S., *Myths from Mesopotamia: Creation, The Flood, Gilgamesh and Others*. Oxford, 2000.

Donner, H. and Röllig, W., *Kanaanäische und aramäische Inschriften* 15 erweiterte und überarbeitete Auflage. Wiesbaden, 2002.

Drower, E.S., *The Mandaeans of Iraq and Iran*. Oxford, 1937.

Fadhil, A.A., *Eine kleine Tontafelbibliothek aus Assur (Ass. 15426)*. Inauguraldissertation zur Erlangung des Doktorgrades an der Philosophischen Fakultät der Universität Heidelberg. Heidelberg, 2012.

Farber, W., *Lamaštu: An Edition of the Canonical Series of Lamaštu*

Incantations and Rituals and Related Texts from the Second and First Millennia B.C. Winona Lake, 2014.

Finkel, I.L., 'The Dream of Kurigalzu and the Tablet of Sins', *Anatolian Studies* 33 (1983): 75–80.

Finkel, I.L., 'Necromancy in Ancient Mesopotamia', *Archiv für Orientforschung* 29/30 (1983/1984): 1–17.

Finkel, I.L., *The Ark Before Noah*. London, 2014.

Finkel, I.L. and Taylor, J., *Cuneiform*. London, 2015.

Finkel, I.L, and Rey, S., *No Man's Land*. London, 2018.

Flückiger-Hawker, E., *Urnamma of Ur in Sumerian Literary Tradition*. Orbis Biblicus et Orientalis 166. Freiburg, 1999.

Foster B., *Before the Muses: An Anthology of Akkadian Literature*. 3rd edn. Bethesda, 2005.

Frahm, E., *Babylonian and Assyrian Text Commentaries: Origins of Interpretation*. Guides to the Mesopotamian Textual Record, Vol. 5. Münster, 2011.

Frymer, T.S., 'The Nungal-Hymn and the Ekur-Prison', *Journal of the Economic and Social History of the Orient* 20 (1977): 78–89.

Gadotti, A., *Gilgamesh, Enkidu and the Netherworld and the Sumerian Gilgamesh Cycle*. Untersuchungen zur Assyriologie und Vorderasiatischen Archäologie 10. Boston/Berlin.

Gansell, A.R., 'Dressing the Neo-Assyrian Queen in Identity and Ideology: Elements and Ensembles from the Royal Tombs at Nimrud', *American Journal of Archaeology* 122/1 (2018): 65–100.

Geller, M.J., 'Udug', in E. Ebeling, E.F. Weidner and M.P. Streck (eds), *Reallexikon der Assyriologie*, Vol. 14: 274–5.

Geller, M.J., 'Very Different Utu Incantation', *Acta Sumerologica Japonica* 17 (1995): 101–26.

Geller, M.J., 'The Last Wedge', *Zeitschrift für Assyriologie* 87 (1997): 43–95.

Geller, M.J., *Healing Magic and Evil Demons: Canonical Udug-hul Incantations*. Die babylonisch-assyrische Medizin in Texten und Untersuchungen, Vol. 8. Berlin, 2016.

George, A.R., 'Sennacherib and the Tablet of Destinies', *Iraq* 48 (1986): 133–46.

George, A.R. and Al-Rawi, F.N.H., 'Tablets from the Sippar Library VI. Atra-*ḫasis*', *Iraq* 58 (1996): 147–90.

George, A.R., *The Epic of Gilgamesh*. New York, 1999.

George, A.R., *The Babylonian Gilgamesh Epic: Introduction, Critical Edition and Cuneiform Texts*, Vols I and II. Oxford, 2003.

Gray, C.D., *The Šamaš Religious Texts*. Chicago, 1901.

Grayson, A.K., *Assyrian and Babylonian Chronicles*. Texts from Cuneiform Sources 5. Glückstadt, 1975.

Gurney, O.R. and Hulin, P., *The Sultantepe Tablets*, Vol. 2. Ankara, 1964.

Heessel, N.P., 'The Hands of the Gods: Disease Names, and Divine Anger', in I.L. Finkel and M.J. Geller (eds), *Disease in Babylonia*. Cuneiform Monographs 36. Leiden and Boston, 2007: 120–30.

Horowitz, W., *Mesopotamian Cosmic Geography*. Mesopotamian Civilizations 8. Winona Lake, 1998.

Izre'el, S., *The Amarna Scholarly Tablets*. Cuneiform Monographs 9. Groningen, 1997.

Jacquet, A., 'Funerary Rites and Cult of the Ancestors during the Amorite Period: The Evidence of the Royal Archives of Mari' in P. Pfälzner, H. Niehr, E. Pernicka and A. Wissing (eds), *(Re-)constructing Funerary Rituals in the Ancient Near East*. Wiesbaden, 2012: 123–36.

Jiménez, E., 'Highway to Hell: The Winds as Cosmic Conveyors in Mesopotamian Incantation Texts', in G. Van Buylaere, M. Luukko, D. Schwemer and A. Mertens-Wagschal (eds), *Sources of Evil*. Ancient Magic and Divination 15. Leiden, 2018: 316–50.

Johnston, S.I., *Restless Dead: Encounters between the Living and the Dead in Ancient Greece*. California, 2013.

Jonker, G., *The Topography of Remembrance: The Dead, Tradition and Collective Memory in Mesopotamia*. Leiden, 1995.

Katz, D., *The Image of the Netherworld in the Sumerian Sources*. Potomac, 2003.

Katz, D., 'Death They Dispensed to Mankind: The Funerary World of Ancient Mesopotamia'. *Historiae* 2 (2005): 55–90.

Katz, D., 'Sumerian Funerary Rituals in Context', in N. Laneri (ed.),

Performing Death: Social Analyses of Funerary Traditions in the Ancient Near East and Mediterranean. Chicago, 2007: 167–88.

Katz, D., '"His Wind is Released" – The Emergence of the Ghost: Rite of Passage in Mesopotamia', in A. Mouton and J. Patrier (eds), *Life, Death and Coming of Age in Antiquity: Individual Rites of Passage in the Ancient Near East and Adjacent Regions*. Leiden, 2014: 419–37.

Kenyon, K., *Digging up Jericho: The Results of the Jericho Excavations, 1952–1956*. London, 1957.

Kilmer, A., 'The Mesopotamian Concept of Overpopulation and its Solution as Reflected in Mythology', *Orientalia* NS 4 (1972): 160–77.

King, B., *How Animals Grieve*. Chicago and London, 2014.

Köcher, F., *Die babylonisch-assyrische Medizin in Texten und Untersuchungen*, Vol. 3. Berlin, 1964.

Köcher, F., *Die babylonisch-assyrische Medizin in Texten und Untersuchungen*, Vol. 4. Berlin, 1971.

Kottsieper, I., 'Aramaic Literature', in C. S Ehrlich, , G. Beckman, B. R. Foster, S. Tower and I. Kottsieper, *From an Antique Land: An Introduction to Ancient Near Eastern Literature*. Lanham, 2009: Chapter 8.

Kwasman, T., 'A Neo-Assyrian Royal Funerary Text, in M. Luukko, S.S. Svärd and R. Mattila (eds), *Of God(s), Trees, Kings and Scholars: Neo-Assyrian and Related Studies in Honour of Simo Parpola*. Helsinki, 2009: 111–25.

Kwasman, T., 'Some Remarks on the So-Called "Bird Text"', *Isimu* 20–1 (2017–18): 205–20.

Lambert, W.G., *Babylonian Wisdom Literature*. Oxford, 1960.

Lambert, W.G., 'Enmeduranki and Related Matters', *Journal of Cuneiform Studies* 21 (1967): 126–38.

Lambert, W.G., 'The Gula Hymn of Bulluṭsa-rabi, *Orientalia* 36/2 (1967): 105–32.

Lambert, W.G., 'The Theology of Death', in B. Alster (ed.), *Death in Mesopotamia. XXVIᵉ Rencontre Assyriologique internationale*. Mesopotamia Copenhagen Studies in Assyriology 8. Copenhagen, 1980: 53–66.

Lambert, W.G., 'Exorcistic Mumbo Jumbo', *Revue d'Assyriologie* 77 (1983): 94–5.

Lambert, W.G., 'A New Babylonian Descent to the Netherworld', in T. Abusch, J. Huehnergard and P. Steinkeller (eds), *Lingering over Words: Studies in Ancient Near Eastern Literature in Honor of William J. Murnane*. Atlanta, 1990: 289–300.

Lete, G. del Olmo, *Canaanite Religion According to the Liturgical Texts of Ugarit*. Bethesda, 1999.

Levene, D., 'Calvariae Magicae: The Berlin, Philadelphia and Moussaieff Skulls', *Orientalia* 75 (2006): 345–79.

Levine, Baruch A. and de Tarragon, Jean-Michel, 'Dead Kings and Rephaim: Patrons of the Ugaritic Dynasty'. *Journal of the American Oriental Society*, Vol. 104, No. 4, Oct.–Dec. 1984.

Lewis, B. and Jewell, E.R., 'Sumerian Economic Texts from the Robert Hull Fleming Museum of the University of Vermont', *Acta Sumerologica* 4 (1982): 53–68.

Lewis, T.J., 'Dead', in K. van der Toorn, B. Becking and P.W. van der Horst (eds), *Dictionary of Deities and Demons in the Bible*. Leiden and Grand Rapids, 1999: 224–8.

Lewis, T.J., 'Dead, Abode of The', *Anchor Bible Dictionary*, Vol. 2: 104. Yale, 1992.

Livingstone, A., *Court Poetry and Literary Miscellanea*, State Archives of Assyria 3. Helsinki, 1989.

Livingstone, A., 'To Disturb the Dead: Taboo to Enmešarra?' *Nouvelles Assyriologiques Brèves et Utilitaires* 1 (1991): 1.

Livingstone, A., 'Ashurbanipal: Literate or Not?' *Zeitschrift für Assyriologie* 97 (2007): 98–118.

Loktionov, A.A., 'An "Egyptianising" Underworld Judging an Assyrian Prince: New Perspectives on VAT 10057', *Journal of Ancient Near Eastern History* 3 (2017): 39–56.

Luukko, M. and Ponchia, S., *The Standard Babylonian Myth of Nergal and Ereškigal*. The Neo-Assyrian Text Corpus Project. Helsinki, 2013.

MacGinnis, J., 'A Neo-Assyrian Text Describing a Royal Funeral', in *State Archives of Assyria Bulletin* 1 (1987): 1–11.

Maul, S., *Zukunftbewältigung eine Untersuchung altorientalischen Denken anhand der babylonisch-assyrischen Löserituale (Namburbi)*. Mainz, 1994.

Maul, S., 'Totengeist und Vögel: Eine Vogelliste aus dem neubabylon-ischen Grab 433 in Uruk', in R.M. Boehmer, F. Pedde and B. Salje (eds), *Uruk: Die Gräber*. Mainz, 1995: 218–20.

Melville, S.C., *The Role of Naqia/Zakutu in Sargonid Politics*. State Archives of Assyria Studies, Vol IX Helsinki, 1999.

Messerschmidt, L. and Ungnad, A., *Vorderasiatische Schriftdenkmäler der Königlichen Museen zu Berlin*, Vol. 1. Leipzig, 1907.

Novák, M., 'Das "Haus der Totenpflege" zur Sepulkralsymbolik des Hauses im Alten Mesopotamien', *Altorientalische Forschungen* 27/1 (2000): 132–54.

Novotny, J. and Singletary, J., 'Family Ties: Ashurbanipal's Family Revisited', in M. Luukko, S. Svärd and R. Mattila (eds), *Of God(s), Trees, Kings, and Scholars: Neo-Assyrian and Related Studies in Honour of Simo Parpola*. *Studia Orientalia* 106: 167–77. Helsinki, 2009.

Novotny, J., and Jeffers, J., *The Royal Inscriptions of Ashurbanipal (668–631 BC), Aššur-etel-ilâni (630–627 BC) and Sîn-šarra-iškun (626–612 BC): Kings of Assyria, Part 1*. The Royal Inscriptions of the Neo-Assyrian Period, Vol. 5/1. Pennsylvania, 2018.

Ogden, D., *Greek and Roman Necromancy*. Princeton and Oxford, 2001.

Ogden, D., *Magic, Witchcraft, and Ghosts in the Greek and Roman Worlds*. Oxford, 2002.

Oppenheim, A., *The Interpretation of Dreams in the Ancient Near East: With a Translation of an Assyrian Dream-Book*. *Transactions of the American Philosophical Society* 46/3 (1956): 179–373.

Oppenheim, A.L., *Ancient Mesopotamia: Portrait of a Dead Civilization*. Revised edition. Chicago and London, 1977.

Otero, A.P., 'Who Names the Namers? The Interpretation of Necromantic Terms in Jewish Translations of the Bible', in A.P. Otero and P.A. Torijano Morales (eds), *Textual Criticism and Dead Sea Scrolls Studies in Honour of Julio Trebolle Barrera: Florilegium*

Complutense. Supplements to the Journal for the Study of Judaism 158. Leiden and Boston, 2012: 241–76.

Paget, R.F., *In the Footsteps of Orpheus: The Discovery of the Ancient Greek Underworld*. London, 1967.

Panayotov, S., 'Healing in Images and Texts: The Sickbed Scene', in *Patients and Performative Identities: At the Intersection of the Mesopotamian Technical Disciplines and Their Clients* (ed. J. Cale Johnson). Pennsylvania State University Press, 2020: 129–58.

Parker, H., *Ancient Ceylon*. London, 1909.

Parpola, S., *Letters from Assyrian Scholars to the Kings Esarhaddon and Ashurbanipal*. Alter Orient und Altes Testament 5/2. Neukirchen-Vluyn, 1983.

Parpola, S., 'The Neo-Assyrian Royal Harem', in G.B. Lanfranchi et al. (eds), *LEGGO! Studies Presented to Prof. Frederick Mario Fales on the Occasion of his 65th Birthday*. Leipziger Altorientalische Studien, Vol. 2: 613–26. Wiesbaden, 2012.

Peled, I., '*assinnu* and *kurgarrû* Revisited', *Journal of Near Eastern Studies* 73/2 (2014): 283–97.

Pettit, P., *The Palaeolithic Origins of Human Burial*. London and New York, 2011.

Porter, B.N., 'Noseless in Nimrud: More Figurative Responses to Assyrian Domination', in M. Luukko, S. Svärd and R. Mattila (eds), *Of God(s), Trees, Kings and Scholars: Neo-Assyrian and Related Studies in Honour of Simo Parpola. Studia Orientalia* 106: 201–20. Helsinki, 2009.

Potts, D.T., *Mesopotamian Civilization: The Material Foundations*. London, 1997.

Potts, D.T., 'Elamite Ula, Akkadian Ulaya and Greek Choaspes: A Solution to the Eulaios Problem', *Bulletin of the Asia Institute* 1999, New Series 13: 27–44.

Ragavan, D., 'Entering Other Worlds: Gates, Rituals and Cosmic Journeys in Sumerian Sources', in D. Ragavan (ed.), *Heaven on Earth: Temples, Ritual and Cosmic Symbolism in the Ancient World*. Papers from the Oriental Institute Seminar Heaven on Earth Held at the Oriental Institute of the University of Chicago 2–3 March 2012. Chicago, 2013: 201–22.

Reade, J.E., 'Rassam's Excavations at Borsippa and Kutha', *Iraq* 48 (1986): 105–16.

Reid, J.N., 'The Birth of the Prison: The Functions of Imprisonment in Early Mesopotamia', *Journal of Ancient Near Eastern History* 3/2 (2016): 81–115.

Reiner, E., *Šurpu: A Collection of Sumerian and Akkadian Incantations. Archiv für Orientforschung, Beiheft 11.* Graz, 1958.

Richardson, S., 'Death and Dismemberment in Mesopotamia: Discorporation between the Body and Body Politic', in N. Laneri (ed.), *Performing Death: Social Analyses of Funerary Traditions in the Ancient Near East and Mediterranean.* Chicago, 2007: 189–208.

Sanders, S., 'The First Tour of Hell', *Journal of Ancient Near Eastern Religions* 9 (2009): 151–68.

Schwemer, D., *Akkadische Rituale aus Ḫattuša. Die Sammeltafel KBo XXXVI 29 und verwandte Fragmente.* Berlin, 1998.

Schwemer, D., 'Die Hochzeit des Totengeistes. Babylonische Magie am hethitischen Königshof'. *Alter Orient Aktuell* 2 (2001): 23–5.

Schwemer, D., 'Any Evil, a Stalking Ghost, and the Bull-Headed Demon', *Zeitschrift für Assyriologie* 110 (2020): 141–60.

Schwemer, D., 'Entrusting the Witches to Ḫumuṭ-tabal: The ušburruda Ritual BM 47806+', *Iraq* 72 (2010): 63–78.

Scurlock, J., 'Taklimtu', *Nouvelles Assyriologiques Brèves et Utilitaires* 1 (1991): 3.

Scurlock, J., 'Death and the Afterlife in Ancient Mesopotamian Thought', in J.M. Sasson, J. Baines, G. Beckman and K.S. Rubinson (eds), *Civilizations of the Ancient Near East volume III.* New York, 1995: I 883–94.

Scurlock, J., 'Soul Emplacements in Ancient Mesopotamian Funerary Rituals', in I.J. Ciraolo and J.L. Seidel (eds), *Magic and Divination in the Ancient World. Ancient Magic and Divination III.* Leiden, 2002: 1–6.

Scurlock, J., *Magico-Medical Means of Treating Ghost-induced Illnesses in Ancient Mesopotamia. Ancient Magic and Divination III.* Leiden, 2006.

Sibbing-Plantholt, I., 'Visible Death and Audible Distress: The

Personification of Death (*Mūtu*) and Associated Emotions as Inherent Conditions of Life in Akkadian Sources', in S.-W. Hsu and J.L. Raduà (eds), *The Expression of Emotions in Ancient Egypt and Mesopotamia*: 335–89. Leiden, 2021.

Simpson, S., 'Annihilating Assyria', in I.L. Finkel and S. Simpson (eds), *In Context. The Reade Festschrift*: 140–65. Oxford, 2020.

Sjöberg, Å. W., 'Nungal in the Ekur', *Archiv für Orientforschung* 24 (1973): 19–46.

Smelik, K.A.D., 'The Witch of Endor: I Samuel 28 in Rabbinic and Christian Exegesis Till 800 A.D.', *Vigillae Christianae* 33 (1979): 160–79.

Stol, M., 'Fevers in Babylonia', in I.L. Finkel and M.J. Geller (eds), *Disease in Babylonia*. Cuneiform Monographs 36. Leiden and Boston, 2007: 1–39.

Temple, R., *Oracles of the Dead: Ancient Techniques for Predicting the Future*. Vermont, 2002.

Tropper, J., *Nekromantie. Totenfragung im Alten Orient und im Alten Testament*. Alter Orient und Altes Testament 223, Neukirchen-Vluyn, 1989.

Tropper, J., '"Seele" oder "Totengeist"? Erwägerungen zum Begriff *eṭemmu*', in Atrahasis I 215–17. *Ugaritische Forschungen* 19, Neukirchen-Vluyn: 301–8.

Tsukimoto, A., *Untersuchungen zur Totenpflege* (kispum) *im alten Mesopotamien*. Alter Orient und Altes Testament, Vol. 216. Neukirchen/Vluyn, 1985.

Volk, K., *Inanna und Šukalletuda: Zur historisch-politischen Deutung eines sumerischen Literaturwerkes*. Arbeiten und Untersuchungen zur Keilschriftkunde 3. Wiesbaden, 1995.

von Weiher, E., *Spätbabylonische Texte aus Uruk Part I*. Ausgrabungen der Deutschen Forschungsgemeinschaft in Uruk-Warka, Vol. 10. Berlin, 1976.

von Weiher, E., *Spätbabylonische Texte aus Uruk Part II*. Ausgrabungen der Deutschen Forschungsgemeinschaft in Uruk-Warka, Vol. 10. Berlin, 1983.

Wan, S.-K., 'Where Have All the Ghosts Gone? Evolution of a Concept in Biblical Literature', in M.-C. Poo (ed.), *Rethinking Ghosts in World Religions*. Leiden and Boston, 2009: 47–76.

Wasserman, N., 'The Susa Funerary Texts: A New Edition and Re-Evaluation and the Question of Psychostasia in Ancient Mesopotamia', *Journal of the American Oriental Society* 139/4 (2019): 859–91.

Weissert, N., in K. Radner (ed.), *The Prosopography of the Neo-Assyrian Empire*, Vol. 1 part 1A. Helsinki, 1998: 162, 163, 227.

Westenholz, A., '*berūtum, damtum,* and Old Akkadian KI.GAL: Burial of Dead Enemies in Ancient Mesopotamia', in *Archiv für Orientforschung* 23 (1970): 27–31.

Wiggermann, F., 'Scenes from the Shadow Side', in M.E. Vogelsang and H.J. Vanstiphout (eds), *Mesopotamian Poetic Language: Sumerian and Akkadian*. Cuneiform Monographs 6. Groningen, 1996: 207–26.

Wiggermann, F., 'The Göttertypentext as a Humanistic Mappa Mundi: An Essay', in G. Van Buylaere, M. Luukko, D. Schwemer and A. Mertens-Wagschal (eds), *Sources of Evil*. Ancient Magic and Divination 15. Leiden, 2018: 351–70.

Acknowledgements

That this book has finally staggered to completion allows me to thank very appreciatively and alphabetically those who have been of such help and encouragement along the way with references, books and discussions. I am especially grateful to Peter Blakebrough, Chris Cobb, Amy Gansell, Jemima Gazzard, Mark Geller, Becky Lao, Olivier Lebleu, Odette Murray, Gale Peterkin, Radek Tarasewicz, Christopher Walker and Mark Wilson. At Hodder, Rupert Lancaster, Becca Mundy and now Louise Court have sustained the author magnificently through the elusive afflictions that pursue all ghost writers. The clear and gentle expertise of my copy-editor, Nick Fawcett, at such times is unique. Likewise, warm thanks go to my most supportive and valued agent, Gordon Wise. My esteemed British Museum colleagues formerly or still have been indispensable, especially Gareth Brereton, Rupert Chapman, James Fraser, Imran Javed, Julian Reade, Sébastien Rey, Felicity Cobbing and St John Simpson. I owe a special expression of gratitude to Jamie Fraser, who coolly produced three desperately needed computer-drawings at a very late stage with panache and aplomb and, together with Chris Cobb, brought our most venerable ghost to new life out of the old clay. Finally, I can delay no longer in thanking my dear and long-suffering family, Joanna, Theo and Julia, who have had to cohabit with this book so protractedly.

Picture Acknowledgements

Pictures in Text

Relief of Ashurnasirpal II: © Bowdoin College Museum of Art, Brunswick, Maine, Gift of Dr. Henri Byron Haskell, Medical School Class of 1855. Critical support for the Assyrian Collection at the Bowdoin College Museum of Art is provided by the Yadgar Family Endowment.

Reconstruction of the funeral scene in grave PG 789, Illustration by Amédée Forestier, 1928: © Illustrated London News Ltd/Mary Evans

Old Babylonian house innovation planned on a clay tablet, British Museum 86394: © The Trustees of the British Museum.

Neo-Babylonian house plan from the Merkes quarter at Babylon; after Baker, H. D., 'House size and household structure: quantitative data in the study of Babylonian urban living conditions,' in H. D Baker and M. Jursa (eds.), Documentary Sources in Ancient Near Eastern and Greco-Roman Economic History. Methodology and Practice. Oxford 2014: 2-23.

Middle Bronze Age House at Jericho, reconstructed after the grave goods in Tomb B35: © The Trustees of the British Museum.

CBS 8235, Penn Museum: Author's drawing.

The Boghazköy 'wife' as reconstructed in Schwemer 1998: 65: Schwemer, D., Akkadische Rituale aus Ñattuåa. Die Sammeltafel

KBo XXXVI 29 und verwandte Fragmente. Berlin, 1998.

Author's half-serious sketch map of Ishtar's passage de rite: Author's informal sketch redrawn by James Fraser.

Schematic identification of the equipment for the game so enjoyed by Gilgamesh: Redrawn by James Fraser.

Diagram of the temple plan with its statuary after the reconstruction in Wiggermann 2018: 356 Figure 2 : Redrawn by James Fraser.

Pictures in Inset

Shamash, god of Justice and Chief Ghost-Arbitrator, Code of Hammurabi (ca. 1792-1750 BC): © DeAgostini/Getty Images

Ghost amulet of clay no. 1 British Museum 59322: © The Trustees of the British Museum

Ghost amulet of clay no. 2 British Museum 54990: © The Trustees of the British Museum

Ghost-banisher amulet in obsidian British Museum 127371: © The Trustees of the British Museum

Zimzilaḫ the dog warden (lines 3-4). A 1575 (obverse): © Fleming Museum of Art, University of Vermont, Museum purchase 1910.3.124

Indispensable manual of anti-ghost magic, British Museum K.2175: © The Trustees of the British Museum

The illustrated tablet par excellence and details, British Museum 40183: © The Trustees of the British Museum

Stela of Nabonidus, king of Babylon, British Museum 90387: © The Trustees of the British Museum

The Persian Verse Account of Nabonidus, British Museum 38299: © The Trustees of the British Museum

The magic tablet, reverse showing the colophon line at the end, British Museum K.6073: © The Trustees of the British Museum

Any Evil as drawn on BM 47701 at Babylon After Anu-balassu-iqbi of Uruk, British Museum 47701: © The Trustees of the British Museum

The world's first depiction of a ghost. Tablet drawing in clay, reverse of British Museum 47831 © The Trustees of the British Museum

Enhancement of drawing on British Museum 47831: Drawing by Chris Cobb and James Fraser

The *Queen of the Night*, British Museum 2003,0718.1: © The Trustees of the British Museum

Necromancy Manual 1. The Assyrian talking-ghost tablet from Nineveh, British Museum K.2779: © The Trustees of the British Museum

Skull: © Baimieng/ Shutterstock

Necromancy Manual 2. The ghost-interrogating tablet from Babylon, British Museum 36703 © The Trustees of the British Museum

Index